U0059737

美麗之島

北部教會宣教禧年回顧與前瞻

（中英雙語版）

The Island Beautiful
The Story of Fifty Years in North Formosa

作者—— 劉忠堅 Rev. Duncan MacLeod

譯者—— 林昌華　　總策劃—— 謝大立

審訂—— 鄭仰恩

主流人物系列 8

美麗之島：北部教會宣教禧年回顧與前瞻
（中英雙語版）

The Island Beautiful: The Story of Fifty Years in North Formosa

原　　著：劉忠堅（Duncan MacLeod）
譯　　者：林昌華
校　　對：蔣茉春
審　　訂：鄭仰恩
總 策 劃：謝大立
贊助單位：溫哥華台灣基督長老教會
出版顧問：鄭超睿
發 行 人：鄭惠文
主　　編：李瑞娟
封面設計：海流設計
排　　版：旭豐數位排版有限公司

出版發行：主流出版有限公司 Lordway Publishing Co. Ltd.
出 版 部：臺北市南京東路五段 123 巷 4 弄 24 號 2 樓
電　　話：(02) 2857-9303
傳　　眞：(02) 2857-9303
電子信箱：lord.way@msa.hinet.net
劃撥帳號：50027271
網　　址：www.lordway.com.tw

經　　銷：
紅螞蟻圖書有限公司
臺北市內湖區舊宗路二段 121 巷 19 號
電話：(02) 2795-3656　　傳眞：(02) 2795-4100

華宣出版有限公司
新北市中和區連城路 236 號 3 樓
電話：(02) 8228-1318　　傳眞：(02) 2221-9445

The original English version of *The Island Beautiful, The Story of Fifty Years in North Formosa* by Duncan MacLeod was published by the Board of Foreign Missions (now the Life and Mission Agency) of The Presbyterian Church in Canada.
Complex Chinese Edition © 2021 by Lordway Publishing Co. Ltd.
All rights reserved.
初版 1 刷：2021 年 12 月
1st Edition：Dec., 2021
書號：L2109
ISBN：978-986-06294-4-6（平裝）
Printed in Taiwan

國家圖書館出版品預行編目資料

美麗之島：北部教會宣教禧年回顧與前瞻 / 劉忠堅 (Duncan MacLeod) 作；
林昌華譯. -- 初版. -- 臺北市：主流出版有限公司, 2021.12
　　面；　公分. --（主流人物系列；8）
　　中英對照
　　譯自：The island beautiful : the story of fifty years in North Formosa.
　　ISBN 978-986-06294-4-6（平裝）

1. 傳教史　2. 教牧學　3. 臺灣

248.33　　　　　　　　　　　　　　　　　　　　110019860

溫哥華台灣基督長老教會設教35週年紀念

目錄

4

5

6

總策劃序 ◆ 台灣北部教會最重要的「禧年史冊中文版」問世！

謝大立牧師

加拿大長老教會於一八七一年六月在魁北克召開的總會年議會中通過接納馬偕成為海外宣教師，九月十九日，禮拜二晚上在多倫多的 Gould Street 教會為封立馬偕為牧師暨授職海外宣教師。一八七一年十月十九日早晨，馬偕在家鄉 Woodstock 車站與親友道別後，朝著宣教禾場邁開步伐。隔年三月九日起，馬偕踩踏北福爾摩沙土地，遍撒福音種子在大大小小的鄉鎮，培育出北台灣許多初代愛主忠心事主的基督徒和傳道人，立下教會擴展的基石。一九〇一年六月二日，馬偕在畢生忠耕耘的園地被主召回，當時北台灣宣教面臨空前的危機，一代領袖的離去，帶給許多信徒、傳道人無助徬徨的憂慮，甚或有人會問：「教會還有明天嗎？」然而，歷史證明了教會是上帝的，不是馬偕的，上帝的教會不會因為一個領袖的倒下黯然結束。反而是，因著領袖的無私奉獻在主的祭壇上，而激勵更多受召的奉獻者前仆後繼地跟隨他的腳蹤，承接宣教的火炬繼續福音的使命。正如保羅所說：「恁著學我，親像我學基督。」（你們要學我，如同

我學基督一樣。」（哥林多前書十一章一節）

一九二三年，台灣北部教會慶祝設教五十週年之際，宣教師與本地牧者於隔年分別出版了重要的史冊，一本陳清義用白話字編寫《北部台灣基督長老教會之歷史》，該書後由陳宏文翻譯成漢字於一九九七年出版。另一本，則是出自宣教師學者劉忠堅（Duncan MacLeod）之筆，由加拿大長老教會海外宣教委員會於一九二三年出版的 The Island Beautiful, The Story of Fifty Years in North Formosa，該書內容豐富紮實，是北部教會首個禧年最重要的史冊，可惜此冊面世近百年卻遲遲未見中文譯本。

二〇二〇年欣逢溫哥華台灣基督長老教會慶祝設教三十五週年之際，阮決定通過文字出版來回應上帝的疼，藉由雙語的出版品做為台灣與加拿大的橋梁，讓這本歷史性的著作得以嘉惠中、英文讀者，並喚起 PCC 和 PCT 共同關注、記念這段上帝在歷史中成就的福音行動。

此次《美麗之島：北部教會宜教禧年回顧與前瞻》得以順利出版中英雙語版，幸得各方協助。感謝加拿大長老教會 The Life and Mission Agency General Secretary Ian Ross-McDonald 牧師，無條件讓與中文翻譯以及英文再版；感謝台灣神學院鄭仰恩教授費心促成與譯者的合作，並協助審閱、校對的工作；感謝玉山神學院林昌華教授詳實的翻譯，並加上豐富的註釋，幫助讀者掌握內文的精髓；感謝本會潘立中弟兄協助提供翻譯修訂的建議；最後要感謝主流出版社的出版顧問鄭超睿弟兄以及編輯李瑞娟姊妹的用心。末了，願以此作為加拿大長老教會差派海外宣教師前往北台灣一百五十週年紀念的獻禮。

（加拿大長老教會 Westminster 中會，溫哥華台灣基督長老教會小會議長）

推薦序 ◆ 壯哉！美麗之島！
——劉忠堅寫北台灣教會初期史

鄭仰恩牧師

加拿大長老教會來台宣教師劉忠堅（Duncan MacLeod, B.A., B.D., D.D., 1872-1957）於將近一世紀前（1923）為慶祝北部教會設教五十週年而撰寫的《美麗之島：北部福爾摩沙五十年的故事》一書[1]，在溫哥華台灣基督長老教會為慶祝該教會設教三十五週年的全力贊助下，將要由主流出版社印行、出版，真是一件值得慶賀的美事。

劉忠堅和台灣北部教會的創建者馬偕（George Leslie Mackay, 1844-1901）同為蘇格蘭裔，同屬清教徒傳統，又有共同經歷的加拿大經驗，在設教五十週年的歷史時刻提筆撰寫這段初期的開拓及發展史，應該是最適當的人選了。一方面，他可以非常貼近馬偕和其他宣教師以及早期本地信徒的心靈與世界，另一方面，他也可以保有適度的歷史距離感，以稍具客觀的角度來述說這段歷史並提出對本地宣教的建言。我想，各位讀者在閱讀本書時，應該可以感受到這樣的雙重角度和觀點，在一世紀之後，讀來仍有一定的溫度和張力！因為在本書中較少提到劉忠

堅自身的故事，我藉此序文簡要描繪一些他在台灣所遺留下來的歷史圖像和身影。

毫無疑問的，劉忠堅是繼馬偕及吳威廉（William Gauld, 1861-1923）之後北部教會最重要的領導者，也是當時最有能力也最積極從事佈道工作的宣教師。[2] 事實上，自從一九○七年底抵台以來，他就積極參與佈道、巡視教會，以及神學教育的工作。他的台灣話非常流利，具雄辯之才，因此以漢人為主要宣教對象，更組織北部教會佈道團。[3] 到一九二二年為止，在他和吳威廉的努力下，北部增加了十八間新教會，主要是在大甲、客家地區、東部蘭陽區，以及基隆一帶。自一九一九年起，在他的領導下，北部教會也積極響應由加拿大母會所引介的「前進運動」（Forward Movement），並推展大規模的佈道事工，成績卓然可觀。[4]

劉忠堅出生於蘇格蘭西北方赫布里底群島的小島琉圍（Isle of Lewis），在一個具有深厚清教徒傳統的家庭長大。在蘇格蘭完成高中學業後，他前往加拿大中西部的曼尼托巴學院（Manitoba College）讀書，後來還到英國劍橋大學的西敏寺學院研讀神學，最後又回到曼尼托巴封牧並開拓教會，因此帶有加拿大西部草原的拓荒者特質，也懷抱著強烈的合一思想。隨後新婚的劉忠堅夫婦也決意投入海外宣教，並於一九○七年十一月來到台灣。[5] 在來台的加拿大宣教師中，他的信仰偏向保守，帶著強烈的靈性特質，經常主張台灣的傳道人需要強化靈性操練，因此也曾經和神學思維較為開放的約美但（Milton Jack）發生爭執，直到後者於一九一七年轉往韓國京城（今漢城）擔任朝鮮基督教學院的教授為止。[6]

自從約美但離開台灣後，劉忠堅就擔負起神學教育的重任，除了一九二一至一九二三年間因例假返國由吳威廉接任外，他於一九一七至一九二六年間兩度擔任台北神學校的校長。值得

注意的是，自從台灣大會於第三屆會議（1914）中決議「台灣應只有一所神學校」且建議南北

神的學生「暫時兩年受業於北部，兩年受業於南部」，又於第四屆會議（1915）中票決台北為

聯合神學校的校址以來，他對南北神學校的聯合問題特別關心，更於一九二五年四月停辦台北

神學校（以兩年為條件），並率領十一名神學生前往台南神學校就讀，希望在兩年後能順利在

台北成立「聯合神學校」。不料此事於一九二六年生變，台灣大會於四月舉行的第十三屆會議

中議定變更「聯合神學校」之校址為台中。為此，北部教會在「聯合神學校」成立無望的前提

下，於一九二七年六月自台南招回學生，並於該年十月在淡水龍井目舊「偕醫館」重新開學，

由明有德（Hugh MacMillan, 1892-1970）出任復校後首任校長。[7] 面對南北神學校聯合事件的

風波與重挫之後，劉忠堅似乎突然從歷史圖像中消失了。

在這段期間裡，對劉忠堅造成巨大影響的就是「加拿大教會聯合運動」。簡單地說，經

過將近四分之一世紀的協議過程，加拿大的衛理公會、公理會和佔三分之二比例的長老教會

於一九二五年聯合組成了「加拿大聯合教會」（United Church of Canada），而其他佔三分之

一比例的長老教會成員則因不屈從而延續原本的「加拿大長老教會」（Presbyterian Church in

Canada），雙方對其法定地位和財產分配的要求與主張更引發了長時間的立法爭執，兩教會間

的緊張與敵意也持續幾十年之久，北部宣教事工因而大受影響。原因是大多數在台宣教師都贊

成且歸屬聯合教會，但在一九二六年六月北部教會這個加拿大宣教區卻被裁決歸屬加拿大長老

教會，導致大多數宣教師於其後數年當中紛紛離開，包括劉忠堅在內。宣教師的大批離去，造

成領導階層的獨裁及「集權化」，這也影響到北部教會後來的所謂「新人運動」。[8]

在這過程中，原本劉忠堅已於一九二六年二月第三十回的北部中會裡被選為中會議長，他也樂意接受。然而，在同年九月「北台灣將歸屬加拿大長老教會」的消息傳來後，他就沒有出席一九二七年二月十五日的第三十一回北部中會，僅在議錄第六條記載著：「劉忠堅牧師辭長老中會議長、傳道局理事長職，並言明四月以後要長久在南部工作。」[9] 鄭連明明確指出，這是「加拿大教會聯合的風波影響到北部台灣教會的一頁正式記錄」。[10] 等到一九二七年四月間劉忠堅再度出現在台南神學校時，他已經成為加拿大聯合教會的宣教師，且準備於8月間接替巴克禮（Thomas Barclay, 1849-1935）擔任台南神學校代理校長。[11] 這樣戲劇化的過程實在令人難以想像。另一位加拿大宣教師蘇若蘭（James E. Sutherland, 1922-2001）就認為，劉忠堅是馬偕之後最出色的演講家和佈道家，他的「被迫南下」是北部教會最大的損失。[12]

整體言之，從上面的簡要描述，相信各位讀者應該可以感受到本書作者劉忠堅是一位熱情、堅毅且願意毫無保留地付出的宣教師。事實上，本書出版於一九二三年，正是他即將被捲入巨大風暴之前，但我們在他的文字裡所讀到的，卻是真誠、溫暖與熱情，這都讓我們對這位宣教師充滿著感激之情閱讀本書。

最後，請容許我稍微說明一下本書的翻譯歷程，也算是為這本書的出版歷史留下紀錄。自從我於一九九四年從美國學成返國之後，每年都要教授「台灣教會史」的課程，當時就發現劉忠堅這本《美麗之島》還沒有漢文譯本，深覺可惜。後來，曾經一度邀請幾位英文能力不錯的學生進行集體翻譯，其中好幾位也交出了譯稿，但並不完整。經過幾度延宕，我就將這些譯稿交給林昌華牧師，請他協助校譯並完成其他部分。沒想到，他卻是選擇全部重譯。後來他出國

— 13 —

讀書，之後也曾討論過出版的事，但總覺得仍未妥當。一直到兩年前謝大立牧師代表溫哥華台灣基督長老教會向我提起想要翻譯並出版本書時，我們才將這些過去的努力兜在一起。經過幾個月的校譯與審訂，總算「事已成了」，真的要感謝上帝的美好攝理！

（台灣神學研究學院 教會歷史學教授）

譯者序 ◆ 望向未來：如何利用外國宣教師眼光，作為將來發展台灣教會的參考？

林昌華牧師

一九八九年筆者以神學生的身分協助整理台灣神學院故孫雅各牧師（Rev. James Dickson D.D.）宿舍中清出的舊文獻和史料，可算是與台灣教會歷史資料邂逅的開始。當時所見的文獻史料內容相當豐富，除了從一九一九年到一九四五年間台北神學校與台北州廳或台灣總督府往來的公文書信之外，就是一批宣教師所撰寫的台灣教會史英文文獻資料。這對當時「台灣史」還被當成是政治上禁忌的年代，真可以說是讓筆者開了眼界，這批英文資料大部分是一九七〇年代台北成文出版社所發行的複印書冊，但是也有少量的原始版本，當中印象較深刻的是 *The Island Beautiful* 以及 *From Far Formosa* 這兩本書。筆者以當時有限的英文閱讀能力，只知道這兩本書大概是北部台灣教會相關的歷史著作。當時筆者期望有一天能夠有能力詳細閱讀甚至研究這些英文文獻的內容，讓這些英文文獻成為無法閱讀英文的台灣歷史研究者參考的資料。

十五年後筆者的期望成為現實，二〇〇四年筆者受邀參與當時政府教育部所屬的「國立編

譯館」出版計劃而成為「青少年歷史文庫」的作者之一。筆者根據《馬偕日記》手稿和書信的原始史料加上翻譯 From Far Formosa 的內容編寫成為《來自遙遠的福爾摩沙》一書（本書在二〇〇六年出版），著作之餘筆者也希望能夠順便將 The Island Beautiful 翻譯成為中文，除此之外當時的筆者希望能夠繼續精進荷蘭文的閱讀翻譯能力（因為在前一年筆者才譯著出版一本名為《黃金時代：一個荷蘭船長的亞洲冒險》。一位曾經立足台灣的荷蘭船長相當具有文學意味的回憶錄），所以著手翻譯一六七五年荷蘭東印度公司駐台末代官揆一所撰寫的荷蘭文著作 't Verwaerloosde Formosa（中譯《被貽誤的台灣》），所以在那個時候的上班時間，筆者辦公桌上同時攤開這三本書，一下英文一下荷蘭文的翻譯和撰寫過程，讓現今回想仍感覺當時的企圖心實在驚人。後來，兩本英文著作寫作和翻譯完成，荷蘭文的部分翻譯到最後一章時，因筆者負笈前往美國密西根威士登神學院求學，加上沒有找到恰當的出版社，於是就中止翻譯工作一直到現在還沒有完成。倒是這本《美麗之島》在翻譯完成十數年後有機會出版，讓筆者感慨頗深。

《美麗之島》有一個孿生姊妹 Pak-pō Tâi-oân Ki-tok Tiⁿ-lô Kàu-hōe ê Lek-sú《北部台灣基督長老教會的歷史》，兩本書出現的時間都是為了紀念北部教會設立五十週年的目的而寫，只是一為加拿大教士會，而另一本為台灣基督徒的觀點，也因為如此而有其關注的焦點。對《美麗之島》而言，如何透過與日本政府合作來促進教會長老教會在北部台灣的發展，是本書寫作的基本出發點。當然作為一位加拿大的宣教師，劉忠堅牧師能夠更清楚詳細的以西方人的角度敘述馬偕以及後來服事宣教師的工作經驗，這是本地人所撰寫的歷史紀錄無法著墨之處。另外，

在撰寫本書之時，劉忠堅牧師已經在台服事至少十五年，因此對二十世紀初期的北部教會一定有相當程度的理解，甚至他可能利用本身的宣教學專業協助金包里教會，或苗栗大甲地區的教會發展。所以對北部教會的擴張有其親身參與的記憶，因此撰寫本書自然有其說服力和臨場感。說到這裡自然無法不對劉忠堅牧師，這位因大環境變遷而先後有機會參與北部和南部教會神學教育者的簡短介紹。

本書的作者劉忠堅牧師（Rev. Duncan MacLeod）是加拿大長老教會派駐台灣的宣教師，他在一九〇七年開始在台服事。他在一八七二年六月二日誕生於蘇格蘭，一九五七年過世於加拿大。他在台灣的服事根據吳清鎰牧師在《北部台灣基督長老教會九十週年史》的介紹可分為三個面向，也就是佈道、教會事務以及神學教育等。在佈道方面，由於他的台語講得非常好加上頗有辯才，是個不可多得的佈道人才。所以除了受邀前往北部各地教會佈道以外，他更成立「北部教會佈道團」，經常旅行各地作巡迴佈道的工作，該團的團員有：劉天來、楊彰、石安慎、呂芳全和郭先琴等人。再來，教會事務方面，他曾經擔任「北部教會傳道局」局長。所謂「傳道局」所掌管的業務基本上可分成兩部分，包括傳道師的聘派、以及教會紛爭問題的處理。根據教會實際運作的模式，傳道局可以說是掌握了北部教會內部運作動力的咽喉要津，可以說是了解北部教會的重要職務。神學教育方面，劉忠堅牧師曾經擔任台北和台南神學校校長的職位。他之所以能以加拿大長老教會宣教師的身分擔任台南神學校校長，與加拿大教會在一九二七年的巨大變革有關。一九二五年加拿大的衛理公會、公理會和佔三分之二比例的長老教會組成了「加拿大聯合教會」（United Church of Canada），而其他佔三分之一比例的長老教會

— 17 —

則因不支持聯合而延續原本的「加拿大長老教會」，雙方形成對立的緊張關係。恰巧那年贊成和參與「聯合教會」的劉忠堅牧師正帶領台北神學校學生在台南神學校上課，劉忠堅牧師也因歸屬聯合教會而失去長老教會宣教師的身分，並留在台南當地成為台南神學校的校長。一九三九年二戰爆發，在台灣的西方人全部被逐離台灣，也終止了劉忠堅牧師與台灣的關係。

正如先前所言，本書是作為北部教會設教五十週年的紀念，但是對劉忠堅牧師來說，本書撰寫的目的不僅止於複述歷史的過程而已，事實上他的問題，在於如何利用過去五十年的經驗與成果作為將來發展台灣教會的參考。換句話說，長老教會如何了解當時快速轉變的台灣社會並提出恰當的回應。基本上，本書可以分成三個主題，首先是對台灣地理與歷史的一般性介紹，這是十七世紀以來關於台灣的慣常性作法，由此顯見，儘管偶而有著作提及此處，這個地方對西方社會來講，一直是個陌生的所在。再來本書介紹了北部教會創立者馬偕牧師的傳記，加拿大教士會的發展以及北部教會在台灣極北地區、苗栗三義以及台中大甲地區設立教會的故事。在這個基礎之上，作者問：那將來呢？作為整本書的結束。從本書的結構和作者的意圖來看，歷史的回顧只是作為將來發展的註腳，作者的目光是望向未來的。因此若純粹以歷史敘述的角度閱讀本書，就無法掌握住本書的旨趣。然而，作者在最後一章所分析的問題對現在的教會來講仍是艱鉅的挑戰，廿一世紀的教會與基督徒是否有決心和能力解決呢？

（玉山神學院教會歷史助理教授）

原著推薦序 ◆ 公義的浪潮，閃耀福爾摩沙

偕彼得博士（Rev. R. P. Mackay D. D., 1892-1925）

馬偕牧師寫回母會的最後一個信息是，「基督是否會贏得台灣？」不管最後這個目標是用什麼方式達成，最後的勝利將會如同上帝存在那樣的確定。我堅定相信到時將會只有一種聲音高呼：「永遠讚美祂榮耀的名字，願全地都充滿祂的榮光，阿們。」

雖然這個目標還沒達成，但是北部台灣宣教五十禧年紀念日已經接近，過去五十年的歷史證明，馬偕博士的信心並沒有成為羞愧。福爾摩沙總有一天會充滿上帝的榮光。在這個需要拯救與榮耀的世界，福爾摩沙將如同明星閃耀天空。只要比較過去與現在的情況，就可以知道公義如同湧現的浪潮覆蓋全地，正如海洋覆蓋洋底一般。

馬偕登陸時，只有孤單一個人，沒有家庭朋友，生活在不友善的族群當中。基督教被當成是邪惡的儀式，而外國宣教師被稱為「番仔鬼」。找到切入點就好像攻打一座城市一般，《台灣遙寄》中「攻克艋舺」章節，生動描述一般人的態度和他所面臨的危險。當地人認為只要機會來臨就可盡情對外國人發洩仇恨和暴力，例如一八八四年法軍侵擾事件。如今一切都已經改變，官員友善，有些本身不是基督徒的人承認基督教的社會價值，因而協助基督教會的擴展。

—19—

書中歸信的感人故事裡，有一段故事提及一位官員邀請宣教師開設教會，因為他發現自己沒有能力壓制社會中邪惡的勢力。教會在這種情況下設立起來，而福音實在法律無法達成的目標。過去幾年台灣的教會不斷請求派遣更多宣教師，如今這三目標大多已經實現，成員獲得強化；而服務於教育和醫療機構裡的廿名外國宣教師，是由五○年前一粒種子培養出來的。這個結實纍纍的種子，獲得多倍的成長。希望將來在人事、設備和群眾的反應都能有良好果效，甚至異教徒也願意承認基督教比他們所知的宗教更好。

一九一九年霍亂肆虐期間，馬偕紀念醫院被政府徵用，基督徒和非基督徒都獲得一視同仁的治療，每天仍有許多人過世；值得注意的是，非基督徒儘管遵守指示卻仍難逃一死。基督徒在當時還被允許聚會，而其他宗教被禁止聚集。

雖然死亡迫在眉睫，但基督徒仍以欣然、自信和盼望的態度面對；而異教徒焦躁、恐懼、迷信的心情，而使得自己更暴露於險境之中。異教徒承認基督徒家庭氣氛比較快樂，不會有吸食鴉片和賭博的惡習，而周圍環境比較清潔衛生。在這種基礎之上，當百週年紀念之時，難道不會有豐富的收成？儘管目前有這些優勢，但是將來的發展仍取決於是否維持創建者和繼任者聖潔生活的品質而定。

對作者劉忠堅牧師來說，這卷書的撰述是出於愛心的作品，他的加拿大人性格，讓他比其他人更瞭解和欣賞馬偕博士與其他宣教師同工。

休假原本是休養生息，以及為將來工作預作準備，但令人遺憾的是宣教師的假期當中卻排滿難以拒絕的演講聚會，並且他們都是欣然以赴。

— 20 —

書中一系列恰當結束於每段篇章的禱文，是由加拿大宣教學校（Canadian Mission School）校長羅莫瑞牧師（Rev. J. Lovell Murray, D.D）所準備的，感激他為本書所增添的內容。

這些有趣故事的編輯和出版都是由樸李斯特牧師（Rev. H.C. Priest）負責，少有人能夠超越他的能力。樸牧師參與年輕人的宣教教育是廣為人知的事情，但是他在這本為年輕人準備的宣教文獻出版所做的貢獻卻少有人知道。藉著這些詳細和正確的編輯，本卷書已將教會置於更大的責任和使命當中。

（加拿大長老教會海外宣教委員會總幹事，1892-1925）

卷
一

第一章 ◆ 福爾摩沙：美麗之島

遙遠的過去有一些暴戾的龍群潛居於福州附近，經過長遠的世代甦醒了過來。中國地理風水師告訴人們，它們在一日的嬉戲之後，由不可見大洋的深淵滑行出來，到達現在的台灣，這時龍變得極端的活躍，鑽入地底深處，向上衝成為基隆頂端的懸崖，再一路翻滾，直到台灣尾。激烈的扭動形成一長列的高山與峻嶺，最後牠們拍擊巨大的龍尾，升起三個懸崖，形成台灣的最南端。

台灣自然風貌

座落於一片無止盡巨浪中的島嶼

台灣被葡萄牙水手們稱為福爾摩沙（意指美麗之島），他們是在十六世紀末首先拜訪台灣

的歐洲人。這個島嶼的形狀或許可以拿來和一顆造型奇特的西洋梨相比，特別在台灣南部，有著較長的果梗，看起來更形似。福爾摩沙這個島嶼座落於一片無止盡的巨浪、湍急的大海洋流且經常發生地震及暴虐的颱風中；地層經過千萬年活動之後，巴士海峽不斷擴大，將福爾摩沙這個島嶼與南方的群島隔離開來。

這座島嶼位於中國東南沿海，形貌南北狹長，隔著台灣海峽與歐亞大陸相望，北端寬約一百四十四公里、南部三百廿二公里。從廈門（古稱 Amoy）搭船到台灣約廿四小時，從香港來台則需時三天，從日本的門司港（十九世紀時是日本的國家港口）來台也需時三天的航程。

早期的台灣被歸屬於琉球群島，也曾經以此命名著稱於世。許多世代以來中國人稱這個島為台灣（意為由台地構成的海灣），這個名稱令人與「東番」聯想在一起。或許也因如此，荷蘭人向來稱呼島上的人為「東印度番」。

在台灣島嶼的西部海岸九十七公里外，陳列著六十三個島嶼的群島，稱為漁翁群島（澎湖群島）。台灣東邊也有一些島嶼，當中的兩個島嶼住著漢族殖民者，以及占有人口三分之一較為原始的人種，群島人民的智力以及異教崇拜的熱切度比台灣本島的原住民更低。

台灣長近四百公里，寬約一百四十公里，擁有一千一百卅九公里的海岸線，總面積有三萬六千一百九十三平方公里。大約等於半個蘇格蘭的面積，稍微大於溫哥華島，是安大略湖的兩倍大。台灣三分之二的面積是屬於絕美的山脈地形景觀，形成一列由北到最南端，形勢壯觀連續不斷的山脈，這些多山的區域自有歷史紀錄以來就與「獵頭族」的惡名有關，其他的三分之一是南北走向狹長可供耕種的土地，寬度從卅二公里到四十八公里不等，這些土地在過去三、

三百年來被漢人的殖民者所占據。這些沖積平原的地勢由山腳逐漸向外擴充沉降，成為西部沿海附近的低矮平原，最後沉入海中。

台灣內陸地勢陡然升高，成為相續不絕的山脈地形，地形不斷的往上爬升，直到高度超過近四千公尺的最高峰，之後山脈地形陡然下降，直到太平洋浪濤拍擊到的峭壁為止。許多旅行家以各種方式描述台灣這個島嶼壯麗的懸崖景觀，詹伯藍教授（Professor Chamberlain）在《日本事情》（*Things Japanese*）如此描述：

台灣東岸的懸崖是世界上最高和最為垂直的峭壁，由水平面陡然聳立一千八百廿八公尺的高度，景觀是少見的美麗，由岸邊直到山頂，可以見到大小的森林，各樣的灌木與草叢，這些植物生長極為茂盛。有些地方可見到坍方的山壁，當原住民狩獵水鹿和野豬時，很少有他們找不到的路徑或是立足之處。

高聳的山脈

在島嶼內陸那些高聳的山脈之上、位於北回歸線附近，矗立著海拔高達近四千公尺的「新高山」（或稱馬禮遜山，今玉山）是台灣的最高峰。很少人能夠登頂，沿路地勢除了非常危險、以及原住民出沒的關係以外，當時攀登玉山需要龐大的日本警衛隊伍隨行保護，所以旅行的花費實在太高。一年當中的大部分時間，山頂都被冰雪覆蓋。

伴隨著高聳山脈的是深谷和湍急溪流——台灣的地形也不例外。當旅行者站在山頂，眼前所見的是伸展直到天邊的寬闊景象以及高聳的山嶺，這都是大自然之母靈巧雕飾的作品；山間飛濺的瀑布，低深的山谷，風景秀異的草地分佈在低矮的山腰間，四周包圍著綠色竹叢或原始森林。

天然的湖泊

台灣只有若干湖泊，當中最著名的是甘治土湖（今稱日月潭），用以紀念荷蘭來台的第一位宣教師[1]。這座淡水湖泊位居台灣中部風景最美麗的地方，海拔六百零九公尺高，由於電力開發設計畫，台灣政府於一九一八年進行一項規模龐大的工程，在上方開鑿運河，引導附近溪水流入湖泊，升高水位十八公尺；由於湖泊和底下的山谷三公里的距離就有大約三百公尺的高度落差，因此可以藉此高度興建巨大的發電廠，生產的電力足夠供應全台的照明和電力使用。

湖泊之外已有一條鐵路通車（今稱集集線），因此開發的腳步可向內延伸直到原住民聚居的區域。

具傷害力的颱風

台灣以其週期的颱風聞名於世。有很多人把這個擁有巨大破壞力的災難歸因於台灣造成的——然而事實卻剛好相反。台灣超過三百多公里綿延的山脈，經常會絆住直撲中國沿海的颱風，讓它們由北轉西或南方，奇特且奧妙的阻擋住颱風的行進路線，因而讓颱風消失，但台灣

人焦慮舉目所見的卻是颱風肆虐後留下的大量殘骸、山中瘋狂的急流以及淹水的平原[2]。在颱風之後，台北盆地經常成為一片汪洋，而台北市變成了一座漂浮於其中的島嶼，湍急的山溪漫過堤防，沖走橋梁和稻田，因此台灣政府一直努力於嘗試要利用鉅額的經費去保護人民生命財產的安全，以減輕這些颱風所帶來的災害。一九二〇年，台北經歷到四十年來最嚴重的淹水，整個盆地包括教會的建築都浸泡在約一公尺深的水中，房屋浸水之後，當地居民搭著竹筏，搜索被水漂走的身家財產。而日本警察則是忙碌的拯救災戶並將他們送往安全的地區，而醫院的守衛站在及腰的水中，手裡抱著豬隻，努力將他寶貴的財產鎖入醫院樓上的浴室中，想等到積水消退才去進行救援災民的工作，這種把動物（財產）看得比人還寶貴的想法（在其他國家會受到鄙視），在台灣很常見。

頻繁的地震

台灣位於日本和菲律賓島列當中，接近地震帶中心，因此經常發生地震。這裡的地震很少令居民驚慌或是帶來嚴重的災害，但在數個月以前——當時筆者尚未到台灣——一個非常強烈的地震襲擊位於中台灣的嘉義市，造成許多房屋的損毀和人命的死傷。而當年夏天，另一個地震也發生在北台灣，造成了更嚴重的傷害[3]。日本當時著手進行地震學研究，歐洲頂尖學者受到日本政府邀約，前去進行地震現象的觀察。研究的成果也為日本全國的建築和營造業帶來許多幫助，而我們的教會也因此獲益不少。因為所有的教會建物興建之時，都將會使用更有效的方法來確保教堂的安全。雖然會花費較多的經費，但是最終的結果會發現這是一個比較經濟

的做法，並且可以免除一般地震日後造成損害的憂慮。

溼熱的氣候

台灣的天氣類型差異很大，從潮濕、嚴寒、寒冷到極熱的天氣都有。除了高山以外，大部分地區都不會降雪或結冰，整體來說，台灣的天氣整年潮濕炎熱。北部的天氣與南部極為不同。北台灣一到三月是涼爽的冬天，而南部在這段時間是最理想的好天氣。六月到九月，整個島嶼都是極為炎熱的天氣，而十月到十二月是比較溫和舒適的天氣。冬天的平均氣溫是攝氏十度，夏天是攝氏廿九度，但是因為空氣比較潮濕，所以比起空氣乾燥的地區，台灣的夏天令人更難忍受。但是有許多宣教師或是生意人，住在這裡已經卅年到四十年不等的時間，因此這裡的氣候也許真的不是那麼令人難以忍受。為了躲開夏天極端炎熱的天氣，宣教師們都會搬到山上的木屋居住，那裡距離海平面約六百公尺，而加拿大長老教會的住宅距離淡水或台北只有二到三小時的車程而已。夏季別墅對於宣教師們（特別是對他們的妻子和小孩）極有助益。

瘴癘疾病

容易造成各種流行的疫病中，以「瘧疾」讓所有外國人感到最棘手[4]。瘧蚊是這種疾病的傳播者，除了特別喜歡叮咬未曾感染過瘧疾的人，對於其他曾感染過的對象也一視同仁。在日本政府的努力之下，感染瘧疾的死亡率降低許多。如今除了少數沼澤地區外，這個疾病已經不再是台灣人生活和工作的障礙。

危害建物的白蟻

白蟻是宣教師無法忽視的問題。為什麼要浪費時間在這些蟲害身上？那是因為它們比其他所知的生物更有效率的破壞宣教師的時間和財產。它們最具破壞性，但卻最不引起人們注意。它們不分晝夜，安靜而隱密的在地下或地面進行破壞工作，對於高貴的建物或最好的宅第也毫不客氣。

這些看起來蒼白，柔弱和簡單的生物，本領實在驚人。它們似乎很能用非常奧妙的方法探知目標的置放地點。先由一位領袖找到路徑（它們能夠輕易的通過混凝土地基缺口，穿過木頭或甚至堅厚的灰泥），一旦有一隻白蟻打開通路，那麼隨之而來的是整個的族群，安靜但卻是源源不絕的向著攻擊的目標邁進。精準的在地板上鑽洞進入箱子、書桌、飯桌的腳柱，或是五斗櫃當中。顯然這群白蟻的領袖能夠自信的指揮其他白蟻熟練的進行破壞工程。當整群白蟻離開之後，成為空殼的家具就是它們工作的成果。台灣政府已經利用許多年的時間仔細的研究這些極具效率的小生物，試圖找出何種化學物質或油脂能夠有效的防止白蟻的破壞。雖然本地人由經驗學會如何有限度防止白蟻的破壞，但這些白蟻也已經對宣教師的房子造成嚴重和複雜的問題。

母會的海外宣道委員會必須瞭解，這三大自然的毀滅性力量，如白蟻、颱風和地震，在無法完全克服的情況下，興建一座堅固的建築物是唯一明智的方向。

豐富的農產品

台灣的農產品非常豐富，一年當中有兩次的稻米收成，這些收成當中有數百萬蒲式耳（bushel）稻米出口到日本去，自從日本占領台灣之後，稻田灌溉渠道的興建有很大的進展。

重要的產品包括樟腦、甘蔗、茶葉、小米、玉米、大麥、各式的馬鈴薯、靛藍植物（主要用於藍染）、豌豆、豆子、花生、麻、黃麻以及其他的纖維植物。主要的水果有柑橘、香蕉、柚子、柿子、鳳梨、梅子、桃子、芒果以及其他許多只有台灣本地才能長成的植物。

樟腦王國

台灣的樟腦生產可以追溯到二百年前，是現今最有價值的產業，全世界的樟腦產量有超過百分之九十從這個島嶼中產出。當漢人移民的先祖用好奇的目光發現了樟樹的原始森林之後，這個製品的生產就此開始。因此在很久以前，台灣就知道提煉樟腦的技術，不久後，較為善戰的客家人從中國南方移民到此，他們先選擇靠近「獵頭族」邊界——狹長而未經開墾的山地種植茶葉、甘蔗、蕃薯以及水稻，這些具有開創能力以及健壯的客家人就在此從事樟腦的提煉工

作。

5. 許多世代以來，客家人壓迫原住民遷往內山，因此與原住民鄰居結成世仇。所以有許多漢人成為「被獵頭」的對象，原住民可以潛伏在淺山地區數日之久，直到狩獵獲得成果為止。他們拔出配在腰間的番刀迅速斬斷受難者首級，然後驕傲的帶著象徵成功和英勇的戰利品回去番社，而客家人也逐漸成為這種狩獵遊戲的專家，他們也會偷偷潛入山裡，報復襲擊原住民，帶回來的不是頭顱，而是整個身體，然後滿足的舉行歡宴來享用原住民。當年他們相信原住民的肉是最為滋補的聖品，有許多客家傳道師還記得當時的食肉經驗。[6] 客家人的土地不斷擴張，也擁有許多原本法律上屬於原住民土地的永佃權，由於這些殖民者肆無忌憚的砍倒樟樹，因此日本政府決議將樟腦的生產收為政府的專賣事業。樟樹提煉樟腦油的方法簡單但是非常有趣，所需的器械並不昂貴，提煉的工人首先利用鋸子和斧頭砍倒樹木，拿出半圓形的短柄斧頭，交叉的刨下木片，然後放入蒸餾鍋中。汽化上升的樟腦油通過管子，進入冷卻作用的桶子裡，進行純化成為結晶，如同灰白色的冰霜一般。未經加工的樟腦放入缸中沉澱提煉樟腦油。提煉完成結晶狀的樟腦丸裝袋，而樟腦油裝入罐子送往台北的工廠。為了永續發展所需，日本人也進行樟樹大規模的造林運動，因此台灣似乎將來仍然會是世界上樟腦生產的領先之地。

台灣糖業

蔗糖的生產是在十六世紀時由漢族的殖民者率先開始的，史料顯示十七世紀荷蘭統治時期獲得極大的進展，後來中國首位統治者國姓爺家族，也非常鼓勵甘蔗的種植。在日本專家規劃

之下，製糖事業已經成為這個島嶼最為興旺的工業之一。日本的製糖公司快速增加，並有許多土地變成甘蔗種植農場。有鑑於此，當時的台灣政府頒佈法律，保護台灣私人的農業對抗那些不公義的強勢私人企業[7]。有許多龐大的製糖工廠配備最為先進的英國機器，而外國專家被分派到企業營利最豐厚的部門當中。在山上，可以發現仍然有少數客家人經營較為古老和原始的糖廍，這種甘蔗粗製工廠是由水牛所推動的鐵滾輪榨取蔗糖。由漢人原始的製糖方法發展到現代化的日本蔗糖工廠過程，可以看到日本人的企業精神。

茶葉文化

台灣最早種植茶葉的人是漢人的移民，而最為普遍的茶種是烏龍茶，第一位發現這個茶種價值的歐洲人是鄔和先生（又譯斯文豪、史溫侯）[8]，他是淡水的英國領事。一八六七年第一艘裝載著台灣茶葉的船隻開往美國，最初的茶葉出口都是掌握在英國、美國和中國茶商手中，但是後來幾年日本人也進入這個行業競爭。他們嘗試（但是沒有成功）發展綠茶的貿易，也有許多家工廠，最大的是三井公司，從事紅茶的貿易。之後，台灣農民對茶葉的生產缺乏興趣，他們發展別種生計，因種植別種農產品會有比較高的利潤。農民也發現，由於台灣的茶葉中間商不需要負擔茶葉的種植成本，因此中間商獲得極高的利潤；但也在這種情況下，農民也聽說在台灣經商超過六十年以上的英國（或美國）茶葉公司，一直擁有「以公道價格收購茶葉和誠實經商」的名聲，內心頗感欣慰。筆者經常聽見農民感嘆，如果華人貿易商能擁有和外國商人一樣的公道和榮譽心，那麼農民們就沒什麼好抱怨了。

鴉片毒癮

阿拉伯商旅在第九世紀將鴉片帶進中國，十二世紀時，從印度載運鴉片的帆船進入中國大陸，十九世紀中葉，中國被迫開放口岸以允許鴉片進口。漢人殖民者也將鴉片和吸食的習性帶進台灣。日本占領台灣時，本地有百分之七的人口是鴉片煙的吸食者。

政府經過一段時間研議後，對於如何在將來治療毒癮患者這個問題，決定引進照照制度，以便逐漸禁絕人們去吸食鴉片。在那之前仍會繼續發給吸食鴉片執照，一旦過渡時期結束之後，就不會再發鴉片吸食執照。因此，之後隨著吸食者的過世，吸食鴉片的人口也將逐漸減少。儘管有嚴厲的管制（只要有人無照吸食鴉片，都會面臨監禁或是鉅額罰款的下場），但台灣仍然有許多人吸食鴉片。

台灣的鴉片市場是隸屬於政府當中一個利益豐厚的專賣部門。當時只能期望未來國家進步後，激發道德的覺醒而產生強烈的公共意見，讓政府部門知道「販賣鴉片的不可行」，以致最終完全禁絕鴉片的吸食。雖然中國自一九一七年起，吸食鴉片成為非法的事，但中國政府卻沒有能力去執行這道法律，鴉片煙田也不斷出現在這個廣大共和國，雖然還是可以見到「禁絕鴉片」一些令人鼓舞的行動，但是不幸的是，鴉片被英國和美國人大量煉成嗎啡之後，仍賣給日本人走私進入中國。

阻絕任何型式的鴉片流通已經成為國際上的重要議題，並在海牙和華盛頓會議當中被討論。經過各方努力之後，禁絕鴉片流通的《米勒法案》（Miller Bill）在美國國會通過。在國際聯盟（League of Nations）鴉片流通顧問委員會努力之下，獲得鴉片生產國的保證：「鴉片種植的

数量只能夠供應在醫療的用途」。世界各國也樂意看見日本洗刷名聲污點，讓一般人除了醫學用途以外，沒有辦法用其他方法去取得任何的毒品來源。

香菸殘害

台灣的菸草工業已經是政府的專賣事業。或許人們花在香菸的金錢要比吸食鴉片最嚴重的時期還多。人民不分男女，日人或台人都染上這個習慣，有些人受香菸惡魔的轄制就如同那些吸食鴉片成癮的人一樣。而西方各國就如同住在玻璃屋當中，不敢對日本投擲石塊。西方的菸草和香菸公司竭盡所能的在中國努力進行貿易活動，而台灣極有效率的政府專賣制度也將這些菸商關在門外。然而，人們在這個過程當中，對於道德和身體健康的傷害，卻一點也沒有受到阻攔與影響。

傲人的礦產

台灣除了在農業的生產之外，也擁有相當傲人、豐富且寶貴的礦產資源。

豐富的煤礦

在台灣可以找到極為豐富的煤礦資源，這是一種新形式的資源，雖然大部分都是以家庭用為主，但是煤礦卻更適合當作汽船、工業生產以及發電之用，豐富的煤礦使得台灣各地興建發電廠，等到原住民居住的區域被完整探查之後，有可能在未知的高山當中，可以發現更大的

煤礦礦藏資源。

著名的海盜——國姓爺鄭成功——深知煤礦的價值，但迷信的漢人卻拒絕挖掘土地，因害怕冒犯沉睡於地底的惡魔而干擾了一般無辜的居民，所以連帶反對雞籠港（今基隆）附近第一座煤礦的發掘。文章一開始說了，千百年前，那些喜好運動的巨龍，歡鬧滑行離開福州港，潛入台灣海峽之中，而讓長滿龍角的頭困在北山之下，一路狂野痛苦的扭轉身體，向上升起而形成現今台灣崇高的山脈，成為如今這座美麗島嶼的背脊。事實上，現存大部分煤礦的所有權人都是台灣人那麼愚蠢、迷信、妥協」的日本政府所主導。台灣煤礦工業的發展是由「從來不像台灣人，且第一次世界大戰時期，台灣生產的煤礦也遠銷到遠東每一個港口。

蘊藏天然氣與石油

這座島嶼也蘊藏有天然氣與石油，但是當時沒有進一步去加以開發。三年以前，台北近郊有一群鑿井工人挖到天然氣礦脈，有一位迷信的老婦人懼怕地底世界的毒氣從那裡傾洩而出，就拿一疊紙錢放在洞口，點火祈求神明保佑——顯然她的祈禱沒有獲得神明垂聽，因為紙錢點燃了天然氣歿及老婦人頭髮，若非這群鑿井工人的解救，老婦人早已喪命。台灣的石油被一位美國人在苗栗縣發現到，有幾口日本公司的油井在開採，而同一地點生產的天然氣也作為油井的動力來源。台灣這裡的石油品質不如西方國家，或許是因為欠缺較好的煉油技術之緣故。

大屯山溫泉

在北部台灣的大屯山脈附近，發現許多溫泉，從台北市搭乘火車，可以在半小時之內到達大眾化的北投旅館，每日有數百人在那裡享受溫泉浴。

挖掘黃金

儘管台灣東部金礦的發掘已經有相當的成果，但是花蓮平原上性情難料的獵頭族原住民的出現，使得金礦挖掘成為一份冒險的事業。台灣黃金的主要產地在基隆附近，早期有許多人蜂擁前往台灣的「金山」（Klondyke）挖掘金礦，這股熱潮雖然已經消褪，但是金礦的挖掘工作仍在進行當中，也生產相當數量的黃金。如同世界其他國家一樣，黃金的發現會帶來地理自然環境，經濟以及人性道德上的敗壞。

這個地區有許多各式各樣災難的故事，流傳在日本和漢人的年輕人當中。

貿易與工業

十九世紀末期，台灣的貿易和工業快速的發展。當年基隆港有著無比的重要性，因為大量的出口以及轉口物資都是經過這個海港才完成的貿易。

以上我們簡單介紹台灣這座島嶼的美景、地理位置上主要的風貌以及自然資源。這些內容實在有趣，但是我們主要關注的焦點是在於「如何促進台灣這座島嶼與基督王國的關係」，因台灣尚不是等待上帝律法的島嶼。早先那些勇敢的旅行者，沿著這個海島的海岸航行，瞥見島嶼的山巔、模糊的瀑布以及彎曲的台地平原，用極為驚訝的聲音大聲喊出：「美麗之島，美麗之島！」難道我們這些較晚到達的人，不能也同這個時代的先知一樣，用相同的話語來讚美這座島嶼？當台灣人民成為基督的跟隨者、當「連千萬人中最微小的人」能夠知曉上帝的美善時、當基督教思想普遍且深入影響人心時，台灣就真的可以被稱為「美麗之島」！

禱告詞

噢！上帝我們豐盛的造物主，請接納我們為這個美好世界向祢獻上的感恩，祢將我們放在其中，讓我們透過對美麗的感受來認識祢，祢的一切受造者都讚美，我們雙眼由祢手指所形塑一切奇妙歡喜與美好的事物，得到愉悅的感受，也要向祢表達我們愛的禮讚。

願世界上所有尚未認識祢──特別是福爾摩沙島上的人民都能夠知道──是祢為了自己的緣故創造他們，也只能藉由祢拯救的功效，才能將一切醜陋與混亂的罪惡移開，讓上帝形象的榮光照耀而成為他們自己的一部分，當他們張開雙眼和心靈，看見上帝知識的榮耀顯現在耶穌基督的面容，願祢聖潔的美善進入他們生命當中。

噢！主耶穌基督願祢允許，祢的信息在美麗之島上廣傳，祢的靈快速的在生命與生命之間流通，直到整座島嶼閃耀著祢的美麗與聖潔，並且綻放在屬祢的花園當中。為了祢自己的名，允許這一切蒙應允。阿們。

第二章 ◆ 台灣人，統治者與宗教

台灣島上的居民屬於什麼族群？他們的歷史和宗教又為何？（這些問題一旦被提出，在進入宣教工作的主題以前必須先回答。）無疑地，首先進入我們腦海的就是台灣的原住民。

....

原居於台灣的民族

....

多樣的福爾摩沙人

台灣島上的原住民可以分為三個主要族群：

第一個族群稱為「生番」或是「青番」：他們因為獵首的習性而聞名於世，他們又可劃分為九族。各族在風俗和語言有相當程度的差異。

第二個族群是由「阿美族」和「南勢番」所組成：他們活動的區域是台灣東海岸的花蓮港

和卑南平原，屬於半文明的社會，他們在日本人統治台灣後從事的是農業耕作。

第三個族群稱為「平埔番」或是「熟番」：這個族群已經相當文明。儘管部分族群的平埔族曾在荷蘭統治時期接觸基督教，但大部分人都是受到現代文明洗禮之後才接受基督教福音。英國長老教會在南部的平埔番（或熟番）的佈教工作有比較大的發展。台灣北部的平埔族在馬偕博士時代就已經接受福音。後來這些接受基督教的平埔族隨著社會政治的變遷因而迅速消逝，倖存下來的族人也因為與漢人通婚，而逐漸被漢化。

迷霧般的起源

原住民的起源向來隱身於迷霧之中，現存的文獻並沒有告訴我們究竟是哪一個族群？有些族群宣稱他們的祖先是來自菲律賓島嶼的「矮黑人」（Negritos），也有部分族群受到傳統理論的影響，意即他們祖先原居南方島嶼，因為遭遇颱風而來到台灣。台灣島上族群複雜，風俗、傳說和語言各異的現象，目前仍是民族學者難以解答的問題。或許比較保險一點的說法就是島上原住民族混雜著蒙古族（原始馬來族）和印度尼西亞族的血液。無庸置疑的，一波波向北移民的南方族群到達本島定居，他們占領菲律賓到日本南部島嶼的廣大區域——部分的證據顯示，他們與日本南部的島民有著血統上的關係。無論如何，日本與台灣在史前時代就有所接觸，因為早期就有歷史記錄了日本海盜騷擾太平洋沿岸的島嶼居民，最南到澳門，因此不難推斷他們怎會獨漏這個大島於不顧？

— 41 —

原住民的自我孤立和殘酷的行為

雖然我們沒有確切的紀錄可以說明原住民最初與外界接觸的情形，但是有大量的考古資料證明，這些族群自古以來就已經習於互相殺伐。他們一致頑強的抵抗外來政治或勢力的介入，無論是日本、中國、英國以及美國，只要在台灣岸邊遭遇風浪強烈的船難，那些不幸的船員不管是遭遇凶猛的海浪或是殘暴的原住民，都只有極少數人能夠倖存於世。截至目前為止，外人尚未在原住民族當中進行宣教工作。多年來，台灣南北兩個教會不斷呼籲在英國和加拿大的母會，重視這個最為急迫的任務——傳揚福音給台灣這些原住民族，將是我國（加拿大）勇敢年輕人的一項艱鉅的挑戰。

荷蘭統治時期

一六二四年，荷蘭東印度公司占領台灣，荷蘭人對於殖民地的政策，不僅僅是派出長官來管理行政以及政治的事務而已，他們也派出宣教師來照顧本地人在宗教上的需要。一六二七年，荷蘭首位宣教師甘治士牧師到達台灣，他是第一位在台灣傳揚基督教信仰的傳道人。十七世紀前半期，西班牙和葡萄牙神父曾經嘗試進入台灣宣教，卻徒勞無功。荷蘭東印度公司主要

的目的是為荷蘭共和國在東方建立貿易據點，於是他們很快就發現宣教師具有重要影響力，之後，荷蘭當地教會與國家的政策就成為在台灣推行的政策。

在台宣教師卓著的成果

這些宣教師傳福音的成果極為卓著，荷蘭統治台灣的卅七年間，有超過卅位宣教師以及學校教師被派來台灣，他們使用特別為較原始的民族編著而成的教理問答，進行講道和教育的工作[1]。他們也將語言抄錄成羅馬字，藉著這個方法來教育部分的本地人可以閱讀和寫字[2]。有些本地年輕人甚至進一步學會荷蘭文。宣教師也要求在地居民於禮拜天穿著荷蘭服裝，以及遵守其他相關規定。

撤台後，教會的銷聲匿跡

「沒有辦法在道德上帶來長遠的改革」是荷蘭在台宣教師苦惱的根源。雖然尤羅伯牧師（Rev. Robert Junius）在台宣教期間帶動的變革使他獲得當局的讚美，但值得關注的是，荷蘭官方後來宣稱，在他回去不久後，台灣有數個部落起來反抗荷蘭的統治[3]。荷蘭人被鄭成功趕出台灣數個月之後，原本在原住民當中的教會與學校隨之銷聲匿跡。原住民受到漢人殖民者以及鄭成功士兵們的鼓勵，移除了所有西方宗教的遺跡，數位宣教師以及學校教師遭到悲慘的命運，他們當中至少有三個人被釘死在十字架上[4]。兩百年後（一八六五年），當第一位英國長老教會宣教師到達台灣所發現的早期荷蘭教會的遺跡，也只有手上的幾本書而已[5]。

他們為何失敗

宣教失敗、教會消失的原因，我們可以進一步解釋，至少有部分原因是因為荷蘭教會在台灣的作法所導致的結果。第一點，他們將西方教會與國家體制移植到這些「頭腦簡單」的民族上，這就是一個錯誤。因為大部分時候都是政治的旗幟上打著教會的名字，而不是以福音對原住民進行道德上的勸服——雖然強迫原住民改變了行為，也懲罰他們拜偶像之事，但事實上，在東印度公司的殖民統治下，只不過是荷蘭政府強制推行政務的機構而已。荷蘭宣教師的身分不僅是耶穌福音的宣揚者，同時他們也是荷蘭政府的官員，也受巴達維亞（今雅加達，位於印尼爪哇島）總部的政府官員所督導，這實在是政治組織利用基督教會作為教化工具的典型例證，而政治組織的目的只是要進行貿易的擴張而已。宣教師對原住民的教育除了教導基督教真理之外，也有傳授稻米種植技術以及其它粗淺的的手工藝製作。無疑的，若不是因為和國家權力有所牽連，此一政策將有效促進福音的傳播。著名的博物學家華萊士先生（Alfred Russel Wallace），在他去荷屬馬來半島旅行的時候，曾經針對這個主題撰寫一篇長文，並驚喜的發現宣教師在這些落後族群上的工作成果非常顯著；然而，在給予這些高度肯定的同時，他也批評荷蘭政府的統治是「父權式專制制度」（parental despotism）[6]。

其次，有些宣教師讓自己變成貿易商，他們的薪俸是由自己經手的稅金所支付，而烈酒和菸草的津貼由巴達維亞送去。他們也掌管每年發給漢族獵人狩獵執照的事務。再來，他們浪費寶貴時間去追逐獵物，因為這個誘惑力真的很大——每一位宣教師可以擁有三隻獵犬，每一位教師有二隻[7]，因此可以推斷，他們用於狩獵的時間要高於宣教工作。

第三，其中由荷蘭派來的宣教師有道德瑕疵，有些犯過者被判刑入獄，有些人送回國。

就算已經文明的族群也會有犯罪的事情發生，但如果根據這些原住民傳統的法律，犯過者必須要面對極為嚴厲的刑罰。不過日本官員也承認，有些獵頭族利用夜色突擊殺光該地區所有日本人的那些殘暴行徑，實在要歸因於自己士兵的行為不檢。這些與宣教師身分不相稱的事件不僅讓原住民懷疑這些宗教領導者的動機，也相當程度的解消了原住民原本認為「荷蘭人在宗教上很敬虔」的印象，甚至開始不信任。

第四，荷蘭的宣教師當中，整個村莊的歸信就像個人信仰告白一樣普遍。事實上，不論在任何地方，集體歸信都連帶著巨大又沉重的危險——拯救是個別而非群體的事情，那些對洗禮的水過於隨便的人，往往要喝下自己因悔改而流下苦澀的淚水。荷蘭結束統治以前，那些宣教師還沒有擺脫教會與國家的枷鎖，這種制度在西方的世界都無法幫助使人們獲得靈性的自由了，更何況是在這個更原始的台灣呢？

鄭成功與清領時期

如今，台灣的人口大部分是漢人，與台灣首度的接觸也要追溯到數個世紀之前。荷蘭人到

台灣以前，一些比較勇敢的清朝商人和獵人就已經與台灣西部海岸上半文明的原住民有來往，而台灣與清政府在政治上的關係，則是要到一六六二年才建立——那一年，鄭成功把荷蘭人趕離台灣。但隨著荷蘭人教化台灣的影響，有數千人渡過海峽到台灣開墾建立基地。

國姓爺的到達

大約在一六六一年，由於韃靼的入侵，使得中國局勢陷入極度的不安和混亂當中。著名的中國海盜國姓爺（鄭成功，母親是日本人，父親是中國一位偉大的戰士），堅拒與中國統治者（滿清王朝）和談，因為他的父親在滿清手中被羞辱對待過。他曾幾度在戰場上獲勝，但是南京之役因為寡不敵眾而戰敗，於是率領勇敢的部下逃往鄰近的廈門。

由於他在中國的處境日漸危殆，因此開始和台灣的漢族拓墾者秘密接觸，在一六六二年的某一天清晨，有三百艘中國船載運二萬五千名士兵，在熱蘭遮城要求該城堡人民投降。荷蘭官員、士兵、宣教師以及教師英勇抵抗，九個月之後被迫投降，史書所記，很少人曾遭遇比那些勇敢的荷蘭人更悲慘的命運。宣教師蒙受最嚴厲的苦難，甚至在他們曾極力協助的原住民手下遭難。[8] 國姓爺並沒有長久享受他的勝利，他死於一六六三年。

福佬與客家人

隨著鄭成功的入台，成千上萬的漢族殖民者湧入台灣。移民的浪潮持續數個世代，最初來到的是福建南部廈門一帶的人，他們被稱為福佬人並講廈門話。稍晚進來的是來自廣東省北部

— 46 —

汕頭一帶的人。這些人稱為客家人，說客家話。日本人在一八九五年占領台灣時，島上漢人統計的數目是三百萬人。

從鄭成功死亡的一六六三年算起，直到一八九五年日本統治台灣為止，是一段漢番鬥爭、漢人分類械鬥以及民變不斷的血腥時期，9，島上毫無秩序而且沒有一個穩定的政府，這也是馬偕博士一八七二年登陸台灣北部時的真實景況。

日本統治時期

日荷在台

日本統治了台灣，但引發日本人占領台灣的原因實在是有趣。

我們必須要瞭解，中國人在法律上並不能宣稱擁有台灣的主權，鄭成功是個海盜，他是在「沒有法律依據以及進行補償」的情況下占領這座島的。日本併吞琉球群島之後，台灣在地理上更接近日本；在這之前，日本人與台灣人之間並沒有正式的接觸。根據紀錄，當荷蘭人登陸台灣時，他們發現一群日本人定居在台灣南部，並且宣稱擁有該島的主權。因此荷蘭人只向他們要求「一頭牛的牛皮能遮蓋的土地」，日本人對於荷蘭人如此謙卑的請求都感到意外，因此

同意所請。於是，荷蘭人取出一隻大水牛的牛皮，將牛皮切成長條狀，連結起來成為一條長線，圍起來的面積足夠興建熱蘭遮城10。這個故事敘述了日本人當時離開台灣時是多麼厭惡荷蘭人。因而定居下來的荷蘭人就開始發展台灣這個殖民地。

這時開始，日本貿易商開始對台灣產生了興趣，但是雙方尚未發生任何有關政治上的爭端。一八七一年十二月，馬偕登陸南台灣，一艘由琉球出發的日本船在台灣南部海岸發生船難，船上大部分船員遭到原住民殺害，只有少數人逃脫。當災難消息傳到日本後，日本要求清政府賠償，但是清政府卻回答「對於台灣島上還未降服的原住民，沒有法律上的管轄權。」一八七三年，又發生一起類似的船難，日本政府決定親自懲罰原住民，這個態度的轉變幾乎使兩國發生戰爭，但是最後清朝政府退讓，同意賠償日本遠征軍出擊台灣所支出的費用，並且承諾嚴格管理台灣南部的原住民族群。

併吞琉球

一八七九年發生的事件加深了清政府與日本的裂痕。先前琉球群島向清日兩國納貢，後來琉球決定不再向日本納貢，於是遭到日本政治上的攻擊而被併吞。這件事情讓清朝政府非常惱怒。恰巧當時的美國總統格蘭特將軍（General Grant）正訪問日本，於是在他的協調下，獲得有利於日本的安排，而清朝政府則被迫再吞下一顆列強瓜分下給她的苦藥。

清政府割讓台灣

台灣政治史中，最重要的事件發生在一八九五年，清政府和日本再度發生衝突。那一次是與亞瑟港（今旅順）和威海衛的情況有關，日本準備派遣遠征隊南征並前往澎湖群島（這個地方被認為是台灣軍事的鎖鑰），清政府聽說日本占據這些要塞之後，便與日本展開和談協商，談判的結果是簽訂《馬關條約》，內容規定將台灣以及澎湖割讓給日本，而條約文本在一八九五年四月十八日於基隆港外的日本軍艦上簽訂。戰勝國日本藉著精明和自信的外交手腕，在很短的時間內崛起，並躋身於世界主要強權國之一。得到台灣之後，日本不斷周旋，讓自己在東西方的國際社會中建立了高度的政治威望。

福爾摩沙人的反抗

條約的簽署是一件簡單的事情，但是要安定島上因為清政府怯懦的作為而激憤的島民，那就不是一件簡單的事情。然而日本人並沒有因島民全面性的反抗而畏縮，他們的軍隊安然登陸，並且在極短的時間內占據台灣北部，再往南推進直到舊府城（台南）。一年之內，島上的漢人差不多已全部歸順，但客家所在的地區性反抗持續一段時間，最後的一次反抗是發生在一九一三年，鎮壓之後有將近一百名客家人被砍頭。根據日本官方的聲明，基督徒與這些地區性的反抗行動沒有關連。

— 49 —

理蕃政策

日本政府仍然面對了一個艱鉅的任務，那就是要綏靖人數超過十萬並且居住在深山中的獵頭族原住民。那些尚未順服的原住民族，自數千年來就一直是台灣這塊土地的主人，他們先前未曾受過道德勸化或是被武力所降服過，反倒是激烈地抵抗侵占他們土地的入侵者。日本軍事總部針對「最好的壓制方法」產生了極大的歧見，有些日本軍認為這些原住民並不是人類，然而最後仍是「頭腦清楚以及有人性的看法」占上風，因此日本逐步以武力占領加上外交的協調，使得原住民逐漸的降服。在這當中，有許多台灣人和日本人喪失性命。另外還花了大量的經費在這個困難的任務上。儘管日本的士兵勇敢無懼，但攀登原始森林、陡峭高聳的山脈並通過深不可測的山谷和渡過那些谷中湍急的溪流，是他們不熟習的任務。因此，征服原住民的行動中，日本失去的士兵大約有一萬人。在半夜時，原住民通常會攻擊進行巡邏任務的士兵，將他們全部殺害殆盡。然後帶著他們「英勇行動」的戰利品——儘可能的帶走所有頭顱。因此，日本人為了自保（正如一些報告所說的，不是為了消滅原住民），於是興建通電的圍籬。

西方國家關注日本殖民政策

日本政府逐漸降服台灣原住民，而歸順的原住民則是以五十或一百人為一組，被帶到大都市見識島上城市、市鎮與鄉村文明生活的風情，日本政府更進一步教導原住民耕種以及其他謀生方法，並且在部落當中也設立許多學校。期待在很短的時間內，日本政府能夠毫無限制的允許上帝恩典的福音傳揚在這些原住民當中。

日本政府對於傳福音的限制會在稍後章節再談。筆者相信，最好的政策是請日本基督教會來進行傳福音的工作，成為他們的本地宣教事工。

當台灣割讓給日本時，全世界的目光都注視著日本政府，西方的各國很想知道日本要如何殖民不同的種族。

日本政府占領台灣不久後，便設立擁有軍事與行政雙重統治權力的總督。統治初期，國外許多流通報告書中說到台灣在日本統治底下的情況。當中最令日本人難堪的是「記述台灣土匪屠殺日本的男女與孩童而政府隨後進行殘酷報復」的事件。那段時間，宣教師寫回加拿大的報告書中，對於日本政府有兩方不同的觀點。一八九五年，當時負責加拿大長老教會在台灣宣教事務的是吳威廉牧師，他寫道：「台灣現在是日本天皇領土的一部分，當整個局勢恢復安定之後，我們相信這裡將會分享這個偉大帝國的文明」。馬偕博士在一八九五年結束休假，次年回到台灣，寫下如此的報告：「許多日本的士兵和苦力表達出對耶穌的厭惡，並且有許多日本基督徒為我們的主基督勇敢作見證。就個人來講，我受到許多日本基督徒苦力、士兵以及軍事或行政官員的尊敬和善待，我所熟識的一些官員，在這段黑暗時間當中的作為和風度，實在是應該受到最高度的讚揚。」

但無疑的，也有一些單獨個案，某些特定階層的日本人的行為讓西方人極為惱火，也讓較高層台灣人無法忍受，因此掠奪與謀殺的土匪一一出現，煽惑一般平民百姓去暴動以製造紛爭，就連日本士兵也無從分辨何為善民、何為惡棍？加上敵對基督教的人，就藉著這種機會來發洩他們的仇恨，以不實的事情去指控基督徒，因此有許多人喪命。後來，不論何時，只要有

報告指出「遭到逮捕的人是基督徒」身分，被逮捕的人就可以立刻恢復自由，結果是有許多異教徒都拿著聖經或聖詩本裝扮成為基督徒以規避刑責。社會上混亂的狀況持續了最初的幾個月，之後就逐漸安定下來，台灣社會逐漸建立秩序，一個新時代的發展也隨之開始。

日本刑法當中最糟糕的部分就是一個嫌犯在還沒找到證據證明自己無辜之前，是被法院推定為「有罪的人」的。在這種情況之下所造成的後果就是許多嫌犯為了逃避刑求的痛苦，就依照警察要的內容招供。日本官員也承認這基本原則的錯誤所造成的後果非常嚴重。

日治下的台灣教育

日本人占據台灣不到一年，就引進一套教育系統來教育台灣的年輕人。然而，就當時台灣落後的情況而言，令人遺憾的是，當時楫取道明（Katori）以及五位同事在辦公場所被一群受到誤導的台灣人所殺害。[11] 值得關注的是，儘管在這種悲劇的環境之下，在同一年，一套「國家教育系統」也被建立起來。自此之後，有關教育制度維持下來，如今，在台灣的學校有「師範學校」、「中等學校」、「女學校」、「技術學校」、一間「農業學校」以及一間「實驗農業以及山林管理學校」。當時台灣人抱怨日本人沒有意願對青年提供高等教育，這是事實，因為在總督府裡面主管教育系統的官員有些認為台灣人是被統治的民族，所以並不需要優等的教育。但後來台灣行政部門官員籌備較好的教育機會，提出一套新的教育方針去提供男生就讀附加的中等教育，讓日本人和台灣人入學。這對於舊式的種族分離政策來講是一大進步，也讓數百位男孩和許多年輕的女孩在日本的主要教育機構就學。

醫療現代化

日本統治之下的台灣，沒有一個部門的發展比醫療進步得更為迅速，大約在廿年前，台北市成立一間醫學校（今台大醫學院），成立不久後，許多台灣人就開始思考以醫生的工作來作為職業，這間學校每年有四十到六十位學生畢業。在台北市內有兩間大醫院，當中的一間醫院就規模、從業人員以及醫療器械來講的話，可以比美西方國家城市當中的醫院。在台灣主要的城市當中，有許多日本人或台灣人醫生所主持的醫院；而在小鄉鎮當中，則是由日本政府和台灣人醫生設立許多令人誇耀的診療所。在這些本地醫生當中，有一些是基督徒，其中也有在教會擔任服事的工作。

獎勵農業

先前，清政府所採取鼓勵農業以及一般工業最重要的步驟，就是「提供土地給部分人作為永久的產業」，這些土地在清國人統治時期是屬於地主所有，而租佃者的佃權並沒有受到任何保護，但日本政府提供土地使用者聲明土地產權以及登記的機會，於是農民知道在日本政府統治之下，使用的土地產權歸屬自己所有並且受到法律保障之後，就立刻進行土地改革工作。雖然，有時還會在偏遠地區聽見有人抱怨日本人比台灣人受到政府更多的保護，不過整體來講，在政府仔細的監督之下，這種情況都得以避免。

物質生活的好轉

一般人都承認，日本統治台灣廿八年後，物質生活都大步進展，只要將一般人的財產狀況與過去加以比較的話，就必須讚揚日本政府的高明之處。物質生活的進步——特別在台灣資源的開發、郵局、電報、電話系統的建立、鐵路和汽船運輸的推動、貿易、工業以及商業，這些快速的進步使得台灣人的生活變得更為舒適。港口、大面積的灌溉系統、乾淨水井的開放、城市中自來水的供應、發電設備的建立、公共衛生的進步、數千哩道路的開通以及其他各個層面的事務，都是發展國家邁向進步的證明。

台灣知識分子的期望

但是仍然不能忽視的是，台灣人對於自己作為「次等民族」感到無比的遺憾，雖然台灣人相信在日本統治下的生活情況是富裕許多，卻仍有受到外族統治的痛苦感，這種感覺已日漸浮出檯面。台灣人並不是反抗統治者，而是希望「被承認是公民」：擁有與日本人一樣完整的參政權，因此受過較多教育的知識分子開始表達出台灣人心裡的期望。受過教育的年輕人在與日本人頻繁接觸之下，不論在舉止、語言以及穿著上都已經快速日本化，因此可以預期的是，在台灣，這兩個族群最終會融合為一。日本政府也移除台日雙方通婚的限制，也加速了同化的過程。

社會和道德的錯誤

物質生活有長足的進展，使得台灣居民獲得極大的利益，但卻在道德和精神生活的層面上，除了基督教會對社會和宗教的某些影響外，整體來說，恐怕是沒有什麼進步。特別是在當時所引進台灣的一些新興行業（這是先前沒有的），對於台灣人在道德上的提升是沒有什麼助益的。娼妓業，這個在日本合法，但是採取隔離政策的行業被引入台灣本島，造成了日本人和台灣人在道德上的許多災難。如果西方人能夠免除許多社會和道德上的罪惡，那麼我們就有立場去批評日本政府那些倫理上的問題，但我們自己「也在玻璃屋當中」（譯者按：意指作者所處的西方社會也有相同的問題），或許我們不應該急於對他們投擲石頭。

宗教的自由

從宣教師的觀點來看，台灣享受極大範圍的宗教自由。基督教會的傳教工作並沒有受到日本政府與官員的阻礙，宣教師與政府官員之間也的確從來沒有發生誤解過，有時候，由於日本警察不知道基督教的傳教自由是受到政府保障的，所以與基督徒會產生一些糾紛，但那些紛爭都被上層官員用令人可接受的方式化解掉了，部分警察也被調職以避免再產生更多糾紛。我們要指出的是：如今有哪一個地區的國民享受到比台灣更多的宗教自由？以前，台灣總督就任時曾下令開始進行台灣宗教調查，調查結果出來之後，他（總督）公開的表達想法說：「台灣宗教當中，只有基督教對於道德的提升有所幫助。」在頭腦明智與能力極強的台灣總督田健治郎（Baron Den）的執政下，台灣各方面有更大進步的發展將是可以預期的結果。

日本人的教會

為了提供在台日本人在精神生活上的需要，日本基督長老會、公理會和聖公會在台灣當地組織了教會，有些已經超過廿年，然而他們並沒有對非基督徒進行宣教工作，雖然沒有倚賴外在的協助自給自足，但也沒有盡到對自己同胞在台灣傳福音的使命。我們認為日本基督教會恐怕還沒有體認到他們自己必須肩負的宣教責任。

能力過人的詹姆士·庫伯森（James Curthberson）所率領的日本福音隊（Japan Evangelical Band）提出一個可行且令人印象深刻的方向：他與另外三位佈道家進行三個月全島性的佈道活動，在日本人和台灣人中獲得了顯著的成果。

台灣的多元宗教

台灣人缺乏宗教的精神

在台灣停留愈久的時間，就會對台灣人的宗教精神評價愈低，他們對於宗教的道德要求不是忽視就是不感興趣，而當中最熱誠信仰宗教的人，卻往往是當地最沒有道德的人——別的地方很難找到比台灣將宗教與道德分離得更徹底的地方。賭徒會去廟宇祈求，不像稅吏，甚至也

不像法利賽人，他們就像一個人懇切地祈求神明去幫助他「搶奪別人所有的金錢」。雖然賭徒知道那意味的是要毀掉一個正常家庭；還有一個生活在恥辱中的年輕女性（特種行業婦女），她穿戴金項鍊、短襪、誇張的戒指、頭髮裝飾著金飾，但卻以毫不羞愧的面容前往廟宇，請求神明賜她富裕。令人感到可悲的是，只有少數人想到宗教與道德明顯不一致之處。

如同中國一樣，台灣三個主要宗教是道教、佛教和儒教，這三個宗教完全的融合在一起，因此，這些信徒們擁有相似的宗教生活與崇拜儀式。

泛靈信仰

在談到台灣人的信仰前，我們應該先介紹原住民宗教，一份研究原住民宗教信仰的報告指出，儘管原住民各族崇拜的對象極不相同，但他們卻都是精靈的崇拜者，有些族群認為這些精靈是住在太陽或月亮當中，而有些族群認為是住在高山上；少數人對著神像膜拜——雖然這種現象在原住民當中並不普遍。這些原住民的宗教信仰當中最特殊的是阿美族的宗教，他們相信靈魂不滅，以及天上安息之所的存在，然而進入天堂的條件就是他們必須要進行特定的儀式才行，包含由他們正式的「祈禱教師」噴灑清水和祈禱。每年的九月，阿美族人會召集「祈禱教師」舉行儀式，藉著這些儀式，保證他們能夠在將來進入這個永遠歡樂的國度。

原住民族由獵首風俗顯示其暴虐的本質，也幾乎遍存於每一支族群當中，這就是為什麼他們沒有接受基督教的原因，加上他們認為執行這個野蠻的風俗是遵照祖先的教導，具有很深的宗教意涵。

儒教

與儒教接觸的時間愈久，就愈無法將這個宗教歸類於世界的傳統宗教。孔子一再提到「天」，但「天」本身對於孔子自己來講卻沒有什麼特別的意義。儒教實在沒有什麼宗教的精神存在，如同存在於佛教中的那種宗教感。

道教

道教就如同汙穢含有毒素的溪流般，帶著中國的各種迷信，在溪水順著下游行進時，收納更多的髒汙，直到最後，滲透毀壞整個族群的宗教信仰，形成一種精靈信仰、鬼魂信仰、巫術、魔法、占卜以及其他綑綁人心、讓人盲目無知、以及精神死亡的混合體。事實上，道士是台灣島上最無用以及墮落的群體，他們藉著宗教儀式，例如讀咒文，嘗試拯救靈魂脫離地獄的煉火，不論男女老幼，必須在夜間花數小時的時間聽他們念咒語，也當成具有娛樂效果的表演。

佛教

與前述宗教不同，佛教是在中國急需精神慰藉的時代進入中國。儒教並不能讓人心得到安慰，在其教義當中也沒有將來的盼望或拯救的信息。而佛教剛好符合人心渴望的各種要素。它提供罪的赦免和靈魂的淨化，它傳佈普遍的拯救、恩典、憐憫和愛的觀念，讓人從痛苦和煩惱當中得到解脫並傳佈「西方極樂世界」的盼望。它的倫理教育遠高於中國曾經產生的教條，而

與基督教十誡的道德律有驚人的相似性。佛教尼姑和尚出家的行為，被看成是自我犧牲的典範，如果台灣的宗教信仰可以找到成為基督徒的預備信仰，那就是佛教。

許多男女嘗試要脫離迷信的重擔，而且他們的心靈渴求當地宗教是不是還能再給他們更多心靈上的飽足，那他們就是那些羊——準備好隨時回應基督福音的恩典、榮耀的救贖與勝利盼望的人。

本地的人口以及我們的責任

加拿大教會對台灣當地人有什麼責任，讓他們能夠順服復活主的誡命、光明的福音以及愛與自由？根據日本政府在一九二〇年的統計，台灣人口總共三百七十萬四千八百九十九人，在這當中有三百四十五萬人是台灣的漢人，八萬五千人是原住民，十五萬三千人是日本公民，其他是來自中國的華人，還有八十位西方人，包含有領事官、生意人、教師、天主教神父以及英國和加拿大的宣教師。在美麗的福爾摩沙島上，加拿大長老教會的目標是讓基督徒人數增加到五十萬人，教會能夠充份地盡到她的責任嗎？

禱告詞

◆ ◆ ◆ ‥‥‥‥‥‥‥‥‥

噢！上帝祢以一本血統造出萬國，幫助我們承認和其他種族的血脈關係，將台灣人當成我們自己的兄弟姊妹，讓我們這些已經得知祢的恩典，智慧和福音，生命也因此獲得提升而豐富的人，以愛與謙卑的心思念他們。

幫助我們免除族群的優越感，避免看輕那些不如我們幸運的人，以祢的憐憫觸碰我們的心，因為我們的心靈與肉體呼喚祢這位真活的上帝，除非在真道上，在生命的真理上與祢相遇，否則只能空空的探索，讓我們領悟每一位成為祢子女無比的價值與終極的可能性，而不區分距離以及與我們的差異。幫助我們尊重每一個生命，尊敬上帝賦予每一個靈魂的能力，祢思念每一個單獨的生命，期望將自己顯示在他們面前，請為祢兒子的緣故應允此事，祂是萬國的盼望，是世界的光。阿們。

第二章 ◆ 台灣人，統治者與宗教

第三章 ◆ 加拿大長老會差派馬偕到遠東

正如先前的章節所見，加拿大教會並不是第一個在台灣島上進行宣教工作的教派。在肇建者馬偕到達此地的二百年前，荷蘭的宣教師就已經開始在南部工作了，而台灣也因為他們所流的血而聖化。一八六五年，英國長老教會已在南部開始佈教，北台灣卻是宣教工作的一塊處女地[1]，而加拿大長老會也是在上帝的引導下才進入這個地區的。

馬偕的早年時期

加拿大長老會在北台灣的設立者：喬治‧列斯里‧馬偕牧師。一八四四年三月廿一日，他誕生於加拿大安大略省牛津郡的左拉村。一八三〇年，他的雙親從蘇格蘭的蘇特蘭郡前往加拿大[2]，馬偕的祖父曾經參與過滑鐵盧戰役，是一位蘇格蘭高地士兵[3]，這個殊榮無疑的影響

了家中的六個小孩，而這位將來的宣教師是孩子當中年紀最小的。在這當中，伴隨馬偕一生的不僅是一位蘇格蘭（高地）士兵的榮耀，更是一位高地人族長的權威。那段時間是長老教會界騷動的時代，就在馬偕誕生的同年，加拿大長老教會也經歷與前一年相仿發生在蘇格蘭境內令人難忘的「大分裂」[4] 經驗。許多信徒由「老教會」（Auld kirk）退出來，組成「自由教會」，就像其他許多人一樣，在主日禮拜當中是以蓋爾語以及英語講道。在那個時代，只有少數地方有主日學或青年會，但這並不表示左拉村的小孩子沒有接受宗教教育的機會。事實上，完全相反，馬偕的雙親從蘇格蘭高地帶來的信仰傳統以及堅強的宗教情操，在安大略省蠻荒森林的新造木屋裡給了子女們更多的教育，那個時代，一般人家裡最普遍的書本就是《聖經》、《信仰告白》、《小教理問答》、波士頓（Boston）的《四重的國家》（Fourfold State）、《永遠安息的聖徒》（Saints Everlasting Rest）《渴望的詢問者》（The Anxious Enquirer）辛特列（Guthrie）的《極大的利益》（Great Interest）撒母耳‧路特佛（Samuel Rutherford）的《書信集》（Letters）以及《馬琴恩的回憶錄》（Memoirs of Robert Murray MacCheyne）。

台灣的英雄就是在這種環境下誕生的，被養育以及為一生的工作受到了造就。在他還年幼時，馬偕就已經對永恆的真理打開心門。假如你問他為何成為一位宣教師？他會提到上帝永恆的目的和計畫。他年幼的時候就已經告訴你：當你問他為何成為一位宣教師？或許他不會告訴你：；當你問他為何成為一位宣教師？他會提到上帝永恆的目的和計畫。他年幼的時候就已經對神聖的事物有很深的感受，馬堅志牧師忠實的教誨和雙親敬虔的宗教訓練之下，讓他決意將這一生完全奉獻給萬王之王使用。在那段日子裡，這個敬虔的蘇格蘭高地家庭訓練孩子產生堅

定和健全的人格，而家庭禮拜的祭壇就是主要的基石，家庭環境充滿朝氣和莊嚴的氣氛。在那裡，安息日（主日）是個快樂的日子。或許沒有思想的人會將那天看成是漫長又令人厭倦的時刻，但是對於馬偕來講，那是一個他特別享受的時光。然後，就是令人難忘的「聖餐節期」（Communion Season），那時「高地的」牧師與「男性」一起討論「問答」[5]。在這個節期當中，安大略省布魯斯菲爾德（Brucefield）的約翰·羅斯牧師（Rev. John Ross）經常前來協助馬堅志牧師，透過這個敬虔人的協助得以將基督轉化為個人經驗。

就在這些人的引導之下，馬偕深深的啜飲宗教真理的活泉。對他來講，《聖經》是一本敞開的書籍，而古老的先知是活生生的。透過他生動的想像力，在性靈的戲劇當中，他看見他們，就如同巨人一般盡立於山頂，他總是期望能夠攀登山巔，再由那裡望向未來，以及腳下向外延伸的平原。他也是《詩篇》的愛好者，他將《詩篇》與其他經節記在腦海裡，在邁入青少年以前，他也專注的背誦《小教理問答》。

他完成公立學校的課程之後，跟隨他的老師蕭先生（Shaw），一位優秀的學校教師，一起前往位於奧美美（Omeme）的一所高中就讀，馬偕對於運動沒有太大的興趣，他喜歡讀書以及散步鄉間小路，他愛草地更甚於運動場。

宣教的抱負

十六歲時，馬偕得到了第一級教師證書，於此同時，他也已經聽見了遙遠異國對他的呼聲，而擁有比當老師職位更高的夢想。只有永恆的上帝瞭解，馬偕在那段平靜但卻準備不懈的數年當中他心裡的想法。他不是一位普通的青年，因此不喜歡跟隨一般人的腳步。

他有一對敏銳的雙眼，但是他來自靈魂深處的目光卻更為尖銳，藉著性靈的雙眼，他可以看見無形的上帝，以及上帝為他一生工作所規劃的藍圖。他已經將決心寫在臉上，也聽見神聖的呼聲，因此決定不管上帝賜給他什麼能力，為了服事，都願意將他的恩賜毫不保留的放在祭壇上。儘管年幼，承襲了蘇格蘭高地的神秘氣質的馬偕，在當時以及後來的一生當中都深深影響著他，雖然很少人知道他內心的想法，但是更少人知道他的下一步。

雖然他只是一位教書的青年，他卻利用空閒的時間研究神學和醫學。很少人能夠像馬偕一樣，雖然不是以醫療為業，卻在他服事的場域有那麼傑出的表現[6]。在這當中，特別有趣的就是他的拔牙紀錄。每當人讀到他在擔任宣教師時期拔牙的數目——在數年當中就拔掉超過一千顆牙齒，總會不禁去想像，當他站在一群漢人面前，就會不由得產生「將牙齒拔光」的怪異渴望。

成年之後，馬偕的內心一直被異教世界所發出的深沉需要所攪動——那不就是在一八五四年由偉大的宣教師亞力山大‧杜夫博士（Alexander Duff）經過安大略省時（當時馬偕十歲）所講的印度故事嗎？那不就是在他童年時期，經過左拉村的著名宣教師賓威廉（William Burn）[7]將這位來到台灣的宣教師的心靈轉向那個擁擠的百萬靈魂的故事嗎？這絕不是偶然，而是上帝的計畫，在他的心靈深處日夜燃燒著。他絕對不會忘記前往印度宣教的杜夫、前往中國宣教的賓威廉以及中國的百萬靈魂。

普林斯敦和愛丁堡時期

在多倫多諾克斯學院修業一年後，馬偕離開該校，前往普林斯敦神學院深造，在修讀期間，他曾經有兩個暑假在多倫多北方的亞伯山（Mount Albert）教會實習，對於馬偕服事的經驗，當地有些人還存留部份的記憶。

那段時間當中，一般人不需要在普林斯敦待很長的時間，就會聽見許多有關蘇格蘭神學家甘德立希博士（Dr. Gandlish）與辜特立博士（Dr. Guthrie）的事蹟。因此也難怪馬偕自普林斯敦神學院畢業之後，就立刻啟程前往蘇格蘭愛丁堡[8]，向兩位自由教會知名的人士學習。同

年的冬天，他再度去到杜夫博士底下研究，當時的杜夫教授是一位退休的宣教師，他長滿雪白、修長又平順的鬍鬚，看起來像是一位令人尊敬的先知一般。當時他正在蘇格蘭巡迴佈道，希望能夠重新點燃海外宣教之火——那不是一件容易的事情，但是只要有心，就能隨時回應他那火焰般的信息。年輕的馬偕跟隨杜夫教授上山下海，就像以利沙跟隨在以利亞的腳下一般。

馬偕已經決定將生命奉獻給未曾聽聞福音的土地。他的下一步是回到加拿大，將自己奉獻給母會做宣教工作。雖然在那個時候，他所屬的教會只有少部分的人瞭解這位年輕實習生的使命。

任命與封立

前往海外宣教的申請書已經填寫妥當並且投遞給委員會，而「是否能夠儘速成行」的答覆完全取決於一八七一年六月在魁北克市召開的總會的決定，這位年輕的實習生也受邀參會。當年的總會已為了聖詩與教會機構、老教會與自由教會的諸多問題以及新教會的聯合運動而爭辯不休。年輕的馬偕對於這些問題並沒有什麼興趣，他的內心充滿了為宣教事業而奉獻生命的憧憬。

委員會的報告書中敦促總會「贊同對異教徒的宣教工作」，當中指出「有一個人已經奉獻，而教會看起來準備接受這個責任。馬偕先生是教會的一位學生，去年冬天，他在杜夫指導之下做研究，現在已經在這個城市當中準備接下這個教會將要任命的工作」。

總會接納委員會的報告，也做成以下的決議：「竭誠的歡迎喬治．L．馬偕獻身作為異教徒的宣教師，因此，他將會由這屆總會選派成為加拿大長老會的宣教士，前往海外工作」，「而中國將會成為馬偕先生派遣宣教之地」，「授權多倫多中會封立馬偕先生成為牧師，並且根據海外宣道委員會的安排，任命他前往派遣之地」。

一八七一年九月十九日傍晚，多倫多高德街長老教會舉行封立典禮，而金恩牧師（Rev. John M. King D. D.）擔任主禮人。那是個令人難忘的傍晚，除了馬偕以外，當天也按立另外一位年輕的實習生喬治．布利司牧師（Rev. George Bryce），他已經接受金恩博士的推薦，在溫尼伯（Winnipeg）設立曼尼托巴學院（Manitoba College）。本地宣教（Home Mission）與海外宣教（Foreign Mission）的兩個委員會都有人出席封立典禮，前者任命喬治．布利司前往西部工作，而後者任命喬治．列斯里．馬偕前往遠東服務。上述三位，每一個人的工作成果極為卓著，也先後獲得總會議長的榮耀。

馬偕總算可以著手進行長年來的夢想。他在一個月內拜訪了加拿大各地的教會，並稱呼這時的長老教會仍處於「冰河時期」。許多長老教會的牧師並沒有把他當一回事，自然的，他們的會友也不會對馬偕有什麼熱情可言。然而馬偕並沒有因此而洩氣，事實上，他早已將「氣餒」這個字眼由他的字彙當中刪除——他已經見到天國的遠景，到達那個目標之前他絕不能失

望——他已經誓言忠實順服耶穌的使命，前往遙遠的國家，他的教會也接受他的獻身。

出發與離別

出發前往海外宣教之地，意味著與故鄉和親人的離別。以馬偕家人的性格來看，他們或許會將憂慮埋藏於內心深處而強顏歡笑，但是馬偕迴避了這個嚴峻的考驗。

十月十九日，在他接受任命的一個月後，他告別了故鄉，離開的那一天也成為故鄉人談話的重點——某一個人聽到了，或許就對另一個人說：「喬治‧列司里‧馬偕要去中國了，不曉得他會遇到什麼事情？」而這人可能更靈敏於海外宣教的重要性：「你永遠不知道馬偕下一篇報告會是什麼樣的內容，對我們來講總是一個謎。」是的，出發到中國去！在那個時代，海外宣教不是一件簡單的事情，象徵的是一個很大的冒險，對上帝拯救計畫展現了偉大的信心，以及對上帝完全的信賴，而這個憑藉就寫在他內心當中的「大使命」，也在海外宣道委員會送給他的《聖經》扉頁當中。

— 69 —

一八七一年十一月一日，馬偕在舊金山港登上美利堅號，成為船上的乘客。船駛離港口，遠方的山巔也逐漸消失在水平面下，他有一種從來沒有經歷過的深沉孤獨籠罩在身上。離開了朋友、許多的朋友，那是真的，但是因為這樣而深陷孤獨，那就真是誤解他了。在他前方是一個嶄新而陌生的國家，住著一群更為陌生的人民，當時他的部分心情，用筆寫了下來：「不論是早或晚，」他寫道：「每個人都會進入客西馬尼園，在那一天，我發現自己在那個園子當中，因為在小小的艙房裡，我的靈魂動搖，畏縮了一段時間。」

當船隻即將在香港靠岸時，這件事讓他的心情感到愉快，因為飄揚的英國國旗代表著英國式的自由與保護。在旅程當中，他用很長的時間研讀中國地圖以及幾本宣教師的著作。數年前他也曾讀過賓威廉所寫有關汕頭和廈門及當地宣教工作的故事，英國長老教會在上述兩個地方都成立了深具發展潛力的宣教中心。那些故事對他來講，實在非常新奇。當他到達中國領土時，他也知道了部分有關福爾摩沙的事情，因為島上的許多探險故事早已名聞整個東方。

到達香港時，一位英國宣教師，愛特爾博士（Dr. Etel）前來接待他。第二天，他們前往廣東，在那裡遇見兩位美國宣教師，其中一位是馬偕在普林斯敦神學院的同學。回到香港數天

後，他啟程前往汕頭。汕頭的宣教師已經得知馬偕被任命為前往中國的宣教師，也聽到他已經抵達香港的消息。他們盼望馬偕在宣教工作上願意與他們合作，但是他們並不知道馬偕的意願如何。但是馬偕很快就認定這裡並不是他要尋找的地區，於是朝向北方，前往廈門，拜訪那裡的教會[9]。

來自台灣的呼喚不停在他耳中迴響，馬偕的心靈在沒有見到這個島嶼之前，無法在其他地方安頓下來。他被神秘的命運之索牽引著，登上一艘前往台灣南部打狗（今高雄）的小汽船。他堅定認為「是台灣，而不是中國」，那將會是他宣教工作的場域，他也將這個結果寫回的第一封報告書，化解了他們的疑慮，並且相信這是上帝引導他前往東方成為第一位宣教師的結果。

一八六五年開始，英國長老教會在台灣南部進行宣教工作，馬雅各醫生、李麻牧師以及其他人在打狗成立極具發展潛力的教會。在馬偕到達打狗時，他們正於舊府城台南開設一間新的教會，原來數年前，他們曾經在那裡被趕離開過。當馬偕在打狗港登岸後，得知李麻牧師全家正在四十一公里外的地方巡視教會。在一位信徒帶領之下，他前去尋找這位英國宣教師。當時是一八七一年十二月，到一八七二年三月七日，他接受招待，住在這位英國宣教師家中。

我們一路跟著馬偕由故鄉來到南台灣。現在他正坐在李麻先生家中的角落，有一位漢人老師坐在他旁邊，一邊學習會話，同時仔細研究整座島嶼的狀況。他得知台灣北部尚有百萬靈魂未曾聽聞過福音，也感受到帶領他的那一雙神秘之手催促著他起身前往台灣北部。最後，他將

— 71 —

心中的決定告訴李麻牧師，他英國朋友歡喜的回應，「上帝祝福你，馬偕。」於是就在初春時節，馬偕和李麻在德馬太醫生（Dr. Dickson）陪伴下，在安平（今台南）登上一艘北行的小汽船「海龍號」，三月九日他們抵達淡水港。

開始在台灣北部的工作

不論從海上或陸地來看，北台灣都沒有一個地方比淡水港口更加美麗了！這樣的景致，觸碰到這位加拿大宣教師的內心深處。李麻牧師宣布，「馬偕，這裡就是你的教區。」這個聲音在他的內心不停迴盪，那裡的確是他用廿九年的熱情去積極工作的教區。

從港口可以看見舊荷蘭城堡、英國領事館，海拔一千多公尺高聳的大屯山脈；河對岸，海拔六百多公尺的美麗的觀音山更是居高臨下。淡水小鎮有五千個居民，從淡水河邊延伸到後方丘陵。這位年輕的宣教師內心充塞著冒險的感覺混雜著奇異又吸引的魅力，對他來講，這個地方是同工們經過祈禱和祝福後交在他手中的，很難想像這是上帝帶領人去到祂自己掌管的地上的作法。

馬偕站著，舉目遙望，有山脈往南伸展，河流蜿蜒，看起來像是巨大的蛇怪。河岸村落，

碧綠的稻田一級級往上攀爬——當他想到此地尚有許多人不認識基督，他的內心就燃起奇妙的火焰。這個地區是上帝交付給他的使命，這片自然美景已遠遠超越他期待的，並呈現在他眼前等待他前去撒種、耕種以及收成。對馬偕和加拿大長老會來說，那實在是一個歷史性的時刻。

那個時代，淡水這個城鎮除了坐落在一片美景，但事實上它卻是一個巷弄狹窄、喧鬧、髒汙、飄散惡臭、鼠輩橫行和毒蚊肆虐之地。他們禮拜六到達淡水，而禮拜天則是在一位英國商人的貨倉中度過。禮拜一早上，他們步行啟程南行，好更認識這塊土地。這三位宣教師無疑享受了一段充滿歡樂愉快的旅行，他們不會想要將這個機會與「住在西方宮殿當中的舒適經驗」做交換。因為沒有任何文獻提到馬偕的幽默感，因此人們容易論斷說他沒有幽默的美德。在外國人或漢人面前，馬偕都是一位嚴肅的人，個性也極為敏感。然而各種跡象顯示，他的心情極為愉快，因為工作的場域已經安頓下來，而先前的緊張情緒也已緩和，他可以毫無牽絆的四處旅行。根據他所留下的旅行紀錄來看，他們三位宣教師的相處對剛抵台的宣教師必然極為有趣且新奇。例如他們盡其所能的逃避漢人的氣味、吞嚥漢人烹煮的碎肉、對抗蚊蚋、教訓豬隻使之遵守規矩，並與這間漢人旅店裡的常客變成朋友等情形。旅行數天之後，他們到達南台灣教會最北方的據點，在那裡，南方與新教會的界線就此劃定。在與平埔族信徒相處幾天之後，馬偕與一位漢人啟程北上回到淡水。開始在憎恨和排斥「野蠻人」（西方人）的群眾當中工作。

— 73 —

早期當地人對基督教的觀感

馬偕最初幾個月的宣教紀錄可在其他資料找到——想必這位新來的加拿大宣教師、一位本地傳道兼廚師，必定引起淡水當地居民的騷動，也激起不小的敵意，或許也讓部分居民感到意外。馬偕到達以前，有關「耶穌教」的荒唐謠言四處流傳，說外國的宣教師挖出過世信徒的眼珠和心臟去製藥，也派人到市場將毒藥撒在肉品和青菜當中，除了這些以外，還有更荒唐的謠言到處流傳。另外還有一種引起居民們憤慨的謠言，那就是外國人到淡水的目的，是要占領台灣這座島嶼。馬偕還沒到淡水前，有南台灣的漢人被頭人慫恿去拆毀天主教與英國長老會的禮拜堂，駐在香港的英國領事接到受攻擊的報告之後，立刻派遣英國軍艦砲擊安平港，使得漢人心生恐懼，懇求英國宣教師繼續留下來進行傳教的工作，並保證不會再有攪擾宣教的事情發生。

最初的果子

當馬偕橫渡太平洋時，曾經祈禱上帝「賜他一位擁有才能和恩賜的年輕人，成為第一位信徒」，幫助他更有果效的傳福音。而上帝也回應了他的祈禱。當馬偕在淡水的小屋安頓下來之後，某日下午，一位看起來斯文且聰明的年輕人走進房間，希望能夠與這位宣教師談話。原來他早年曾經遊歷中國，因此願意和馬偕這位外國人交談。當他們二度見面時，馬偕送給他一本《聖詩》。與他數度接觸之後，這位宣教師完全相信，這個人就是他曾向上帝祈求的這位信徒的名字是嚴清華，他的故事記錄在《福爾摩沙紀事》當中，他能夠勝任基督徒各個層面的工作，也是一位優良的教師，在講道時能夠清晰表達他的想法。不管是在談話或在講台上，年輕的宣教師馬偕都能夠輕易瞭解嚴清華說話的內容，他的表達能力也遠遠超過其他本地人。阿華（嚴清華）對於教會的法規與體制有極為優越的知識，似乎對宣教工作的所有細節都非常熟習。馬偕完全信賴阿華，將他當成是一生的友伴。馬偕用以下的文字敘述記錄阿華的第一次禱告，「他不曾在別人面前祈禱，而這個要求似乎讓他感到意外，但是他立刻跪在一張搖晃的舊竹椅面前，以迫切的言詞，以及不完善的語詞和斷續的請求，表現出最為熱切的情感。他的雙手緊緊握住椅子，用力的壓在不平的地板上，發出可怕吱吱嘎嘎的聲響，伴隨他那結結巴巴的語句，禱告結束之後，椅子已經移動半個房間的距離[10]。」

不久之後，有三個同伴加入阿華，他們在往後年間提供教會極大的幫助。這三個人，其中一位是陳火[11]，他成為第一位牧師，後來受聘成為駐在當地的牧師。另一位是吳寬裕[12]，他在往後四十年間在北台灣服事教會。這些年輕學生追隨他們的新老師馬偕，在他的指導下，對於基督教真理進入更深的瞭解。一八七三年二月的第二個禮拜天[13]，大概是馬偕來到北台灣

的一年之後，五位信徒在驚訝和狂亂的暴徒面前，藉著洗禮，公開對耶穌基督的信仰告白。隔週，受洗的年輕信徒一起參與主的聖餐。透過聖禮典的舉行，基督教會在北台灣正式成立。連串的事件持續記錄下去，馬偕與信徒在五股坑的小村落開設第一間基督教會，也在這裡主持第一次漢族信徒的婚禮，這件事情到現在仍然讓人津津樂道。

援軍同工來到

台灣北部教會成立之後，對眾人佈道的方法逐漸也變得重要許多，一般居民對醫療的需求，相信一定讓馬偕印象深刻──進行醫療工作或許會比其他方法更容易消除一般人心裡對基督教會的疑懼，前文提到，因為他來到台灣不久之後就寫信回母會，請求派遣一位醫療宣教師來台灣服務。母會快速回應他的請求。一八七四年，隔年一月廿九日，一位具有醫師資格的華雅各牧師（Rev. J. B. Fraser, M. D.）接受任命，成為馬偕的同工。我們不難想像，當他們到達時，受到馬偕什麼樣程度的歡迎啊！華雅各醫生當時寫回母會的書信表達的不僅是工作的價值，他也藉著敏銳和精確的目光，表達對於醫療宣教的高度評價。而馬偕博士的書信中，對於華雅各個人的特質以及醫療技巧也極為激賞。然而令人遺憾的

是，由於華醫生的夫人過世，使得他必須在一八七七年帶著兩位失去母親的幼女，黯然回到加拿大。

第二年，閨虔益牧師（Rev. Kenneth Junor）來台。這位先前曾在百慕達地區有著成功服事經驗的人，被任命為馬偕的同工。閨虔益牧師夫婦以及小孩法蘭克（Frank）在一八七八年四月一日由舊金山登船。到達不久後，馬偕寫了一封有關這位新宣教師的書信，內容中說道：

「我不用告訴你，你也知道，我永遠無法忘懷閨虔益夫婦的友善，他們在這裡，一切都很好，願上帝祝福我的同工以及伙伴，因為他們極力照顧我這個不配獲得如此對待的人。」

而閨先生則對於馬偕堅強的性格，以及他在肉體和精神上的活力印象十分深刻。馬偕在一封書信中無意提到一件事件，表達出他性格當中柔軟的部分：

「就在我生病的時候，閨虔益牧師也為嚴重的高燒所苦。他們可愛的小男孩法蘭克，因為突然間抽搐而躺在地上，並且在禮拜五下午兩點回去天家。可愛的法蘭克在他過世的前一天傍晚，拿著裝食物的盤子來到我的房間，爬到床上，坐在我的旁邊。法蘭克真是一個好男孩，如今他在極為遙遠的那邊，在至高的天堂，千萬的孩童圍繞的寶座旁。」

馬偕的婚禮

同一年當中，有兩件重要的事情發生在馬偕身上：一件是攻克艋舺（今萬華），另一件更為重要，並且對他未來宣教工作的發展有很大的影響，那就是娶得一位漢人妻子（張聰明）。無疑地，對馬偕來講，這個生命階段必須努力的目標是「建立一個自主自養的教會」，以下是馬偕寫給海外委員會的書信，當中記述的方式不讓人感到意外：

「五月，我在淡水的英國領事館與一位漢人的淑女結婚，婚禮過後立刻前往鄉下，與她一起去巡視教會。」馬偕夫人從早年開始，就擁有堅毅和吸引人的氣質，她個人對於經常拜訪她家的基督徒有很大的影響力。她的性格忍耐、謙卑，很有人緣，她也一直都是窮人的朋友；遭逢困難的人總會發現她是一位好幫手。任何有她那樣地位的人，總會變得驕傲和專制，但是馬偕夫人並沒有如此。她仍保有真誠以及友善的性情，受到本地信徒和宣教師的愛戴。對於她丈夫的繼任者，她從來不曾表現任何嫉妒與冷漠。與宣教師有深刻情誼的人，總是會欣賞喬治·列斯里·馬偕的夫人。

美麗之島：北部教會宣教禧年回顧與前瞻

禱告詞

噢！祢依自己的意願和歡喜在人的內心裡做工，我們為那些為祢兒子福音而前往世界各地勇敢獻身的靈魂來讚美祢，特別要感謝祢派遣無畏的傳信者傳揚祢恩典的信息，他們順服祢的呼召，前往遙遠的海嶼，前往那些尚未知曉祢大愛的民族當中，祢並不輕看他們為了福音的緣故而忍受的孤寂和艱難。

幫助我們，藉著這個典範，感激祢兒子的贈禮，祂來到人群當中，謙卑自己，取了奴僕的形象，犧牲自己的生命、受到人們排斥與拒絕，以便讓我們可以得到今世與來生的完全。

噢！上帝請祢允許，讓我們也能夠歡喜的接受祢訓練的方式，日復一日，放棄一切來跟隨祢，肩負祢引領我們承擔的責任，讓我們能夠忍受十字架的苦楚，讓我們為了贏得祢歡喜的緣故而拒絕誘惑，因為這更勝於生命的價值，在上帝的旨意以及耶穌基督的緣故來服事我們的世代。阿們。

第四章 ◆ 馬偕在台事工及安息

打破規則：馬偕的第一次休假

馬偕在台灣不想做的事情有三件：他絕對不坐轎子、他絕對不休假、他絕對不結婚。但是他並不是第一位改變想法卻仍保有偉大地位的人。馬偕來到台灣之後，就不斷提醒加拿大教會，台灣宣教工作的發展是多麼順利，海外宣道委員會幾乎還沒有時間瞭解前一封報告書的重要性時，後一篇更有趣的報告書就已經寄到。一年一年過去，宣教的工作也不斷成長和發展。

在這個卓著的發展情況下，馬偕對於休假返國述職的時間迫近，心裡的感受極為複雜，但是馬偕要回國的消息還是傳回了加拿大。

一八八〇年，當他回到加拿大時曾遭遇一些不愉快的經驗，讓他才剛開始的假期蒙上些許

陰影。最後，他回到故鄉的省分，引起了很大的轟動，特別是左拉地區。那裡有許多人想要目睹這位在台灣原住民族中過夜、在刻不容緩的危急時刻逃離災難、蔑視滿清官吏和漢族暴徒的人，和他那位剛剛結婚的台灣妻子。他們想看這位「黑鬚番」——因為他的親身經驗實在非比尋常。

在加拿大教會中的風采

短暫休息之後，各地教會的邀約紛紛來到。各地民眾都想聽他演講，而他的演講也真的值得聆聽。可以確定的是，在加拿大教會的傳教史當中，沒有別的宣教師可以像馬偕一樣，擁有鼓動聽眾感受的魅力，也很少人能夠只憑藉流利的口才就喚起聽眾的宣教熱情。「我們聽福爾摩沙的馬偕演講，真是令人永遠難忘。」這是當時聽到他的呼籲而內心深感激動群眾的證言。

他在講台上的風采、特有的手勢、那對黝黑又銳利的眼神，加上充滿熱情的說話方式以及完全忘我的的精神，都深深打動聽眾的心。他靈魂深處的熱火點燃了許多人的心靈，當他說出「美麗的福爾摩沙」時，眼神帶著深沉的思念，表達出他對台灣這座島嶼的愛意。

別人描述他在休假時給人的印象，《記錄》[1]有以下的描述：「馬偕博士是宣教師當中高

貴的典範，擁有顯著的犧牲自我、機智、勇氣以及熱情超乎一般人之上的特質，我們實在不需要告訴讀者，有關他的成功究竟到了什麼程度。」一篇總會的報告書記錄了他激發該機構的興趣，內容說道：「由於喬治·列斯里·馬偕牧師在台灣極為卓著的貢獻，他的出席已經成為總會大會當中一個令人關注的焦點，而他那真誠以及激發出每個人去關懷的宣教演講，無疑將會使人們在很長一段時間之後，仍然牢記在心。」在這次休假當中，女王大學（Queen University）適時的頒贈給他一個榮譽神學博士（Doctor of Divinity）的學位。

他的漢人妻子——無論到哪裡都陪伴著他——製造出更多的趣味。他們夫婦受到大家極為熱誠的接待，也受邀前往加拿大東方省分（Eastern Province）拜訪，在那裡，他們受到不亞於故鄉人給他們的歡迎。

離開加拿大前夕，伍斯托克地區的教會為馬偕夫婦在伍斯托克衛理公會舉行送別會。在會中，受到人們尊敬的奧利佛·莫瓦特（Oliver Mowat）出席並且表達了對馬偕以及他的成果感到深刻的關心之意。馬偕夫人被引導到台上，為她在加拿大這些日子以來，經歷過種種奇異且各式各樣的體驗進行簡短的發言，由馬偕擔任翻譯。當天晚上更重要的事情就是教會贈送馬偕博士六千二百一十五美元，用來在台灣建造建築物以作為訓練傳道師的學校。

一八八一年十一月，馬偕夫婦啟航回台。在他即將啟程的第二度遠東之行當中，各樣的想法、回憶和期望都充溢在他的腦海當中，也在他的內心攪動。他已經回過故鄉並領受各樣的善意和榮耀，而且他也感受到母會對他的偏見逐漸移除，虛假的謠言也被更正，同時激起母會對自己責任的瞭解以及熱情。現在他可以滿足的回到台灣，因為他的休假成果豐碩，加上當他們

想到台灣也有人等著歡迎他們回去，內心就感到非常的快樂。

回到台灣受到熱烈歡迎

回到他所擇居的土地（淡水）之後，馬偕就開始計畫建造一所全新的傳道訓練學校。在回航的旅途中，他就已經開始著手規劃這個新的「牛津學堂」的藍圖，他想像自己看見採石工人努力的切割石板，工人在林間砍下木材的聲音，他也彷彿聽見漢人在集中這些建材的吆喝聲。

橫渡太平洋的旅程中，他的心思因即將實現的夢想而充滿了希望。十一月卅日，當船接近台灣時，他用以下的文字表達他的心情：「台灣的高山已經在眼前出現，繼續滾動吧！你這狂野的太平洋！我從來沒有預期會再次橫渡你這大洋，海風和浪濤，請你善待我們吧！」

台灣的基督徒成群歡迎馬偕，極為熱情；淡水海邊有馬偕的屬靈子女們排成一長列，等待迎接他們摯愛的傳道人領袖和妻子返台。當他們登上海岸，歡迎的人群大聲喊叫：「偕牧師平安，偕牧師娘平安！」對馬偕夫婦來講，那真是一段愉快的時光，因為已經回到屬於他們的家和摯愛的人群裡。

思想起回自己祖國加拿大的歸鄉經驗，回台灣更激起這位宣教師的熱情。這位在他回鄉的

那段時間肩負教會責任的閏虔益牧師，他處理事情的方式，獲得馬偕最高的評價。的確，我們可以想像，對於本地信徒來講，這或許不能算是獲益良多的經驗，但不知不覺當中，他們也接觸到兩種不同的領導方式，這樣也有助於讓本地信徒們瞭解，接觸異國宗教基督信仰時真正委身的對象為何？或許這些事，基督徒也可藉此學習，上帝利用不同類型的人物來擴張祂的國度吧！

建造牛津學堂

馬偕回台不久後，山上的採石場開始出現敲擊岩石的聲音，鋸子、斧頭、刨刀也開始就位，為「牛津學堂」這所新的學院切割大樑和門窗。在魔法師的魔法棒觸碰之下，石材與木塊合為一體。而回到駐地的馬偕也立刻把宣教基地從原先安靜平淡的狀態轉化成往日熱鬧的氣氛。奠立地基、牆壁日漸升高，然後安放梁柱，這個建築物就在崇敬者帶著驚訝的眼神注視下漸漸成形，而成為一棟葳爾小屋的微型宮殿。

這棟建築物以「牛津郡」的地名來命名為「牛津學堂」，因為興築的經費是由當地的馬偕友人募集而成的。學院在一八八二年六月舉行正式啟用典禮，距離馬偕結束休假返台已六個

月，典禮中有許多外國人和本地信徒出席，也是北台灣教會歷史性的一刻。典禮當中穿插兩次有趣的贈禮活動，第一是由漢米爾頓的汪澤先生（Mr. Wanzar of Hamilton）贈送給傳道夫人的廿四台縫紉機，第二是當場宣布底特律的馬偕船長夫人（跟馬偕同樣稱呼，並非同一人）贈與一筆興建醫館的金錢，還有五百元美金捐獻給艋舺教會，作為協助建堂之用。

閏虔益因病離台

「牛津學堂」興建完成之後，馬偕比以往更熱衷於工作。當時，雖然閏虔益牧師的台語已經講得相當流利，但他卻不斷遭到瘧疾發高燒的攻擊——相同的疾病也為馬偕帶來不小的麻煩。當時所採用的宣教政策是採取和本地人同樣的生活方式，藉此希望能夠完全瞭解他們——然而大自然的法則是嚴厲的，違犯者就會遭到懲罰——因此，在東方人的方法是如果採取自我保護將可避免時間、金錢以及身體上的損傷。但閏虔益牧師遭受到肉體和精神上的折磨而倒下，於是被迫於一八八二年十二月返回加拿大。

宜蘭平原的群眾歸信運動

同年，馬偕提交一份於宜蘭平原上一篇亮麗的佈教成績工作報告書，他介紹那裡的生活條件以及迫切的需要之後，在該封書信結尾也要求母會支付二千五百元的經費來興建當地的兩間教會，好容納兩千位聽眾，並加上「為了上帝的緣故，不要拒絕，也不要延遲。」想像一下委員會成員聽見東海岸群眾歸信運動的故事，以及馬偕勇敢要求二千五百元經費來建築兩間教會的英勇行徑，如果能看見那些委員的表情，必定是非常有趣的事情——在那種情況下，他們能夠做什麼呢？大概只有儘速照馬偕的要求進行吧？一封電報記錄以下的回應：「錢會寄過去。」關於群眾的歸信，需要在此做個簡短的說明，宜蘭平原上的平埔族人當時正面臨約十萬名漢人將之滅族或同化的危機。早期，福音沒有被台灣漢人接受，但是近年來已經成功打開他們心門，獲致令人鼓舞的成果了。

— 86 —

在台宣教唯一可行之法

先前提過，閏虔益和他的家人因為健康的關係被迫歸國，而黎約翰牧師（Rev. John Jamieson）全家接續於次年來台。大約在這個時候，馬偕似乎已經改變「自加拿大申請宣教師來台」的作法。他比以往更為急切地認為「按立本地人成為牧師」是未來在台宣教惟一可行的作法。一八八四年春天，他藉著「封立兩位本地傳道成為牧師」的方式，將長時間深藏內心的想法付諸實現。封立的兩位牧師都是極具潛力和能力的人——嚴清華是馬偕第一位門徒，陳火是一八七三年春天頭一批受洗五人當中的一員——封立他們為牧師之後，馬偕寫一封信回母會，信裡表示：「海外宣道委員會今後不需要再為派遣別的宣教師來台而傷神。」另一封信當中，他更進一步說：「不要認為你們派遣宣教師來的這個政策比較好，長時間以來，我一直尋求的是在台灣能建立一個能夠自養的教會。」而委員會對於馬偕意見的看法，出現於當時的《記錄》當中，他們顯示出保守的態度：「委員會一致同意，正如《記錄》主編所說的，『我們由衷地瞭解馬偕所認定的看法，亦即封立本地的牧師是解決宣教師問題最快速的捷徑。』不過我們卻都意外地發現，他（馬偕）已經如此迅速的著手進行了。」

馬偕的政策是叫任何一位繼任者都能由衷同意的，因為只依賴一或二位外國宣教師無法

在數年、甚或數代之後達到教會自立自養的目標。值得我們關注的是，藉著男女宣教人數的增加，朝向「自養」目標已經達到五倍的成長。我們可以從北部教士會（the North Formosa Mission Council）的態度看到，從一九二二年在對母會的信裡要求「至少再額外增加十五位宣教師」可知當時的需要。

法軍砲擊封鎖台灣：焚而不熄

當時，監督多數的偏遠地區教會已經成為馬偕和兩位牧師的沉重負擔，因為那裡有需要傳道師去照顧信徒靈性上的需要。除此之外，更有一片烏雲籠罩在北台灣上空。法國軍艦騷擾中國的沿海，一八八五年八月五日，2 流傳的謠言更成了事實——有五艘法國軍艦接近雞籠港口——造成北台灣的騷動，照例來看，基督徒就會因此成為被逼迫的對象。十月，法軍從北部海岸繞到淡水港並封鎖該地，英國領事建議馬偕夫人和小孩、黎約翰夫婦以及兩位英國婦女要立刻前往香港避難。但這位道地的「軍人」馬偕博士卻拒絕讓他的信徒們遭受未知危險的命運。在有些人離開之後，法軍也已經開始砲擊紅毛城及附近地區，這時的馬偕受到瘧疾激烈的攻擊，以致於不省人事達數日之久。因此他被規勸去搭船前往香港養病。自此之後，他就被迫

留在香港直到法軍的封鎖結束為止。對於馬偕和教會來講，那真是極端痛苦的時期，許多信徒的家與教會的財產遭到戰亂的劫掠損毀，等法軍撤離之後，教會才開始著手整修重建教堂的工作。馬偕向滿清官員劉將軍（劉銘傳）提出「一萬元賠償」的要求，才藉著這筆經費去重建艋舺、錫口和新店的禮拜堂，傳教工作才又恢復先前盛況。因此，似乎每一次對立都會激發對黑暗勢力更大的還擊，同時也激起這位無懼的宣教師更大的熱情。當戰爭的煙霧消散之後，馬偕寫回母會的報告書中，寫著：「焚而不燬」（Nec tamen consumebatur）。

年輕熱情的吳威廉來台協助

一八九○年，黎約翰牧師在北部台灣付出六年的光陰之後與世長辭[3]，而他的妻子則回去加拿大。馬偕再度成為唯一的宣教師，他發現獨自監督不斷成長的教會，實在是個沉重的負擔，因此寫信回母會，請求他們另外再派一位同工前來。委員會因此任命吳威廉牧師（Rev. William Gauld）以回應他的請求。他們夫婦在一八九二年來到台灣。吳威廉生於安大略省米得賽克斯郡（Middelsex）西敏斯特（Westminster），在他十六歲時，曾與弟弟喬治（George）聽過馬偕第一次休假返國於倫敦郡聖安德魯教會（St. Andrew）的演講。聽完演講的返家路上，

威廉轉過身來對他的弟弟說：「我立志要當一位宣教師。」成年以後，這個信念更加地強烈，然而他的宣教目標卻轉向印度。公立學校教書的工作結束之後，他前往多倫多大學美術學系以及諾克斯神學院就讀。當海外宣道委員會焦急的尋找一位與馬偕同工的適當人選時，吳威廉的名字首先被列入考慮，委員會的報告書如此寫道：「吳威廉先生以學院的成績、教會服務的成果以及他對於海外宣教的興趣，於是毛遂自薦，因此他是承擔這個責任與職分以及選派的最佳人選。」

馬偕第二次休假，吳威廉扛起重擔

當吳威廉夫婦到達台灣之後，馬偕開始進行第二次休假返鄉的準備工作。而牧師們和傳道師也在規劃表揚馬偕全家的各樣活動。馬偕返鄉的消息迅速在淡水和教區傳揚開來，不管是基督徒或是非基督徒，都有志一同地為馬偕準備暫別的典禮。當時有超過七百位信徒與他們敬愛的宣教師告別。馬偕在當時的一封書信中如此寫道：「異教徒和基督徒、富人和窮人、讀書人和文盲等聚集一起，表達他們的敬意，祝福我們一路平安返回母國，以及期盼我們儘速回來，鑼鼓樂隊向我們致意，也一路吹打，護送我們經過一間又一間的教會，隊伍行進當中，爆竹聲

不斷響起，揮舞的旗幟伴隨燃放的鞭炮聲。有人準備一百磅的牛肉，站在路邊等待我們到達，真是妙極！真是妙極！廿一年來，我的雙眼看到的改變；當我首度巡視整個北台灣時，各階層的居民以他們想要的方式對待我，因此這一次，我就讓他們和其他人用他們感到適當的方式來進行。」

九月六日，就在吳威廉夫婦到達台灣九個月後，馬偕一家人搭乘「印度女皇號」（Empress of India）航向加拿大。他們第一次休假返國的時候，只有夫婦兩人，如今再加上媽蓮、以利和叡廉（George William Maclay），形成一個小小的馬偕家族。當他們穿上蘇格蘭高地短裙，又再度成為眾人的目光焦點。那次旅程由柯玖（維思）同行，他是一位聰明的漢族年輕學生，數年後與馬偕的二女兒以利結婚，並在往後多年的時間裡與宋雅各醫生（Dr. George V. Ferguson）同在馬偕醫院服務，是台北市內最大教會的長老。

對於吳威廉牧師來講，以他區區數個月的工作經驗以及對本地語言極為有限的知識下，單獨面對教會的工作，對他實在是個沉重的負擔[4]。但是馬偕在一封離開台灣不久前寫的書信，卻表達出對這位新宣教師的信心，他說：「吳威廉將會在下禮拜日第一次以台語講道，他也會竭盡所能的探訪信徒和佈道，整修所有教會的財產，按期提供傳道師的需要，主持洗禮和聖餐，我相信他會以理想及精確的方式處理這些事務，因為他所顯現的是熱忱態度以及精確的目光。吳師母非常忙碌，我想她是努力盡自己的本分，她一向都是以低調但熱情且敏感的態度完成她分內的工作，如果她『不是總想要向不可能挑戰』的話，那麼她將會有更大的影響力。」

如今吳師母已經在台灣服務超過三十年，少有女性宣教師能夠像她那樣與台灣人的心靈那

麼接近。她養護他們、安慰他們的痛苦、醫治他們的病痛，以奇妙的方式轉變他們的心。她那快樂又開朗的精神，加上對音樂的熱愛，心靈的慈悲與誠懇讓她贏得大部分基督徒的心。她能將看來毫無天分的人變成音樂家，她訓練年輕男女演奏及歌唱，充份展現她的音樂長才。後來她在許多教會機構當中訓練年輕人，為台灣教會提供寶貴的貢獻。

擔任加拿大總會議長

馬偕家族於九月再回到加拿大時，受到家鄉人熱忱的歡迎，他們也對馬偕和他的家人展現極大的興趣。接下來的冬天，馬偕拜訪了安大略省全部的教會。當時是馬偕人生中的黃金階段，他仍然維持著耀眼的活力、蓬勃的朝氣。他非常沉默但又極為敏感，在母會許多牧師的眼中，馬偕是一個謎樣的人物──儘管他們會認為他是一個古怪或特別的人，但卻崇拜他。

馬偕有很堅強的意志，也很少被打敗過，然而在格蘭嘉利（Glengarry）的一間蘇格蘭高地信徒的教會卻成了他很好的對手。有一位曾經在那間教會服務的牧師，說出馬偕「原先被打敗、但是最後獲得勝利」的故事。有一次他帶著心愛的台灣地圖去拜訪那間教會，當教會長老得知他要在主日崇拜時展開地圖的時候，他們以簡短但堅定的語氣告訴他，那是不可行的事。

因此，小會和馬偕爭論，其激烈程度是可以預期的，最後的結果是高地的馬偕被高地的長老們打敗了——馬偕只好在沒有地圖可展示的情況下，對信徒演講。不難想像那天早上所點燃的居爾特之火（Celtic fire），以及在演講內容當中出現數段批評該小會的言辭。然而，勝利在哪裡？在這些長老當中，有三位指定「捐贈部分遺產」給海外宣道委員會，總數大約一千元美金左右。由此可見，同一宗族成員的權力鬥爭結果也都一如往常有利於馬偕。除此之外，由於馬偕是海外宣教的開拓者，加上他在海外宣教卓越的貢獻，因此很自然的，全教會一致希望讓馬偕坐上教會最高的榮譽職位，作為贈與他的獻禮。

因此在新伯朗司維克（New Brunswick）聖約翰（St. John）教會召開的總會年會裡，馬偕獲選擔任總會的議長。他能夠坐上那個位置，表示他受到教會極大的認同。

日軍占台下教會極為困難

當馬偕和他的家人在加拿大享受兩年的休假之時，台灣的教會工作也是平靜而穩定的成長。海外宣道委員會成員心中的憂慮和誤解，也被一篇篇的報告書所化解[5]，《紀錄》如此寫道：「吳威廉在台灣的工作已經進入狀況，這實在令人滿意，以他的同理心以及判斷力，我

們將可以預期有一個好的結果。由於馬偕的返國，委員會當中出現些許的憂慮，害怕他（吳威廉）肩負的責任超過他所能承受的程度，如今這種憂慮已經消失。雖然曾經出現數次困難，但吳威廉與本地牧師和相關的傳道師，藉著智慧去關照監督，因此我們可以確定教會在他的手中是安然無恙的。」

後來，原本穩定成長的事工卻因為中國與日本的戰爭而陷入混亂當中。日本在一八九五年佔台的經過，已經完整的在第二章描述出來，吳威廉牧師當時是掌理教會唯一的宣教師，他那忍耐、良好的判斷力和常識，對於騷亂以及磨難時期的教會來講實在非常重要；而對於本地教會來講，那也是個極為困難的時代，因為基督徒遭受許多的痛苦。我們可以描繪馬偕遠離他所愛的信徒，在這段時間當中他心裡所經歷煎熬的過程。海外宣道委員會的懸念可以由一八九五年報告書的序言當中看到：「遠東的戰事產生許多的疑慮和不安，由於台灣成為日本的領土，這事對於教會的影響值得關注，在這種情況下我們唯一確定的是，萬國的主宰上帝掌管這一切事件。在此同時我們很安慰得知吳威廉夫婦健康良好，遠離一切的傷害。最近事件的影響是所有外國婦女都受命離開台灣，吳夫人在領事的建議之下前往廈門。」報告書接下來是吳威廉所寫的內容，這也是宣教史當中最好的文獻之一。

一八九五年秋天，馬偕和他的家人回到台灣。可以想像馬偕在經歷深沉的憂慮之後，他急切的拜訪當地和外國的朋友，並且積極想要瞭解整個戰事的真實情況。他的證言當中，對於吳威廉以及本地牧師在危機中堅持下去的態度，表現出他個人深刻的敬佩：「教會事工如常進行，不受影響。」一八九九年，吳威廉和他的家人回去加拿大進行第一次的休假後，馬偕獨自一人在日本新政府之下管理教會，局勢緩慢的改變。日本政府對基督教是友善的，宣教工作的進行也未受阻礙。儘管照常努力工作，但那最終讓這位勇敢的宣教師病故的疾病卻快速進展。吳威廉和他的家人於一九〇〇年秋天回到台灣，而這是馬偕「第一次歡迎休假完畢的同工返回工作崗位」的經驗——他以不尋常的方式和他握手，並且以顫抖的嘴唇對他說：「我很感激你回來台灣。」

不治之症之險惡奮戰

馬偕的病症進入比較危急的階段之後，他接受建議，前往香港尋求專家治療，但卻聽到醫生宣布他所罹患的是不治之症。儘管如此，直到生命的最後階段，馬偕都還不願意接受醫生宣判的事實[6]。在他過世前幾週，加拿大長老教會河南的醫生麥克魯受派前來安慰這位退休的宣

教師——直到生命的終末，馬偕仍像一隻牢籠中激烈的與疾病奮戰的雄獅。有幸在那段時間前往探訪他的人，都宣稱不曾在病人的身上看到如此強烈的生命力。他雖然沒有辦法說話，但是在他的監督下，講師念讀講義的內容給學生聽。有一天，麥克魯醫生暗示他，疾病的擴散頗為快速，那表示他的來日無多。離開之後，麥克魯醫生前往吳威廉的家，從那裡望向馬偕的家。他們看見一位將亡的人在走廊邊上下踱步，與最終的敵人做最險惡的奮戰。馬偕的生命終結於一九○一年六月二日，加拿大長老教會收到通知，整個教會為失去最偉大的宣教士和最著名的英雄而悲傷。對台灣教會來講，那真是一個深沉悲痛卻又極為重要的日子，然而教會並不是孤立無助、毫無盼望。儘管教會肇建者馬偕離開了他們，但是教會的頭——耶穌基督，仍然存在。

在台宣教廿九年成果驚異

馬偕雖已蒙主恩召，然而他的工作卻沒有跟著他一起消失。總結他在台灣廿九年的努力，當中的成果實在令人驚異，因為我們知道他是在什麼樣艱鉅的環境下開始他的事工的。當他過世的時候，在台灣本土已有一位外國的宣教師和他的夫人、兩位本地人牧師、六十位傳道、廿四位聖經宣道婦（Bible women）[7]，將近一千八百位信徒以及六十間教會。這些教會當中有

超過一半是建立在平埔族地區；雖然隨著平埔族的消失，這些教會也跟著不見了，但是我們要記得，這些教會是在僅有一位宣教師和他本地助手共同努力下所建立起來的時候，那麼這個成果就更顯得卓著[8]。

筆者從來沒有見過馬偕。但是我竭盡所能去尋找馬偕和他工作的成果——尤其是從台灣教會中對他們所愛的領袖——那些對馬偕印象既深又久的弟兄們搜集到的資料。而這兩章當中對馬偕的評價是由不同來源所建立起來的。

馬偕並沒有比其他的人更為完美，許多時候他的感情壓過理性的判斷，他可以看見一般人看起來平淡無奇的事物當中的奧妙，他能夠生動的述說一段故事或是描述一個事件。他喜歡高山深谷更勝於平原以及常見的地方，他那烈火般的脾氣在許多時候為他帶來許多麻煩，但是他絕不會因此而縮回他的腳步或是接受失敗的事實。他是天生的軍人，也是一位很少徵詢下屬意見的指揮官。他從來沒有顯示出組織能力的天分，但是他那激勵人的性格，強烈到可以成為整個傳教工作整體的組成要素。或許他所創立起來的事工氛圍是敬畏多於情感，欽佩多於欣賞，但是由於他那沉默寡言的個性，使得他不容易成為別人親近的伙伴。

然而那段時間，他所面對的是中國滿清的官吏、狂暴的土匪、政治上的迫害以及無法無天的社會——因此若維持溫柔親切的態度容易招致外界誤解，而會導致成為失敗的原因。有些人在面臨北部台灣教會創建者所面對的景況時或許會畏縮，但是那段時間所面對的仇恨的對立、根深蒂固的偏見和疑懼都已經成為過去；而且當時看起來成功的方法，在一個已經具有法律與秩序的社會中是完全不合時宜的，且讓我們感謝我們今天的生活環境，然後學習前人遺留下

來、盡忠於上帝賦予的使命的典範，忠實的履行我們的本分。

很少有人跟馬偕見面後沒有留下深刻印象的，許多的接觸經驗都被記錄下來。在本章結束

以前，我們引用部分的內容：

「他對上帝單純的信心，對於福音書毫無懷疑的信仰，他對於一生所從事工作的信念，深刻的相信耶穌基督在人生命中的主宰地位，毫不保留的熱情，將自己完全降服在拯救者以及君王的耶穌基督，使得他能夠克服他的個性，讓他跳脫微渺的命運，使得他的本質變得高貴，使他的信仰有力量而使得他的生命成為教會歷史的要素。」

「英勇的小人物……實在很榮幸能夠認識這等人物，而將他的面容清晰的記在腦海當中，能夠鼓舞人對抗成為凡俗人和凡俗生命的宿命。」

「他的個子矮小，但是堅定而活躍，話不多，擁有堅定的勇氣。擁有豐富的常識，同樣的他也完全獻身於主。」

「對我來講，馬偕的光芒蓋過任何一個時代偉大的宣教師，使我們能為他這個人與他的作為來感謝上帝。」

馬偕的墳墓坐落於「青草堡壘」（Fort Meadow）旁的一個美麗角落，一座新近設立中學（今淡江中學）校園的後方，圍繞著磚塊砌成的牆壁，在他的身旁安息著敬虔的陳火牧師，他是就任於北部台灣第一間自養教會的牧師。

禱告詞

◆ ◆ ◆ ....

噢！祢是收成的主宰，也揀選一粒麥子落入土地，在那裡孤獨的死亡，但是當它死亡之後，卻結出許多果實來，我們要在祢面前陳明，那些前往福爾摩沙的宣教師，他們為祢和福音的緣故奉獻生命，那些健康毀損的人被迫返回故鄉，而那些仍在遠方服務的人，每日毫不吝惜的獻出自己的年華，我們祈禱，祢能實現收成的規則，讓這些為愛犧牲的人，能夠結出豐盛的果實。

讓我們也成為上帝拯救台灣人以及世界所有人的同工，願我們的心靈在裡面燃燒，當我們思量他們對祢盡忠奉獻的事蹟時，願我們自己和人群的生命裡點燃新的愛，願我們被新的服務熱情抓住。

為了順服祢的命令，我們向祢祈禱，驅動許多人前往那裡或是祢的禾場，願屬於祢的子民都擁有收穫工人的精神，為了世人的得救而汗流浹背的奔波，直到祢見到心靈的痛苦獲得圓滿。為了祢名的緣故。阿們。

卷
二

第五章 ◆ 北福爾摩沙新時代教會

新時代宣教政策

教會面臨轉型

隨著肇建者馬偕的過世，教會面臨一個全新卻極為艱困的挑戰。台灣本地的基督徒體認到「不會再有另一位作風像偕牧師一樣的宣教師被派來台灣了」；除此之外，他們現在也能夠比較自由的表達長時間壓抑內心的意見。毫無疑問，這些想法，主要是受到南部教會成立中會建立完整教會體制的事實所影響[1]。他們心想，大概不再需要其他西方的宣教師，只要在吳威廉牧師的協助之下，本地人的領袖可以直接承接教會的責任。很顯然的，他們還沒有完全體認到承擔教會責任的重要和嚴肅的意義。這些問題後來都是由吳威廉牧師明智的判斷，堅定的態

度，以及上帝那良善雙手的指引，讓台灣教會能夠非常平順且成功的度過這一段艱困的時期。

華德羅牧師來台

此時的吳威廉牧師比其他時候更熱切期盼新同工的加入，因此急迫的請求母會立刻派遣宣教師來協助分擔教會的重擔。母會回應他的請求，任命一位女王大學的畢業生華德羅牧師（Rev. Thurlow Fraser）來台成為宣教師，並且在一九〇二年秋天，偕同妻子來到台灣。初來之時，華德羅牧師極為認真的學習語言，他那開放的態度和專注的舉止、活潑的精神，強烈的吸引本地人的注意——特別是傳道師和學生的目光。他很快就學會台灣本土語言，並了解本地教會的問題。在他服務期間，撰寫一篇具有重大意義的教會文獻，提交加拿大長老教會總會參考。

教會內部期盼更多的民主精神

之前在馬偕晚年時，嚴清華牧師是他唯一的顧問，陳火這位敬虔的新店教會牧師已經在數年前別世，嚴清華是唯一能夠協助推動宣教工作執行層面的人選。毫無疑問的，為了讓教會工作順利的推展，嚴清華牧師獲得更多的權力。然而這些權力長期掌握在少數人手中，引起其他人的不滿，而宣教師們也體認到這個難題，因而採取行動，回應這個年輕教會對民主精神的需求。

一份歷史性的文獻

就在這個關鍵的時刻，艋舺教會的信徒提出一份緊急的請求，希望教士會能夠派遣一位年輕並具有進步思想的傳道師陳清義前往該教會服務。他是陳火的兒子，馬偕的女婿。在此同時他們也同意「願意自行負擔一切支出」。這個請求讓當時在台的宣教師們（吳威廉、華德羅、嚴清華牧師等人）深感成立中會的必要性，於是一起花費許多時間仔細研究其他宣教區域的重要政策，並在一九○四年五月九日提出研究成果，這份報告書節錄如下：

由於我們相信，北部台灣設立中會的時機已經成熟，藉以使主內的兄弟能夠熟習參與教會事務中組織和行政的運作，並且藉著練習來學會這些技巧，也獲得自立組織的權力，並且由於我們也注意到有一間地方教會請求封立一位傳道師成為牧師，信中也表達其他教會也有相同的需求。因此，北部台灣教士會的成員，請求海外宣道委員會將這個問題提到總會討論，我們更進一步請求總會設立北部台灣中會，在此同時，區分加拿大長老教會教士會的權限，以及「嚴清華與華德羅牧師」和「嚴清華牧師與耶穌聖教」之間的關係。並且，由於我們的目標是建立本地化的教會，而不是讓教會長時間受到國外掌控。因此我們請求，應該授權成立台灣教會的中會，讓它們對神學院的畢業生舉行考試並且進一步封立他們成為牧師，也賦予中會監督中會體制之下各地方教會以及小會的權力，在本地大會成立以前，不需要向更高的權力機構負責。由此我們相信，設立女學校以及選派適任的加拿大女教師的時機已經成熟，因為婦女教育的需求愈來愈急切。因此我們請求海外宣道委員會

與婦女宣道會（The Woman's Missionary Society）協調，儘快派兩位適任的加拿大單身女教師前來。由於進入牛津學堂研讀並準備將來擔任傳道人的學生，幾乎都沒有研讀神學預備課程，因此我們請求海外宣道委員會允許建造校舍，作為預備學校或中學之用。

以上節錄的內容明確指出，在台宣教師們充分體認到周圍環境的快速變遷，新時代裡，教會各樣的需求，也表達出新的民主精神已經在教會出現的事實。就在中會成立以前——華德羅牧師，這位竭盡心思撰寫上述請求書的宣教師，因為妻子身體欠安，在這個情況下離開台灣和他的宣教工作。

宣教師新陣容

吳威廉牧師申請更多加籍宣教師來台

在結束休假返回台灣之後，吳威廉牧師體認到，為了維持教會穩固的基礎，和對未曾接觸基督教的大眾進行佈道工作，需要更多宣教師來協助事工的推展。於是他向母會提出一項緊急呼籲，請他們派遣宣教師來台：成員要包括一位牧師、一位醫生、以及兩位女性的宣教師。這

是一項偉大並且勇氣十足的請求，同時也可以看見他是多麼深刻的體認到「教會對於宣教政策的需求」。

而海外宣道委員會回應的勇氣也是不亞於他的請求，委員會警覺到北部台灣的需要，因此他所要求的四位宣教師如期來到台灣。

歡迎加拿大新任宣教師

一九〇五年十月，約美但牧師（Rev. Milton Jack）、宋雅各醫生夫婦，金仁理姑娘（Miss Janie Kinney）和高哈拿姑娘（Miss Hannah Connell）來到淡水，他們在那裡受到吳威廉夫婦以及台灣基督徒的歡迎。對於台灣的教士會與教會來說，當五位年輕熱情的宣教師一起搭船前來台灣，那實在是個偉大的時刻。這一群高貴的宣教師來到，讓本地的牧師、傳道師以及信徒們得到很大的精神鼓舞，讓他們知道獲得加拿大教會對本地教會的關心，也讓他們知道加拿大教會打算為台灣的教會建立起一個既寬廣又堅固的根基。

以樂觀態度學習本地語言

在淡水兩間宣教師的住宅現在是充滿活力！這些青年的宣教師展現出歡樂和年輕人的熱情，他們首先面對的問題是台灣話，每一間空房都成為課堂，每天早上和下午，宣教師和他（她）們的語言教師重複練習單調的台語八音。對這些新到的學生在初學階段裡來講，這些音調聽起來幾乎都是相同。然而，隨著對語言能力的瞭解增加後，讓他們獲得很大的鼓舞。他們

認為「別人可以成功學會語言，相信他們自己也不會失敗」。次年，宣教師的人數再度增加，

約美但牧師的夫人也到達台灣，並且熱情的加入語言學習的行列。

運用多元創意方式與本地人溝通

六個年輕人住在「草地堡壘」當中——這裡是整個區域當中最美麗的地方。他們這一群外

國人，引起了當地人的興趣，特別是來台之後，他們養成「每天黃昏在海邊或稻田間散步」的

習慣，總是吸引當地人好奇的目光。而且當兩位女宣教師並行之時，許多人都誤認為她們是一

對夫婦——對台灣人來講，區分西方人的男女性別有些困難。因為在那個時代，漢學老師都會

穿著各色長袍，驕傲的在淡水街道踱步（那些長袍極像婦女所穿的長裙），然而台灣的婦女卻

是穿著長褲。一些有趣的評論（絕對不是恭維）在那些旁觀者當中流傳著，而這些評論幸好那

些西方人聽不懂。

當這些宣教師的語言能力有所進展之後，台灣訪客開始漸漸增加，並且拜訪的時間增長，

有許多時候，會讓這些學語言的學生感到不舒服，因為他們有限的字彙已經用完了。當沒有辦

法用語言表達出來的時候，手勢或身體語言就成為補充的溝通工具。宣教師如果沒有從語言教

師那裡得到鼓勵的話，他們也一定不會缺乏從謙恭的來賓口中聽到那些奉承言詞的機會。本地

人會告訴宣教師他們是多麼聰明、發音又是多麼的清楚，但同時卻又轉身問，「老師，宣教師

剛剛說話的內容是什麼？」由於漢人很少有笑容、甚至連微笑都沒有，因此當宣教師有什麼錯

誤的時候，可以想像他們不會有什麼幽默感。如果跟著他們回到家，只會聽到他們說「這些外

國人是犯了多麼大的錯誤」，然後就可以聽見他們爆出大笑（因為宣教師語言上的錯誤）。如今這些漢人取笑宣教師的笑話很容易就可以寫滿整個章節，並且可以帶來許多的娛樂效果。

醫療宣教師運用看診時間學會本土語言

本地人發現了這些宣教師當中有一位醫生（指宋雅各醫生），之後，似乎整個城鎮的居民「都生病」了。他們在沒有受到邀請的情況下前來拜訪，他們也很快就知道醫生宿舍的所在地，每天大門一開，就擠得水洩不通。由於漢人的居所幾乎沒有隱私可言，他們自然也不知尊重外國人房舍的隱私權。因此那些患病的人會在醫生家中的任何角落、任何時間與他攀談，以便得到治療。

對於宣教師宋忠堅醫生（Dr. Ferguson）來講，要去防備漢人研究他們的家庭狀況，實在不是一件簡單的事情。這位外國醫生的所有時間全都讓本地患者占用了，他能有什麼時間學習語言？因此，他每天下午的看診時間都需要吳威廉牧師娘或柯玖來擔任翻譯，直到後來，他漸漸能夠自己使用這個新的語言與患者溝通為止，才在緊縮的看診時間內學會本地語言。

行政組織的強化

「教士會」成立，經驗得以傳承

由於宣教師人員的增加，因此對於能夠相互討論宣教事務，以便形成共同政策的需求也跟著增加；而比較資深的宣教師是當時唯一在這個國家停留夠久、瞭解本地情況的人，因此他們組成教士會，在會議當中討論問題，提出新的政策並且遵行，會議的紀錄也要保留下來並每個月寄送到母會的海外宣道委員會。因此，比較年輕的宣教師很快就可以瞭解本地的狀況。一九○七年秋天，筆者來到台灣之時，儘管較為資深的宣教師正在加拿大休假，但當時的教士會卻已經非常有效率的指導經常性的教會事務了。

偕彼得博士訪台喚醒「馬偕時代」回憶

海外宣道會幹事偕彼得博士的來訪，是台灣本地教會極為熱衷的一個事件。他的到訪，喚醒本地信徒對於已經過世的「偕牧師」的回憶，因為那是他們「信仰的父親：馬偕」經常提到的人。偕彼得博士在馬偕來台宣教初期常和他書信來往，可謂台灣教會與母會的窗口。或許偕彼得博士在東方國家的探訪經驗中，沒有一個地方像「美麗之島」那樣震撼他的心靈，島嶼高聳的山脈與低窪的平原，以及最讓人震懾的，是本地人對於偉大開創者的記憶仍保留得非常完整。

筆者劉忠堅牧師抵台

一九○七年十二月，筆者和妻子來到台灣，初來的兩年研習語言並拜訪許多地方教會，最

初的同伴是年資最久的信徒和牧師嚴清華，也是馬偕牧師除了家人之外最親密的朋友。

初期觀察仍需積極的佈道行動

在學生陪伴我們拜訪異教的村落之後，筆者認為北部台灣的佈道事業還未達發展的階段，而廣大的群眾多半尚未接觸過福音：比較年長的當地人曾經聽過「耶穌」與「偕牧師」的名字，但除非當地設立了基督教會或有信徒住在那裡，否則年輕的一代對福音一無所知。在馬偕晚年的數年裡，牛津學堂的工作占據他大部分的時間與精力，而一位宣教師和一位本地牧師也無法有效率的巡視六十間教會，更不用說要在六十間教會以外的地方進行佈道工作。在馬偕過世之後，吳威廉牧師也必須在學院教書，協助牧養工作以及照料宣教事業的行政事務，結果就是積極佈道的工作必須從它的根基重新規劃。

北台宣教增添更多生力軍

大約在這個時候，有四位宣教師加入此地教士會的陣容，黎媽美姑娘（Miss Mabel Clazie），安義理姑娘（Miss Lilly Adair）以及馬偕的兒子偕叡廉夫婦的加入。馬偕的獨子偕叡廉以及媳婦（著名的布魯斯非爾德教會的約翰·羅斯牧師的女兒偕仁利）返台服務，對於台灣基督徒來說，這是一件最具深刻意義的事情。偕叡廉在台灣出生成長，並且能講自然流利的台語，他的母親和兩位姐姐媽蓮與以利歡迎他於完成加拿大和美國十年的學院訓練之後回到家，許多牧師和傳道師還記得他童稚時期與他們渡過最愉快的回

憶；但是聚會中最快樂的人是他盡責的母親張聰明，她在兒子離開那段時間，想念兒子，並且也隨時提供他在異國提出的需求。

宣教中心移轉到台北市

一九一一年當中有幾件重要的事情，隨著宣教師人數的增加，必須開始興建宿舍以及其他的機構，經過詳細的研究之後，教士會請求海外宣道會允許在台北首府購置土地，並且決定在必要的工作經過相當發展之後，就將宣教中心從淡水移往台北市。這個要求獲得了允許，在台北市外近兩公里處購置土地，作為興建醫院、神學院以及六間宣教師宿舍之用。購買土地數個月之後，吳威廉牧師被任命擔任監督「馬偕紀念醫院」的興建工作。

醫療事工的進深

醫療事工的價值

宣教工作伊始，醫療工作便是極具吸引力的一個項目。當年，馬偕發現醫療工作在移除一般人對基督教信仰以及對福音機構的偏見兩方面的重要價值，更不用說醫療傳道的即時價值。

華雅各醫生短期在台灣工作的期間建立了淡水醫院，但馬偕過世之後，這個部門的工作受到嚴重的挫折，因為沒有人負擔這個工作。雖然外國人社群的醫生們提供的協助令人感激，但是距離「足夠」還有一段路。

淡水醫院再度開張

宋雅各醫生到達之後，將醫療工作有條理地組織起來。淡水醫院再度開設——雖然內部空間狹窄，但對於每週來就診的千百名患者，提供了許多有效的肉體與靈魂治療。這個工作與現代化的腳步與時俱進，這是歸因於日本醫療科學快速的進步所致。早期的政府官員非常支持這項事工，並對這位新醫生的個性與技術，印象也非常深刻。

宋雅各轉往台北，群眾不捨

宋雅各醫生在淡水進行醫療工作的四年間。每天早上有超過一百位病人耐心地等待這位外國醫生的治療。這些年中，群眾的身體得到醫治，也有許多人因而承認耶穌基督為救主。將醫療工作從淡水移往台北，對宋雅各醫生來講一件是很簡單的事情，但是漢人中有富裕有權勢的人將這件事情當成是「表達對宋醫生高度感激的時刻」——長列的轎子將他載往火車站，宋醫生坐的轎子也用紅布裝飾起來。

馬偕紀念醫院的開設

為紀念北部教會開創者而開設的「馬偕紀念醫院」於一九一二年完成，十二月廿六日正式啟用時是一件很重大的事件。民政長官與數位首要官員出席，他們在致詞中對教會創建者和宋雅各醫生在台北設立這個人道機構表達感激之意，也沒有忘記教會建築與建者的功績。隔日，北部教會超過一千位信徒聚集在醫院，紀念北部設教四十週年，由幾位尚健在而記憶深刻的人回顧創建以來的歷史足跡，這些致詞者當中有一位是吳寬裕牧師，他是最初接受基督教信仰的五位信徒之一，並且在將近四十年間傳揚福音，在這個場合中，再度點燃對馬偕的回憶之情，這個事件恰巧作為慶祝紀念北部台灣宣教第四十週年的大事。

基督教醫療事工的評估

醫療傳道工作對於每一個有興趣於宣教事業的人有著極大的吸引力，它是少數能夠獲得非基督教徒認同的事工之一，是基督教真正的精神和實際特色之所在。同時，對於患病的人來說，也是極為有力的佈道方式。當患者在醫院獲得醫治的時候，他們看見活的福音，並且也熟習福音故事。很自然的，那些留在醫院治療得較長時間的人，比起那些一來到醫院、但只聽過一次福音的人來說，會比較有令教會滿意的結果。理論上來講，這種方法使得數千人原本沒有機會與基督教接觸，但卻因此而聽到上帝的話。這在草創時期更是如此。對於基督教醫院事工成果的評估，不僅只限於每年年終報告中強調有多少位患者前來診治，進行多少次移除患者身體疾病與疼痛的手術而已，也應更進一步的評估基督教的影響力（醫院對於非基督教社會的佈

— 113 —

道，擴張基督教工作盡了多少力量協助）。如果宣教事工在醫院這個地方失敗，那麼它算是在最好的機會當中失敗，而且教士會對它的支持力道將會大量的減少。對於這件事情，非常值得感謝的是北部台灣基督教醫院一直都是強力的佈道機構。有許多醫療技術成功和上帝恩典的故事可以述說。

宋雅各醫生返加休假心繫台灣

馬偕紀念醫院完工，讓教士會（特別是醫療宣教師）感到非常滿意，宋雅各醫生花費二到三年的時間準備醫療計畫和規則，同時不辭辛勞的照顧患者。醫院啟用不久之後，他必須返國休假，讓他非常遺憾──特別是醫院還欠缺在台灣有多年學習、擁有台灣話知識的醫生，讓他沒辦法安然的交託工作。

醫療宣教師過勞

一九一一年秋天，受過護理訓練的烈以利姑娘（Miss Isabel Elliot）來到台灣。一九一二年春天，宋雅各醫生將返國休假的數個月前，倪阿倫醫生以及烈以利姑娘夫婦（Dr. A.A. Gray & Mrs. Gray）到達。當宋雅各醫生返國之後，倪阿倫醫生以及烈以利姑娘（Miss Elliott）接手這座雙連新醫院醫療和護理工作，而柯玖先生擔任倪阿倫醫師的譯員，而馬偕女兒偕以利則是擔任烈以利姑娘的翻譯。這是後來北台教士會不願意再推行這項政策的原因，因為種下的結果就是「宣教師的身體與心靈完全崩潰」，導致醫療宣教師因為無法適任而離職。不過當時倪阿倫夫婦受到宣教

師同工和台灣民眾的喜愛，他表現出對本地人真正的情感，以及真正宣教師的精神，而倪夫人則是成為婦女同工當中最有效率的人。對於宣教師同工來講，他們的永遠離開，實在是一件遺憾的事情。

呂馬烈姑娘到達及生力軍回去

一九一七年秋天，受過護理訓練的呂馬烈姑娘（Miss Margaret Luscombe）來到台灣，兩年之後她通過語言考試，但是因為身體狀況不佳，只好在一九二一年夏天回去加拿大；由於馬偕紀念醫院因為缺乏醫生（一九一九年宋雅各醫生離台）而關閉，呂馬烈姑娘甚至在她短暫停留的時間當中，並沒有機會從事她極有興趣的護理工作。

基督教教育機構的設立

建築宣教師羅虔益來台

一九一三年秋天，一個新的步驟開始，當麥基爾大學（MacGill University）的畢業生羅虔益先生（K. W. Dowie）接受任命監督建築事工，以及利用部分時間組織城裡日本與台灣青年的

基督教工作，成為宣教師當中最有價值的同工。雖然他對於日本語和台灣話有很好的知識，但因為宣教師人數減少，因此只能將自己的活動侷限在既有的工作上，以及財務、教育和新近教會建築工作上。之後，羅虔益夫人前來台灣與他會合，她在日本參與日本基督教女青年會（Young Women's Christian Association）的工作。

開設中學，教會知識水準提昇

一九一四年以前，北部台灣沒有男子中學的存在，本地教會生活中這個極大的欠缺使得宣教工作受到很大的損害。一九〇二年，有一封書信送往海外宣道會，請求開設男子中學，然而鑑於缺乏專業訓練師資的緣故，中學校的組織延後到一九一四年，這時已在宣教地區的偕叡廉牧師也準備好要進行這個重要的工作。他被教士會任命為校長，同年四月，學校就在他父親馬偕度過多年最好、最快樂時光的「牛津學堂」開設了。

宣教機構的價值

牛津學堂創校之初，就充分地顯示出教育存在的意義，顯示出對教會青年的價值，以及成為有效率的宣教機構。學生大多來自非基督教家庭，他們當中的許多人，在幾年求學期間表達對耶穌基督的忠貞。如今急需兩位能力優秀的教師或得到教師資格的宣教師，特別是考量到隨著新校舍建設而帶來學校擴充的需求，台灣政府的新規定當中，對於提高教育標準的要求，更是如此。因為淡水中學校符合這些規定，因此得到政府的認可，將成為教會青年教育有效率的

— 116 —

機構，讓非基督徒學生歸信，以及傳揚基督教知識到達全台灣極有效率的宣教機構。

偕叡廉先生執掌這個學校直到最近休假歸國為止，在他休假這段期間，羅虔益先生負責這間學校的運作。偕先生對於台灣話完美的知識，以及他那受到歡迎的基督徒氣質，儘管他不是受封的牧師，但他成功的指導學生的心靈。對那些學生來講，他所表現出來的是基督教牧養當中的傳福音精神。一九一九年回台的偕叡廉先生對於學校靈性生活的深化。擁有教育專業的偕叡廉夫人對於台灣青年不倦的教誨，花費許多的時間和精力教英文，他們藉著歡迎年輕人前往家中，以及讓他們瞭解英文的樂趣，偕先生夫婦幫助移除「一般人以為學校是西方機構」的誤解。

田健治郎總督的政策

在此要表達對福爾摩沙政府深刻的感激之意，特別是在田健治郎總督主政之下，對台灣青年接受較高等教育有極大的興趣。為本地男女學童設立的小學校和公學校有很大的發展。由於中學校的欠缺，台灣的中學水準和在日本的同級生相比，較為遜色。增加這些教育機構數目的這項新政策，以及提高前述的教育標準，或許暗示福爾摩沙政府計畫興建大學的可能性，如此的機構會讓台灣的年輕人準備在獲得更自由的公民權之後將負起新的責任。如果這項政策實行，台灣的教會將會非常高興，因為這樣會使教會能夠監督教會的年輕人之道德標準。如今有數百位台灣年輕人冒險前往日本較大的教育中心，因此可以肯定的說，台灣的有錢人會更加樂意、自由的捐獻金錢給台灣的大學使用。

約美但牧師派往韓國

一九一七年，約美但牧師被任命成為朝鮮延世基督教大學的教授，和他家人一起遷往韓國工作，在此之前（一九〇七至一九一六年間），他大部分時間是擔任台北神學校校長的工作。

北部教會新時代的開始，政權轉變之時，有許多執行的工作都是約美但牧師以其優秀的行政能力以及對於設立本土教會發展自養的極大興趣，提供無與倫比的幫助，加上約美但夫人耀眼的天賦，協助淡水與台北兩地的婦女工作。

神學校缺乏足夠師資

台北神學校一直都是教會生命成長的重要力量，許多年來，教學工作都是在淡水牛津學堂進行的，組織中學了之後，神學校必須轉往台北市，當學校正在建築時，學生有三到四年的時間在臨時校舍上課，吳威廉牧師被任命計畫新學院的興建工作，一九一七年暑假奠立地基，一九一八年春天啟用，是吳威廉牧師第三次休假返國前幾個月完成的，這所學校的空間寬廣，足夠供應教會將來的需要。然而神學校的事工卻因為缺乏足夠的外國教師而十分艱辛，如果這個重要的機構要提供最偉大、最好的服務的話，任命更多已封立的宣教師是必要之舉。從啟用以來，學院成為牧師、傳道師聚會和中會會議及一般會議極具吸引力的聚會場所。

數年以來，神學院由吳威廉牧師負責運作，再由城裡來的日本及台灣牧師協助教育工作。

現今急需有能力的教師，因為吳牧師他必須奉獻全時間在這個讓年輕人完整準備進入基督教牧會重要的工作之上。

（加拿大總會）「傳道委員會」和「海外宣道會」迫切的渴望，這間學院在最近的將來，必須完整的裝備並提供足夠且適任的教職員。

新設立幼稚園

北部台灣的宣教工作於最近幾年增加一項新的部門。由於日本政府並不允許在境內設立私立小學，教士會決定利用這個機會在大城市當中設立幼稚園，福順姑娘（Miss Jannie Hotson）被任命來台，利用兩年的時間學習台灣話之後，前往日本學日本語。

宋雅各醫生退休

由於身體欠安，宋雅各醫生必須在一九一八年春天前往日本，不過回台之後，他的身體仍然十分衰弱，因此他勢必要在隔年回去加拿大。由於害怕他恐怕無法回到這個組織完備的工作崗位，對於他那些新近設立的機構同工而言倍感憂心。後續的消息是，他將退休回國，這讓教會非常沮喪，宋雅各醫生留給台灣基督徒和非基督教的社會永難磨滅的印象，他得到日本官員

— 119 —

（特別是醫務部門）高度的尊敬，因為他那真誠的個性以及內外科的技術。他沉默寡言加上理性的判斷以及優良的基督徒原則，為教士會各部門以及本土教會在處理眾多且複雜的問題上，帶來極深的利益。

一間設備齊全的醫院卻是關閉的

宋雅各醫生在一九一九年離開之後，馬偕紀念醫院也隨之關閉，這件事情的意義對教士會來講雖然極為清楚，但對於宣教師來講，當他們每天看見這間每天原本可以容納許多病患，需要他們提供肉體和心靈上幫助的建築物時，卻是不斷感受心痛和苦楚。這種情況除非母會責成海外宣道委員會派遣足夠的醫生來重開醫院，否則損害是無法彌補的。

教士會成員增加

一九一九年十月，吳威廉牧師夫婦第三度休假返國，他的心裡因為偕叡廉夫婦以及舜姑娘（Miss Maude Ackison）以及數個月之後的女王大學畢業生的連虔益醫生（K. A. Denholm）的來到而歡喜（連夫人在一九二二年辭職回加拿大）。一九二二年的高華德牧師（Rev. G. Coates）以及一九二二年的高華德牧師娘抵台。他們的來到，為台灣宣教的事工提供佳美的典範。最近來台的是夏瑪利姑娘（Miss Mary Haig），她在一九二〇年抵達台灣。

現在迫切的需要

有關加拿大長老教會婦女宣道會發展與事工的歷史，將會在稍後的章節中處理，下列男性宣教師的需求是北部台灣教士會渴望解決目前缺人的最低要求：

一、四位受封立的牧師：一位負責現有十萬居民的宜蘭平原、一位負責新竹地區、一位負責客家族群、一位負責主日學事工。

二、三位醫療宣教師；在馬偕紀念醫院服務。

三、兩位教師；在中學服務。

四、一位事工經理。

對於這個呼聲，有誰願意說：「我在這裡，請差遣我？」或者如果沒有辦法的話，也可以提出類似的禱告：「我自己沒有辦法去，但是有沒有另外一個人可以代表我去？」

噢！上帝，讓我們為祢奇妙的恩典以及福音在台灣的勝利而獻上我們卑微的感恩。當我們看見祢親手栽種的葡萄園，內心就充滿歡欣，並且盼望自己也在勞苦工人當中，讓我們為更勇敢的信心禱告。

因為祢將自己顯示在耶穌基督身上，讓男男女女每個人和孩子都看見，而他們的生命也因為順服祢而心意更新，因為耶穌照亮並潔淨每個家庭，在祢年輕的教會當中，祢的子民得以享受崇拜讚美時的心靈連結，在學院和學校裡，內心得到啟發而富足、人格更健壯，生命得以形塑、得到造就、得以服事。我們為醫院當中的醫療專業團隊、宣教師們所給予的各樣友善並以基督的靈與聖名服事而感謝祢。

讓這些同工的事工更加豐盛，派遣更多生力軍前往協助，讓我們主上帝的美善降臨在他們身上，以他們的雙手來建立祢的事工，是的，以他們的雙手來建立它，以我們救主的名禱告，阿們。

第五章 ◆ 北福爾摩沙新時代教會

第六章 ◆ 本土教會成長緊扣佈道事工的發展

海外宣教的核心目標

在非基督教的環境當中，海外宣教最重要的步驟就是「達成本土化教會的建立和發展」，作為一位宣教師，必須不斷提醒自己，海外宣教的工作並不是將一個外國機構移植到當地而已，而是去建立一個能讓當地人將自身的特質表達出來，且與這些人的特殊生活處境相調和的教會。所以如果只是表象的設立西方式的教會，那將是可嘆之事。

宣教師和當地教會領袖合作，互相支持，並且瞭解彼此的責任，是達成以新約為基礎來成立教會的必要條件；上層結構必須與當地宗教、歷史和特色以及社會條件和人民的風俗習慣相配合才行。建立本土教會的責任必須不斷在當地領袖身上加重，達成這個目標則是必須訓練配

得上、有資格的人來擔任這個偉大的使命。在此地，有一些令人值得感謝的理由，那就是上述提到的事情上，北部教會躲過了其他宣教區域所遇見的問題。

本土教會的成長不應只是由內部開始，也應該由外部開始成長才是。如果教會要發展，維持其活力與信仰，那必須得建立成員的知識與良善，而且「所有的成員」都必須背負福音的使命。本章節簡單的介紹北部台灣教會在過去五十年來自立、自養和自傳的故事。

「自立」的發展軌跡

奠基的工作

創建者馬偕在世的時候，整個教會形成一個大教區，在實際的運作當中，宣教師是唯一的經營者。當時物質條件尚未成熟到可以讓開創者建立組織。儘管基礎已經打好，但是仍然需要更多加拿大或是台灣的福音工人準備所需的材料。

組織中會

馬偕過世三年之後，第一屆的中會組織起來了，並且在次年舉行第二次會議，會議的程序

— 125 —

規則準備完成，也任命委員會去跟教會生活與事工的各個部門討論，並且提出報告。這一個步驟是一大進步，教會的自立樣貌至此大致成形。

封立牧師

一九〇六年春天，設立了六間佈道所，部分在客家區域。第二年，與此相關的傳道局也組織起來了。由自立自養的觀點來看，更重要的步驟就是將四位傳道師封立為牧師。當中的三位牧師前往有能力自養的教會，而第四位則是代表教士會前往宜蘭平原監督教會的發展。數個月之後，另外一位傳道師（他曾經擔任道士）接受封立，派往教區最大的教會——大稻埕教會。

前述的四位封立牧師之一就是馬偕的大女婿陳清義，他被派往著名的艋舺教會。這些事情在非常短的時間之內發生，傳教工作的穩定和發展跟馬偕一生中締造了令人感到振奮的紀錄相比，一樣有著同樣重要的意義。假若馬偕回來世上，看見幾位先前的學生和傳道師已經被封牧，並且協助教會管理的工作，一定會感到非常高興。

南北合組大會

北部中會組織完成之後，南部教會派遣會使表達兄弟般的問候，而北部教會也好意回謝。在不同場合當中，雙方中會的會使代表均各自表達進一步合作的意願，甚至有意願將兩個本土教會聯合起來。南北宣教師也極力鼓舞聯合運動，因此南北兩個中會各派代表成委員會。在南北雙方一致表達積極的意願之後，南北教會於一九一二年秋天在台灣中部的彰化達成

聯合的目標，教士會主導的「台灣大會」因此成立。

教會聯合的利益

這次聯合運動達成之後，所帶來的好處實在難以列舉，而南北教會採用統一的傳道師謝禮薪級，編製《教會規則與制度》小書，以及教育機構課程的統一等，以上是益處的部分。當中最重要的是，任命常設性的「主日學事工委員會」，到現在該會已經認真且成功運作數年之久，由於這個事工被看成是非常重要的工作，因此教會請求母會海外宣道委員會派遣主日學的專家前來協助這個工作。兩年以前，台北神學校舉行首次「師範訓練學校課程」，有超過卅位主日學老師參加，在十天的課程裡，傳授教學方法以及相關主題的討論。基督教事工在這個新的聯合當中獲得最深的利益，無疑地，傳道局將成為永久性的機構。

最近，「台灣大會」授權要為聯合教會編製第一本《聖詩》，南部教會使用的《聖詩》與北部教會使用的《廈門教會聖詩》，其語言與內容有點差異。這個沒有必要的混淆狀況，如今已經解決了，現在出版的《聖詩》比較豐富，也更適合台灣的教會與主日學崇拜之用。

如今已經在教會組織上獨立的「台灣大會」，在去年春天的紀錄裡提到，所有的基督徒都應禁止烈酒以及任何形式的麻醉藥品。大會也決議在各個教會當中設立「執事」制度。

「自養」的成長

設立發展基金幫助弱小教會

本土教會的自養與自立一樣重要。中會開始運作三年之後，教士會委員一致同意必須鼓吹本地的信徒負擔起「自養」的責任，也感覺到愈大愈強的教會應該去幫助比較弱小的教會。從那個時候開始，這個議題就在每次的中會不斷被討論，直到在一九一〇年設立了一個發展的基金為止。從那時起，「同情與合作的精神」成為整個教會生活的整體性格，因此這個基金的金額逐年增加中。

孤兒寡婦及其他急難基金的設立

過世牧師及傳道師們、孤兒與寡婦的扶助，成為教會關心的另一個目標。這個問題由中會提出，在很短的時間內就設立「寡婦與孤兒基金」，不久之後也另外再設立「年老與衰弱傳道人基金」，這兩個基金在一九二一年合併在一起。在這個時候，台灣的教會這個合併基金的總金額達到三千五百元，減輕了一些逐漸年老的傳道人的內心焦慮，也對他們帶來很大的幫助。

另外，也有設立「本土宣教基金」，這個基金所產生的利息，支付給對教會周邊非基督徒的佈

道會，而且已經有數年的時間。

除此之外，每一年教會收到自由奉獻的金額，都會拿去幫助教會外的急難需求，例如「英國與(海外聖經協會)」或最近中國飢荒的事件，北部教會也奉獻一千元作為救難之用。

教會的奉獻金額增幅大

比較一九〇七年與一九二一年奉獻的金額，我們會發現成長的幅度非常明顯。一九〇七年所有奉獻總額是二千三百四十六元。一九二一年除了對教會設立五十禧年奉獻的兩千元以外，奉獻的總額是一萬四千一百四十元，在十五年間增加了五倍。

佈道會事工的落實

傳福音是教會最重要的事工

教會成長最具有鼓舞作用的，或許就是教會自發性積極推動的佈道會事工。首先，我們必須思考，在宣教區域傳福音的意義是什麼？在台灣，大部分群眾都居住在城鎮當中，其他的人則住在河岸、山邊或竹叢裡的小村落當中，那麼，福音要如何傳到那裡呢？要用什麼方法達成

目標？筆者抵達台灣那年，在中國上海舉行「福音到達中國百週年」會議，在該次會議中，對於傳福音事工的界定，值得抄錄於此，內容如下：

「帶著拯救世界使命的知識，亦即耶穌基督救贖的死與復活以及改變心靈的能力，前往這個帝國傳給每一個人，讓他們接受基督作為個人的救主。」

這個目標包括台灣，中國或日本的每一個城鎮、鄉村與村落的範圍，以及社會的各個階層——包括那些在渡船或礦場當中工作的苦力階層以及基督教或非基督教的機構。呼召每一位基督徒工人，不管當時的地位為何，都要面對這個至高的使命，集中禱告的內容，將目標集中在這個教會最為重要的事工上。

基督是我們傳福音的模範

正如其他的事情一樣，主耶穌是我們傳福音工作的偉大模範，一個鄉村接著一個鄉村，從山上和湖邊，對著少數人或群眾宣講，不論在何處、面對什麼樣的人，祂都傳揚上帝國的福音以及教導「教義」，祂不因困境而失望，也不會因為受到歡迎而自滿。筆者必須面對「傳揚福音直到世界的盡頭」這項事工，就在這裡，帶著耶穌的精神和熱情，也總是會發現最大且最歡迎他投注的工作域上。

對傳統信仰者的佈道與傳福音

或許需要超過一個世代以上的時間去努力，才有辦法孕育出許多「完全體認到基督教事工重要性的人」出現；或許要許多年之後，才能夠讓許多基督徒深刻體認到「自己對於非基督徒鄰舍的責任感」——除非罪的感覺進入到他們靈魂深處，否則他們似乎不會對別人的罪感到有負擔。或許當他們體驗到對於異教徒迷信和拜偶像的憤慨，他們才能夠掌握到基督教信仰的重要性、基督福音的美好與祝福。除非有五旬節聖靈之火將他們心靈的廢物燒盡，否則他們不會對「拯救自己的同胞」產生熱情，如同點燃福音之火一般地將他們推向前。

宣教師在教會生活中的角色

在這個偉大的使命當中，宣教師工作必須引導同工深化他們的屬靈生命，不斷提升同工直到獲得勝利及豐盛的生命為止，宣教師才能在教會的生活中扮演重大而重要的角色——假如失敗的話，其宣教工作也將完全失敗。當一個人呼召世人擁有神聖的生命，過著聖潔和奉獻的生活，使他們不斷渴望更多聖潔的生命、永遠保持靈性上對馬其頓呼聲的高度敏感，這是基督教宣教事工不可或缺的要素。

一間健康的教會需具備的要素

不管擁有什麼樣的特質，宣教的精神是本土教會成長的要素。儘管教會的自立和自養發展非常重要，但是只有這些仍不足。《聖經》當中的老底嘉教會是一間自立自養的教會，但是絕

— 131 —

對不是一間健康的教會，如果教會無法踏出界線之外，她將不會、也無法有重要的發展。中國的部分由上海的季理裴博士（Dr. Donald MacGillivray）做了重要的總結，在會議當中，他的評估強調四個要點：

一、壓倒性的證據顯示，中國本土的教會特色是積極傳福音，也是信徒增加的主要原因。

二、教會所謂的成長，在新的宣教區域必須是進入異教徒群體才能獲得信徒的方式。

三、穩定下來的教會有鬆懈的危險。

四、有被異教社會孤立的危險。

這位精通日本傳統的領導人物所做的證言，可以幫助我們瞭解一件事：如果教會不認為有對自己區域內傳福音的責任，那麼要建立本土化的教會就會非常困難！在最近的會議當中，這種情況被簡短的概述如下：

「我們所移轉的教會，可以推測屬於基督教會的每一個人，很明顯的，每個人並沒有確實的體認到自己作為本土教會的責任，那就是將日本予以基督教化的工作。這件事情，當然沒有最終的解決方案，一間獨立的教會必須負起繼續發展的責任。我們必須要讓每一間本土教會，擁有對自己尚未接納福音的同胞有去傳福音的責任。」

— 132 —

佈道「組織化」的必要

關於台灣教會的情況，最初的宣教工作純粹是佈道的工作，也就是宣教師帶領他的傳道師前往那些基督徒（這些人是在城鎮或鄉村接受福音的人）以外的地區佈道。透過這個方法，許多人被帶進教會。但是當教會數目逐漸擴張後，地方教會和訓練學生的工作占據了宣教師大部分的時間，所以有些地區因為宣教師沒有時間前往他們教會，有數年的時間沒有舉行過聖餐。開拓的宣教師馬偕特別適合於佈道工作，但卻變成了各地教會的總指導者，以致後來沒有人去指導佈道的工作。連在他過世前，傳道師居然都已經失去了在街上或路邊呼召異教人士進入教會的技巧。日本占領台灣之後，有一件困難的情況發生了，那就是本地的傳道師幾乎無法進行佈道的工作，因為很難不引起警察的干涉。

筆者建議的佈道政策

現代的教會首要的工作是必須先組織起來。因為教會當中擁有許多不同部分的工作，而這也隱含著由於教會對牧者有「指導教育工作」的職務需求，或者其他部門也有調度的需要，而造成佈道工作遭受忽視的危險。從中國退休並擁有豐富經驗的宣教師甘吉遜博士（Dr.

第六章 ◆ 本土教會成長緊扣佈道事工的發展

Campbell Gibson）表達他的想法：「如果每一個教會都有相同固定的作法：就是在每個宣教中心，至少要派遣一個人去專門負責佈道的工作，這將會是聰明和成果豐碩的方法。但是我並不認為每個人都有能力去做到這樣的事情，如果將這個工作交給教育程度不高、較沒天分的宣教同工身上，必會產生更糟糕的結果。許多人似乎認為，一位不適任學校和學院工作、牧會工作的人，可能可以做好佈道工作──如果教會將佈道工作看成是給那些較無效率或者在擁有的人選當中挑選最好的，他天生資質優秀，有寬廣的人文素養，透過訓練讓他有廣博和實踐的神學，並將會是一件很可悲的事情──相反的，讓我們鼓勵每個教會任命一位新人或者在擁有的人選當且在上帝的恩典之下，擁有屬靈的深度，來作為教會的佈道者。」

筆者受命為「佈道職分」的宣教師

為了「佈道」這個特別工作，筆者在一九〇七年被任命，並且在過去十四年來盡力做好這個工作。當我到達台灣的時候，閱讀到發表於《中國記錄》（Chinese Record）當中一系列有關佈道的文章，讓筆者的印象非常深刻。不久之後，筆者深信自己工作的重要性，並且知道所謂的「佈道學」只有透過實際的練習與經驗才能獲得。

常保持對佈道的熱情

當筆者接受這個任命之後，已經通過了第二年的語言考試，隨即和同工開始規劃在非基督教的環境當中舉行的佈道工作。我們在很多地方租房子，在那裡，一個禮拜舉行好幾次的佈道

會。筆者和幾位傳道師在城鎮和鄉村、街道的一角、空地、市場、官府前廣場，甚至廟門口都舉行佈道會。由於年輕一輩的傳道師已經很少對異教徒佈道了，因此這些佈道計畫最初並不吸引他們。筆者難以理解（由於筆者是遲鈍的外國人）為何這些本地人對於筆者全力投入的佈道工作缺乏興趣。那些早年曾跟隨馬偕上山下海，但如今已經年老的人，在他們身上仍然能看到宣教的熱情。從他們身上能令人想起過去的時光，筆者曾經聽過的那些草創時期的往事。

區會議及佈道會的支持是佈道成功的關鍵

這幾年成功的因素要歸功於以下這項事工：一九〇七年，中會將教區分為三區，每個區域要半年一次舉行會議來協助牧師與傳道師的工作。在這個會議的前兩天會討論「這間新生教會所面對的問題與需求」，第三天則是在宣教師監督之下，對傳道師舉行《聖經》以及相關主題的考試。每天傍晚，這些傳道師分成幾個小組，外出「傳揚上帝的話語」。由於有我這個外國人在場，因此日本警察並沒有干涉我們的活動。這些傳道師在會議上的熱情實在令人振奮。基督徒的心靈受到攪動，而周圍的異教徒也對福音感到興趣。佈道的心志十分穩定且士氣不斷升高且被讚揚（po-so），「傳揚上帝話語的種子」成為這段時間基督徒最熟習的說詞。

教會牧者關心佈道會並制定新規則

不久之後，教會領袖開始體認到，也有些擔心「基督徒和異教徒鄰居之間有一道鴻溝」存在著，而且在教堂周圍也全都是還沒有聽過福音的人們。最後，中會開始重視這件事情，在經

過深思熟慮之後，決定將前述「本土宣教基金」的利息，用在廿間或更多教會於每年對異教徒鄰舍舉行的特別佈道會之用。為了達到最好的效果，中會佈道委員會決定以下的規則：

一、將每週印行的週報發給一般社會大眾。

二、聘一位敲鑼的人，每天下午繞行城鎮，宣布聚會舉行的時間及地點。

三、邀請幾位口才佳的人：這些人必須將給異教徒聽的佈道主題轉發給特別安排的委員會委員。

四、基督徒必須歡迎他們的異教徒鄰居，並引領他們到位置上，坐下來，並且將《聖詩》與福音單張發給他們。基督徒也必須提供佈道者食物以及歇息的場所。

這些特別的聚會持續了數年的時間，所帶來的影響穩定增加中，大部分的教堂在數週內的時間當中，總是坐滿了人，有時甚至還非常擁擠。

成功的佈道會消弭教會與世人的鴻溝

上述佈道工作的規則實施後馬上看到立即的成效，但是更深遠的影響是「改變一般人對教會、傳道師以及信徒的態度」。信徒和非信徒間的距離逐漸拉近、基督徒不再受到質疑與排斥、牧師和傳道被看成是社會中的傑出人士，各個階層的人自由的與他們交往。地方領袖如城鎮耆老和辦事員，他們雖然不是基督徒，但也常會參加這些特別的佈道會，並且公開勸告他們的朋友要前來聽基督教的「教義」。地方領袖承認這些佈道工作改善了許多人的行為。今天的

台灣，那些比較有受教育的階級人士，他們會嚴肅的思考基督教所傳揚的信仰精神及文化。

細分成更小的佈道團成果卓越

這些年來，少數比較熱心的平信徒會去鼓吹組織「佈道團」，但是有些人認為「推動這個運動的時機未到」。這個議題也成為三個區域的傳道師會議中討論的主題，最後找到了通往這個目標的捷徑。區域會議再分成更小的組別，每一組平均五位傳道師，這些小組組成佈道團，前往沒有教堂或很少基督徒的異教村落去舉行佈道會，每個月有連續五天、還前往更偏遠的地區去佈道。這些佈道團已經如此舉行佈道會達數年的時間，直到一九一九年，外國宣教師才擔任總督導的責任。就一般的感受來看，如果教會進行的是最有效率的事工時，中會應該要將這個事工納入管理範圍內。

....

「向前運動」所帶來的教會增長

....

台灣跟進加拿大展開「向前運動」（Forward Movement）

一九一九年春天，加拿大海外宣道會聯合幹事阿姆斯壯牧師（Rev. A.E. Armstrong）拜訪

台灣，在一個牧師、傳道師、代議長老及執事參與的大型聚會中，阿姆斯壯牧師提到加拿大教會所進行的「向前運動」。後來，一、兩個禮拜以後，中會開會時，討論到北台灣教會要不要展開「向前運動」的提議？與會者熱切接納了這個建議。中會認為，最適合推動這個運動的時間點應該和台灣教會的「設教禧年」結合。於是，「向前運動」開始進行，它的主要目標之一就是「對非基督徒社會進行傳福音的工作」，因此一個常設的「傳道委員會」被任命並專責督導上述的佈道團。

容所說：

達成六萬五千人聽到福音的事工目標

這個事工一開始，就因認真的推動而獲致成功，正如一九二一年的報告書當中所節錄的內

「由於『向前運動』與設教五十禧年時間接近，一開始推動，信徒就熱情的參與。除了在平常的教會禮拜之外，十二個佈道團也在偏遠的村落舉行了三百卅場佈道會，有六萬五千人聽到福音，當中有許多人是首度聽聞。以人數來說，比去年的聽眾多了百分之五十，這些結果雖然無法以圖表顯示，但我們仍知有五十五人決志要成為基督徒，那些人當中，有許多人將家中神像交給傳道師處置並成為固定參加禮拜的信徒。除了這些在異教村落舉行的特別佈道會之外，在北部台灣廿二間教會也一樣舉行。至少有一百零六位非基督徒簽署決志卡，因此『向前運動』的精神逐漸深化，在這當中最令人鼓舞的就是，這是一個本土

運動，從台灣的基督徒發起推動的，他們是這個運動成功的推手。」

信徒人數的增加

這一章如果在「沒有針對教會成長並提出數據證據」的情況下完結，就不能算是結束，首先，必須提出一些解釋，以免將過去與現在做比較的時候，產生誤導的結論——因為這是非常容易去由統計圖表誤認「初創時期的教會數目比現在更多」的誤導——但事實上，信徒人數卻幾乎相等。

信徒造就奠基於教會了解信徒的生活

我們必須要瞭解，在早期的時代，一位宣教師根本不可能對信徒的生活和行為有多少瞭解，對信徒的造就幾乎是不可能的事情——一位外國宣教師極不可能從台灣的基督徒身上獲得什麼資訊。另外，也有許多可以在別的宣教區找到的隱晦動機、加上也缺乏足夠的督導，以致於教會信徒名錄多年未整理，有些已過世多年的信徒，他們的名字也沒有被粗心的傳道師給銷

— 139 —

掉。事實上，宜蘭平原信徒名冊的整理花費了數年的時間，就可以得知整理名冊這個過程是多

麼緩慢而困難了。過去十四年來，東部教會所報告的信徒人數逐漸減少，這是肇因於平埔族的

快速消失，原本超過卅間的教會減少變成八間，而現存的教會幾乎全部設在漢人居住的市中心

裡——漢人信徒的基礎打得較為穩定——在這樣地區條件下的基督徒，是令人感到比較樂觀

的。

再加上，現在已經有多位被封立的宣教師、八位受封立的牧師以及規律召開小會討論教會

信徒的紀律。另外，現在生活和行為的標準，以及對於基督教真理的知識提高了許多，而由舊

有統治者（清朝）特有的政治與社會條件之下產生的隱晦動機，如今已經大量減少。如今有五

十間佈道所（或教會），每一間都有一位本地牧師或傳道師，八位牧師都在有能力自養的教會

當中牧會，其他支出的部分也從他們教會自己去支應。在我們的教育機構當中，原本有幾位是

學生的人，前往日本深造畢業之後仍回到母校成為基督徒教師。

初信者需要一位更有力量的佈道家領袖帶領歸信

一九二一年年底，有二千三百七十四位受洗的成人會員，一千六百廿五位幼兒洗禮會員，

另外也有大約三千人，多多少少也會規律的參與教會的崇拜、接受基督教指導，他們當中有許

多人是站在基督教和異教的界線當中，一些人為了各樣的原因尚未接受洗禮，但已經棄偶

像，承認自己是基督教團體的一分子，雖然異教的迷信與偶像崇拜已經對他們失去吸引力，但

他們仍還沒有完全順服及宣告主耶穌基督作為他們的救主。能夠觸碰人們良心、顯示異教愚蠢

並且同時表達出各各他十字架吸引人心的、有力量的佈道家不多，因此才有那麼多人仍然停留在「初信」的階段，而無法成為主內一家人。

主日學傳道師訓練

主日學有接近兩千位學生以及超過兩百位教師。傳道師方面，雖然沒有特別去訓練，但近年來，他們對這個事工表達出極大的興趣。他們會去督導自己教會的主日學課程，助手當中有許多人曾經在淡水的基督教學校接受過教育──這是最有潛力的事工，因此希望能夠有「曾經接受主日學訓練並已受封立的宣教師」儘速前來這裡。

「美麗島基督化」是全台基督徒的責任

北部台灣的基督徒團體包括受洗的成年人和孩童、追隨者和他們的子女在內，人數大概可到一萬人，這表示總人口中，每一百五十人就有一個人與基督教信仰有關聯。雖然在最近幾年當中發展很多，但本土教會的設立尚未完成，這是一個對台灣人以及外國同工的挑戰。有許多事要感謝上帝，使得過去幾年當中，加拿大宣教師和他們極有效率的男女同工，是在和諧合作的氣氛下完成工作的。未來幾年仍然需要外國宣教師的協助──當台灣的基督徒對自己的責任有更多的體認、當他們敏銳的意識到自己國族社會的需要、當他們發現宣教師愈來愈熟習台灣人的生活與問題後，因此他們更能毫無保留的奉獻自己一生的服事。

如今台灣教會的地位，由於知識，屬靈力量的成長，能夠有效率的組織起來，以及積極的

傳揚福音，我們應該感謝上帝。希望加拿大教會透過禱告，衷心的支持以及派任適當數量的宣教師同工來幫助外國宣教事工，直到台灣教會已經有能力擔負起將「美麗島基督化」的責任為止。

禱告詞

主耶穌基督，我們相信祢以及大公教會，我們感謝祢，因為祢設立信者兄弟般的情誼，我們榮耀祢，因為祢是教會（新婦）的主宰，我們為她的過錯以及徬徨來懺悔，為她的無情與世俗懺悔，為她的爭鬥以及不和諧懺悔，但我們仍要歡喜，因為她是屬於祢的教會。

我們特別要為北部台灣的教會向祢感謝，因為人數增加、活力增強及領袖的明智與獻身精神；因為她謹守祢的真理、熱切的拓展祢的信息。幫助教會讓她成為先人的寶貴傳統，並與世界各地教會互相連結，永遠與祢連結、忠實於祢，讓她絕不阻擋及遮蔽祢，而是忠實的表達祢

的真理，並且讓尚未呼求祢聖名的人群知曉祢，願祢特別祝福傳道師與聖經宣道婦，願教會的每一位成員都能清楚的見證祢福音的大能，通過話語生命顯示祢的救贖。

傾倒祝福在祢普世的教會當中，願她能夠活躍於祢偉大事工當中，因為祢已經在困難或順利的日子裡，將這些擺放在她眼前，期盼她萬事有卓越的成果，我們在此以祢的聖名懇求，阿們。

第七章 ◆ 北部教會非凡信徒的故事

在新時代當中，大家有興趣將教會擴展到新的宣教領域。佈道活動很重要，但當時卻尚未被接納，成為制度化教會的一部分，因此從機構內部去組織和建立教會是很重要的工作，並在已經建立教會的地方開拓新的宣教區域。

一九○五年以後，北台灣教會開設十八間新的佈道所，有幾間在客家區域、三間在大甲區域、七間在宜蘭、兩間在花蓮港平原、兩間在基隆地區，而一間在台北市。這些地方都已經建造教堂，但還有少數地區的信徒仍然在街上租來的禮拜堂裡舉行禮拜。

這一章雖然只談上述提到的大甲這一個地區，但是我們要知道的是基督教信仰在最近幾年已進展很多，而且在那些地區也住著幾位北部台灣有史以來最非凡的信徒。

大甲信主的讀書人陳其祥

台中大甲是個擁有五千人的市鎮，坐落於沿海的農業地區當中。它位於北台灣教區的西南部，城鎮周圍散居著數十個鄉村與聚落，城鎮與鄉村當中住著富有或有受教育的居民。

陳其祥，也是一位信主的讀書人，他的故事成為這一章要談的內容。他生於距離大甲約五公里的馬鳴埔村，父親是一位富裕的農民、也是地方官員。陳其祥受過漢學教育，名聲遠播。

陳其祥是四個兒子當中最小的一位，他的三位兄長研讀儒教經典，但是陳其祥卻被派去放牛。他抱怨自己的歹命，並請求父親准許他和哥哥們一起去讀書和準備考試。他的父親送他去祖父那邊，他的祖父看見這個孫子熱切讀書的期望，於是准許他的請求，但條件是「必須找到另一個人來代替他放牛」。陳其祥找到一位貧窮的少年，少年對薪資的最高期望是「只要能夠餬口」就好，因此少年去陳其祥的家中代替他放牛。

就算陳其祥有什麼缺點，但也絕不是一般年輕人那種喜好浮華的享受。尤其當一般年輕人穿著鮮亮顏色的服裝——特別是參加考試的時候更是穿得光鮮亮麗——但是他陳其祥穿著普通的裝束而已。其他人或許會乘馬或搭轎子，但他寧可步行兩天的時間前往新竹應考。有一次，他在旅途中成了兩位驕傲的年輕人的嘲弄對象。當他們到了城內，主考官注意到那兩位來考

試、懷有大志且穿著滿清裝扮鮮明打扮的年輕人，就尖銳地挖苦他們，然後指著陳其祥並告訴那些人說，陳其祥雖然是富農和地方官員的兒子，但卻可以成為他們日常生活和謙卑的榜樣。

陳其祥對於知識的渴望造就了他非凡的特質。他研讀儒教經典，獲得很大的進步。雖然他有許多值得讚美的優點，但也有其道德上的弱點。他舉止雖然文雅，但是他講話尖酸刻薄。他的個子矮小又單薄，看起來有病容，因為他父母與兄長都有吸食鴉片的惡習，所以他跟隨祖父。早上大部分的時間，他都在床上吸食鴉片，下午才會到農場散步，然後回到房間研讀經書，抽鴉片及吸水煙，直到一天結束為止。年輕的時候他有近視的問題，染上吸食鴉片的惡習只是加重病況而已，最後他由於不斷揉眼，雙眼受到嚴重的影響。

當日本占領台灣的時候，他大約卅歲。由於他擁有資產並且值得信賴，日本政府選擇他擔任地方官員。他在職位上不僅拒絕一切的賄賂，並且因為嚴謹和公正去解決問題而贏得好名聲，甚至連惡人都怕他。他的慷慨也是遠近馳名的。

但是在這個時候，他除了有鴉片癮，也染上了酒癮，這讓他的母親非常苦惱。以下的事是由陳其祥親自告訴筆者的：

日本人習於舉行大規模的宴會，邀請地方領袖參加，我每次都會受到邀請，回到家時都已經喝醉。有一天，我的母親責備我，指控我的行為讓她蒙羞。我因她的言詞感到哀傷，因此決意將酒癮完全戒除。在這之前，我習慣搭乘轎子，但如今我答應母親騎馬，這樣我就比較不會受到飲酒的試探。不久之後，我受邀前往大甲，參加某項重要公共工程完工的慶

祝宴會。因為我對母親的承諾，於是我選擇騎馬前去赴會。宴席中，日本官員表示，雖然菜餚很簡便，因為有很多酒可供應，希望大家盡情喝酒。我記得對母親的承諾，但他希望大家不要吝惜飲酒，因為有很多酒可供應，希望大家盡情喝酒。我從來不喝烈酒，所以我坐在椅子上，感到痛苦又困窘。在我身旁坐著一位老學究，他說：『在我一生當中，我從來沒有喝過烈酒，因為害怕烈酒會傷害他薄弱的身體。於是他戰戰兢兢的站起來，對著官員切請求是否能夠免除喝酒？但是在官員的勸說下，我還是喝了。結果當天，我搭乘轎子回生意人，我確定他一定會樂意喝掉我和他自己的份額。』由於我還沒有觸碰酒杯，於是我懇家，但當我酒醒之後，發現我的母親就傷心的站在床邊。不久之後，她過世了，而我飲酒的惡習仍然不改。

後來，當陳其祥接觸到基督教的時候，他對於知識的飢渴仍然非常深切，但是他的身體已經被酒破壞並且心裡沒有平安快樂。迷信和偶像崇拜這些事對他已經不具吸引力，像他這種對玄秘和宗教有極大興趣的人來講，儒教是一片荒瘠的田地。為了滿足他內心的渴望，他最後開始研習佛教當中的「齋教」。

大甲鎮上有一些信齋教的人督促他加入這個宗教，但是他想找到問題的解答，但是卻被告知「沒有辦法得到解答，除非願意加入這個玄秘的宗教才行」。當他研習齋教系統時，由於上帝的保守，使得基督教真理的大門為他打開。

在那時候，那個地方有兩、三個人曾經在中台灣的彰化基督教醫院聽過福音，這些人當中

的一位就是陳其祥家裡的僕人旭仔。每個安息日早上，在天還沒亮前，旭仔就會和另外一位年輕人走路前往距離約廿公里的三叉河村，因為當地近期設立了一間新的基督教堂。參加完兩場禮拜之後，他們還會走廿公里的路回來。返家時已經日落。他們多次禱告，希望上帝能夠在大甲建立教堂，讓鎮裡的人有機會聽見基督教真理、他們自己也不用走那麼遙遠的路途。有一天陳其祥問旭仔，說他是一位貧窮的年輕人，既不能讀也不能寫，為什麼那麼快樂？而他自己則是擁有家產和受過教育的人，為什麼那麼不快樂？旭仔簡單的回答他：「只要你去聽基督教的教義，你也會快樂。」

下一個安息日來到，在沒有讓其他人知道他們計畫的情況下，陳其祥與旭仔出發前往三叉河村。到達之後，僕人向傳道介紹自己的主人，整個安息日他們就在教堂中度過。傳道師雖然不是學者，但卻是個熱心的人，每個安息日對聖徒和罪人舉行三堂禮拜。然而，這三堂禮拜卻對陳其祥沒有什麼吸引力，因為傳道極力批評他早已經離棄的迷信信仰。當天晚上他留在教堂，詢問問題一直到清晨。他繼續到這裡長達數個禮拜，在這些拜訪當中，他首度遇見一位外國宣教師約美但牧師。約美但牧師對於陳其祥熱切又飢渴追求基督教真理的心，讓他極受感動。不久之後，陳其祥發現基督教赦免罪惡，這個教義深深的刻劃在他的內心當中。

拜訪過許多教會，又整晚與該教會的傳道師討論之後，陳其祥回到最初的性靈指導者三叉河教會那裡，告訴傳道他已經決定要成為基督徒，並且希望租一間房子在大甲設立禮拜堂。傳道師告訴他，不能一邊當基督徒、一邊又是鴉片癮者。陳其祥用他特別的方式回答說：「你講道不是曾經說，上帝是萬能的上帝嗎？如果真是如此，難道他沒有力量幫助我除掉鴉片，給我

力量，逃掉毒癮發作時的痛苦嗎？」於是，傳道與這位受到鴉片奴役的吸食者陳其祥跪下來一起禱告。陳其祥向上帝發誓，就算會死也再不會碰鴉片。從那個時刻開始，就不曾聽過他吸食鴉片。並且在三天之內他就脫離煙癮發作的痛苦。那真是上帝恩典的勝利，於是陳其祥不再質疑上帝的能力或基督宗教偉大的事實。

因祈禱而痊癒，家人相繼成為基督徒

陳其祥比他的妻子早兩個月成為基督徒。他的妻子雖然沒有特別的天分，但是對於處理一般的事務，能力很強。陳其祥在一般事務的處理上都要徵詢妻子的意見，而她對於「丈夫接受新的宗教」這件事，仍需要一段時間才能接納。在得知消息之後，她幾乎不和他說話：安靜的把飯食放在桌上，臉上表露出不悅的神色，而陳其祥只是以微笑來回應，所以他的微笑使得原本許多意見相左的場合，就成為了一股無法抗拒的魅力。而她的歸信要歸因於生病，因為丈夫的禱告而痊癒。最初，她不知道要如何抓住基督教真理，但是後來許多婦女都從她那裡聽到福音。

陳其祥的三個兒子都在公立學校就讀，最大的兒子不久之後畢業，並且尋求進入醫學校的預備課程。他的天資聰穎有自信，雖然對父親非常崇敬，但是卻嚴厲反對父親的新宗教。但母親和他自己生病，都是因為祈禱而痊癒，所以後來他也接受父親的信仰，之後全家人都成為基督徒。

一九〇九年，筆者獲得任命擔任這個地區教會的監督之後，首度拜訪大甲。對於陳其祥他個人所擁有的性格及力量，印象非常深刻，雖然他在外表上看起來不那麼吸引人，但不管人的

階層為何、富有或貧窮、傳道或平信徒、外國人或台灣人，在基督裡，這都沒有差別。陳其祥的個性所帶來的力量、心靈的敏銳以及除了獲得的新信仰以外，他看輕萬物，總是吸引人的注意，贏得別人的聆聽。對那些已經接受基督教信仰的人，他以正統基督教神學的外衣，用具有衝擊性、有時又帶著風趣的方式，以截然不同的方式來表達基督教思想。

租來的教堂和講道熱誠

在陳其祥接受基督不久後，他在大甲的街上租一間房子，而三叉河教會的傳道轉過來這個重要的市鎮牧會，這個消息很快傳遍整個地區。當教堂啟用後，有幾位住在這個地區的男女——他們從「英國長老教會服務超過廿年，並提供極為卓著服務的蘭大衛醫生所屬的彰化醫院」聽到了福音——前來並與歸信的讀書人和新任的傳道師見面。每天傍晚，禮拜堂裡面擠滿了人，有許多人還站在街上聆聽新的教義。儘管遭遇到反對的聲浪，但是追尋真理的人數也不斷增加。

禮拜堂只有約八乘四平方公尺這樣狹小的空間，當中有一塊約一公尺高的布幕隔開男女聽眾，以進行崇拜。女性會友由後門進入，坐在隔絕地區的座位上，兩到三堂的講道結束之後，聽眾散去，而更有興趣的人會留下來聽傳道師、陳其祥和其他人進而詳細講解基督教的信息。有時候，小組的信徒有的會繼續討論到深夜。睡覺的安排方面，只要將椅子並排在一起，就足夠六個人在椅子上面睡覺。至於筆者，則是清出教堂的一個角落睡在放置的野營床上。但是，由於屋子裡面有很濃的韭菜和蒜頭的氣味，加上屋裡極端悶熱，逼得筆者只好將睡床移到屋外

的街邊上，也成了路人覺得有趣和消遣的對象。不管筆者多早起床，都無法避免對街行人好奇的目光。

買地蓋「大甲教會」

第一年，信徒的增長極為顯著，慕道友也穩定的增加，因此信徒發現他們必須考慮租一間更大的屋子或自己來興建一座禮拜堂。他們舉行特別的祈禱會，尋求上帝的旨意，讓他們知道應該要走哪一種方式？陳其祥很快就向一位富有的異教徒購買土地，在上面興建一間長十五公尺、寬九公尺的教堂。雖然有一些信徒還沒受洗，但也與一些新進的擁護者一起募集到將近一千元，加上數百天的義務工作才完成這座新教堂（大甲教會）。禮拜堂後面為傳道師興建的一間宿舍，以及一些巡迴宣教師的住處。

教堂啟用與試煉

教堂的啟用是一件大事情，除了筆者和幾位當地的日本官員以外，還有來自各地的信徒準備了各樣的禮物來慶賀，帶來的東西有掛軸、時鐘以及其他有用處的物品。一位八十歲的女信徒從陳其祥最初聽到福音的三叉河教會那邊，走了廿四公里路來到新教會做禮拜，等禮拜結束後，當天再走回去。她的內心因為在這個異教市鎮的所見所聞而充滿喜悅，而那裡，三年前，不曾出現任何信徒。

隔週，首度舉行聖禮典，陳其祥與另外一位姓林的讀書人，以及其他許多人接受洗禮，一

— 151 —

年之內，大甲教會設立數位長老和執事。雖然信徒成長興旺，但是他們也沒能逃避一些試煉。第二年，颱風毀掉主要建築的部分角落，修理建物花費了數百元。第二次，颱風把宣教師的房間完全摧毀，但是基督徒仍然歡喜的奉獻修理的損害費用。

大甲北部有幾個重要的鎮，它們是苗栗「房裡」、「苑裡」和「通霄」，都是極為有趣的地方，上帝以奇妙的方式顯明祂的恩典。

苑裡福音因陳其祥傳入苗栗地區

「房裡」最初的信徒：理髮師和他的太太

「由鴉片得到拯救——陳其祥」成為大甲附近城鎮居民閒談的話題，有一個村莊稱為「房裡」，當中有一位吸食鴉片的理髮師也開始參與大甲教會的禮拜，每個禮拜六黃昏，他和七歲的小兒子一起走路前往大甲（距離大約十公里），安息日晚上在教會過夜，回到家時是禮拜一早上。這表示他失去禮拜天理髮的收入。他的妻子對於這個損失極為惱怒，這個理髮師不斷述說每個禮拜一回家的時候內心是多麼恐懼，而他的太太是多麼可怕。筆者被激起好奇心，於是決定和幾位朋友一起前往，並在那裡佈道且前往理髮師家中探訪。這個提議並沒有得到理髮師

熱誠的回應——事實上，他回家的整條路上極為不安，不曉得當我們這一群基督徒到達時，惡靈是否會占據他太太？

當我們這群人接近村莊時，先到一間商店前面停腳喝茶，對路人佈道，對於我們這一群訪客的問候與招呼並沒有回應，然後再出發前往理髮師的家。女主人站在門口，儘可能的找椅子坐下來。在幾度尷尬的沉默之後，我們裡面有一位讀書人開始勸誠這位仍站在門口的女主人不要再愚蠢的反對丈夫去聽基督的宗教。她聽了一段時間之後便走開，但拿著一根大約一公尺多、結實的竹棍回來，繼續站在先前的門檻邊，守住大門，然後再安靜下來。但是等到那位讀書人再冒險講一些勸誠的話時，風暴隨即爆發出來，這位結實的婦女在狂怒之下跳到地板上，開始用棍子瘋狂的敲打地板，咒誓她「寧死也不要接受耶穌的教義」。

這時輪到筆者出場，我起來，站到她的身邊，對她講了幾句話。當她聽見我這一位外國人會講她的語言時，她感到一陣錯愕，就忘記生氣，並聽筆者講的內容。筆者說：「到我這裡來……我要給你平安。」「平安。」她回答：「願意。」我們這一群人在一陣特殊的沉默後，站個平安、而且眾人要為她禱告。」「平安」這個字抓住她的注意力。於是，筆者問她「是否願意得到這個平安降臨到這個不安的靈魂身上。」

在一起祈禱，「願上帝恩典的平安降臨到這個不安的靈魂身上。」

當筆者和朋友要離開的時候，這位女主人極力慰留我們吃個飯，但是因為我們還要趕往另一個村莊，所以不可能留下來，然而在離開之前，筆者告訴女主人，希望在下個安息日來臨時，看到她和丈夫、小孩一起出現在大甲教會。當我們轉身離開的時候，才發現門口擠滿了許

多好奇的圍觀者，於是我們就藉著這個良機宣講上帝的話。在群眾當中，有一個顯眼的位置上站著一位臉上長著麻子的人。他最初看起來很憤怒，心想理髮師大概會告訴筆者有關他的惡劣事蹟，但是現在確定我們這群人不知道他的過去，於是才放心地專心聽著講道。下一個安息日來臨了，當筆者在禮拜開始之前進入教堂時，發現理髮師、妻子、小孩和那位麻臉的人，坐在角落，他們整天留在教堂當中，並且答應「下個禮拜還會再來」。他們持續參加禮拜達六個月之久，直到後來他們自己的村莊附近設了一間新的禮拜堂為止。

「苑裡」最早的信徒：富有的讀書人

這些新的信徒居住的「房裡」離「苑裡」不到三公里。當時陳其祥已是一位口才很好的長老，有數位朋友住在苑裡地區。當中有兩位富有的讀書人。有一天，陳其祥在傳道師和筆者的陪伴之下，前往這個市鎮拜訪。他們在朋友家享用餐食。這個朋友是一位年輕的商店老闆，他受到母親的影響，於是對基督教產生了興趣。原來他的母親曾經在住家附近的榕樹蔭下聽過筆者佈道，並且要了基督教福音單張，並希望自己的兒子能夠聽到基督教義的知識，因為她的兒子實在需要革新。當天晚上，這個年輕人清理了一間沒有使用的店鋪，將店裡放滿了借來的椅子，又在後面放了幾個箱子當作講台，「房裡」有幾位新的信徒就可以進來幫忙。

當次拜訪的結果就是開設一間租賃的禮拜堂，並且邀請陳其祥先暫時離開他的家鄉前來苑裡。一九一三年春天，陳其祥搬到苑里鎮。幾個月之後，有一些人決定要成為新的信徒，並且嘗試在鎮內要購買一塊土地，目標是興建一座新的禮拜堂。然而，鎮內有一些人聚集起來想阻

撓此事。儘管如此，但仍然有許多人前來聽道，有些人也放棄了吸食鴉片煙，而且對真道真正有興趣的人也穩定的增加中。

陳其祥長老戰勝戒除水煙管癮

當陳其祥住在苑裡租來的房屋時，有一段「放棄了到那時還在吸食水煙管」的插曲，實在是一段有趣的故事。

有一天，他的三個兒子從學院放假回到大甲的家。大兒子已經能夠流利的演講，二兒子能夠教主日學。於是父親趁兒子休假時，回去大甲看看，在女婿管理之下的農田情況如何？陳其祥不在的那個第一週安息日，當時他的兒子們告訴那裡的基督徒：「牧師即將回去加拿大度假，沒有一樣禮物會比我們放棄無用的嗜好，如吸煙或類似的行為，更讓牧師歡喜，並且若戒掉了，這會讓他們成為更有力的見證者。」於是將近有十二個人回應這個想法。

隔週禮拜六，陳其祥回到家後，一位朋友來家裡拜訪，無端的開始談論有幾位信徒決定放棄吸水煙管的事情。當陳其祥聽見這個提議是由他兒子提出的時候，非常生氣。當天晚上，陳其祥上了床，但是無法成眠。那是他多年來最苦惱的一夜，他的良心控訴著，「繼續吸煙會讓他的身體虛弱」，並且「沒有辦法成為那些決心放棄鴉片和其他有害習慣的信徒的榜樣」。天亮以前，他戰勝了私慾，起床時，已經成為一位更為順服的基督徒，他也發誓再也不會讓吸煙的習慣宰制他。那天早上，他與兒子見面後，告訴他昨天夜裡的事…不安的夜晚以及透過祈禱獲得勝利等等。結果，有幾個人保證自己將來一定完全戒除惡習。那天早上，兒子們快樂的蒐

集將近十二根水煙管，保留下來等筆者再度來訪的時候再展示給我看。

受洗者趣事及奇妙轉變

起初，「房裡」宣教的事工遭遇了許多反彈，那位「原先咒誓就算死、也不願接受耶穌教義的理髮師的妻子」後來歸信了，但是她受到嚴厲的逼迫，甚至因為這個信仰而被打。購買土地興建教堂以及購買泥土製作「土角」的事情也遭遇到困難。這次也是像上次建堂一樣，信徒聚集在一起舉行特別禱告會，一樣也獲得上帝的應允。土地的購買順利完成，有人願意免費提供所需的泥土，不久之後，禮拜堂和傳道師的宿舍興建完成，陳其祥長老也單獨奉獻了數百元的經費。每個安息日的早上和下午，教堂裡面擠滿了信徒和慕道友。

其中最有趣的故事是信徒當中，一位年老的讀書人，他是一位富有的農民，但卻是一位鴉片重度吸食者，他被引導認識基督真理知識後，就成為陳長老的摯友，他是名副其實的拿但業──「上帝的禮物」的意思。他表現出極為有禮和溫和的精神。有幾次，筆者在陳其祥長老和一位大甲長老的陪伴下過去拜訪他，並在他家裡度過了極為愜意的黃昏以及談論與福音相關的主題。陳長老、大甲長老和老年讀書人，這三位都是讀書人，也都曾是鴉片的吸食者，且因為吸食鴉片這個習慣而損害了他們的眼睛健康。如今這三人獲得奇妙的轉變，變得完全的快樂，熱忱的希望將福音的信息傳揚給自己的同胞──筆者與他們相遇的這些經驗，實在令人難以忘懷，內心深處不禁發出由衷的感謝。

筆者休假回來之後，與他們的第一次見面是設立長老執事以及舉行聖餐的場合，大甲的長

老出席協助當天的崇拜，有幾位慕道班的信徒得到接納要施洗。在那當中，有一個人在兩年前因為嚴重的疾病，得到宣教師醫生的治療，而成為基督的信徒。他的妻子跟著他，來到禮拜堂不斷地哭泣。禮拜即將開始，筆者就注意到這一位婦女，她坐在外面的水溝中，頭上披著方巾。詢問之後，才知道她是那位即將受洗者的太太，因為先生即將在今天「入教」，所以她為這件事實而哭泣，因為她將失去他。受洗者丈夫得知妻子所做的事情後，說：「隨便她愛哭多久，我已經為她延遲兩年，我今天決意要受洗。」原來這兩年來，他已是耶穌的門徒，但如今，已經沒有任何事情可以阻擋他公開宣告對基督的信仰。

然而，這不是在那場禮拜中唯一有趣的事件。就在長老執事設立完畢，大家開始吟唱一首適合當時情境的詩歌時，一位身材比一般人高大且滿臉怒容的婦女，聽說自己的丈夫是當天受洗者之一時，她來到禮拜堂門口，請一位老婦進去叫她丈夫出來。當丈夫出現在她眼前時，她立刻抓住他的脖子，先將他推到右邊，然後再推到左邊，每次轉彎的時候就敲一下頭。她用這種暴烈的方式滿足了她的憤怒之後就離開了——她丈夫回到禮拜堂裡面的座位，繼續和其他人一起禮拜，彷彿剛剛沒有發生任何事情一般。

這個事件後續的發展非常有趣。在筆者第二度回國度假之前，有一天傍晚，與一群男女信徒前往苑裡佈道，到達時，發現有一間屋子已經準備好要作為聚會場所之用，並在屋子外院搭建一個台子，好讓人們可以在屋內和街上聽講。佈道完成之後，房屋的女主人熱切的與筆者談論有關聚會的事情。筆者非常意外的發現，她就是當時在教堂門外掌摑丈夫的那位婦女——丈夫的忍耐打破她的偏見——如今她已經是一位固定參加聚會的信徒了。

「通霄」得拯救的勝利

「通霄」是「苑裡」北方約八公里外的城鎮，人口二千人。幾年以前，筆者和助手在通霄這裡一間租來的商店佈道三個禮拜。一九一五年初開始長期租賃一間佈道所，而陳其祥長老同時負責通霄、貓盂和苑裡的事工。

在通霄這裡，有一位漢學先生，他的身體因為吸食鴉片而損害，他的妻子和兒女因為興趣而固定來參加教會禮拜。一天，他的妻子邀請陳其祥和筆者前往他家，希望丈夫因此受影響而得到幫助。那位丈夫聽完信息之後，答應要嘗試改變自己身體和道德上的軟弱。

幾個禮拜以後，有一位身體看起來被毀損的人，來到筆者位於台北的家，他告訴筆者夫人，他來自通霄，希望能夠戒掉鴉片，但由於他是外地人，因此沒有勇氣前往教會醫院去尋求醫生的幫助，因此決定啟程回家。在半路上，他反省自己「不敢找人幫助」的軟弱，並決定要倚賴上帝賜他力量去克服鴉片的癮。後來他將這個惡習完全戒除，也宣告他的身體和靈魂都得到了拯救，自此之後，他告白對上帝的信仰。不久受洗，他也成為當地的基督徒領袖之一。其他在這個中心協助事工進行的人當中，有一位是公立學校的台灣人教師，他是一位虔誠的基督徒，他的妻子是淡水女學校的畢業生。

有一條新的鐵路目前已通車了，經過通霄、苑裡和大甲，讓這個地區的佈道活動更為便

利，也能夠讓筆者方便的前往以前不容易到達的地區。

大甲教會現在能夠自立支持一位受封立的牧師，而且敬虔的長老與執事也將整個大甲地區

看成是自己的佈道區，宣教事工極有潛力，在熱切的代禱下必定有更大的發展。這三間教會的

開拓，這位歸信的讀書人陳其祥是在背後推動的精神領袖。他的工作並不是就此在那裡結束，

因為他的影響力加深到不止整個大甲地區都可以感覺到，相同的也讓整個台灣島嶼感受到了。

他是一個上帝在宣教地區教會興起的堅強、本土的領袖，使得本土教會得以成形的優秀典範，

這也是我們未來熱切祈禱的目標──興起更多本土教會的領袖！

噢！上帝原諒我們，因為我們極為有限，而且沒有在祢的事工上盡力，我們的良心自我譴

責，特別當我們意識到由於自己的不信，以致於失去許多為祢成就偉大事工以及祈禱的機會，

主啊！當我們思想祢在福爾摩沙那些非基督徒群眾當中所行的奇事，就增強我們的信心。

提醒我們，儘管罪惡可以做出許多壞事，但是恩典可以做更多好事，因為福音是上帝的大能。為了拯救世上尊貴和卑賤的人，不管是受人尊敬或遭到遺棄的罪人、是學者或是無知的農民，願我們確信祢的能力和意願是要拯救天下所有的人，而我們也應該藉著信心的祈禱，讓祢能夠隨意的進行奇妙的拯救事工。

我們祈禱，福爾摩沙教會的基督徒們能夠瞭解，自己有對同胞分享上帝拯救信息的責任，幫助他們與宣教師能夠和非基督徒的思想與心靈接觸，讓基督徒在公開或私下的場合、得時或不得時都能闡明祢的真理。更重要的是，幫助基督徒透過愛以及降服於上帝者的行誼來作見證。噢！基督，請繼續拯救台灣人以及外邦人的心靈，直到全地都充滿上帝祢的榮耀，正如大水傾滿大海。以祢的聖名祈禱，阿們。

第八章 ◆ 也到別的城市宣教

基督信仰照亮金包里的黑暗

金包里（今金山）是個人口有三千的市鎮，位於台灣北部海岸，距離基隆約步行三個小時的路程。這個市鎮位居的平原其三面被高山圍繞，第四面正對著海岸。沿岸有一些漁村，在這個小平原及附近丘陵上住著大約一萬人，這是北部台灣最被孤立的一個地方。當日本人來到這裡的時候，教堂被摧毀，留下來的基督徒也都消失不見，有多年沒有一位宣教師來拜訪這裡。曾經在這裡的廟宇擔任油漆工人的吳寬裕，後來成為北部教會最初受洗的五個人之一，曾經多次在不同的場合中告訴筆者「這個被忽視角落的需要」。

美麗之島：北部教會宣教禧年回顧與前瞻

無法遏止的賭博風氣

一九一三年，筆者和兩到三位傳道師在金包里這個城鎮待了兩個禮拜。當鎮民聽到佈道者來到這裡，曾經敵視基督教的態度再度復活！鎮裡的賭徒聚集起來抗拒福音，因此租賃佈道所時就發生了問題，最後只能租到一間「因傳說鬧鬼而廢棄不用」的房子。當這間屋子的大門打開之後，所謂的鬼怪，事實上是一群賭徒，他們偷偷地從後門溜走，於是我們立刻整理這間屋子作為佈道所和居所之用。

在往後的三個禮拜，佈道者盡責的推動工作。每天早上去拜訪這城鎮的各個漁村，下午教導漁村的小孩有關基督教的《聖詩》以及閱讀羅馬字，到了晚上，租屋的客廳裡也擠滿了聽眾。在這當中有三個晚上，一個有組織性的對抗者他們以表演布袋戲的方式在佈道所前面的空地表演——但是金包里的群眾比較喜歡聽基督新的道理。這裡的日本官員因為能夠講非常流利的台灣話，所以能夠毫無拘束的與筆者談話，這位日本官員的態度非常和善，並且對於先前基督教的道理沒有能夠在金包里傳布而表達了他的驚訝之情。他也表示，希望基督教能夠在這裡設立教會，因為他們實在沒有辦法處理本地的賭博風氣，只要能夠在這個市鎮設立基督教會，一定可以幫助改革當地風俗的工作。

再度拜訪但時機仍未成熟

一年之後，筆者再度拜訪金包里，當時陳其祥擔任馬偕醫院傳道，他陪伴我前往。當我們來到鎮外時，一些放學的孩童看見了，他們認得我，於是大聲喊叫：「耶穌來了、耶穌來

了！」，然後立刻跑回家，迅速的將我們到的消息傳達給所有的鎮民知道。當天傍晚，大群的民眾參加了市場佈道會，有兩、三位先前曾經聽過福音，還有其中一位已經丟棄偶像的人也表達出對基督道理的極大興趣，這個人非常希望能在街上租一間房子作為佈道所，但是這個舉動在當時看來時機尚未成熟。他真誠的尋求真理，可以從後來他多次拜訪台北和士林鎮（今士林）聽講道的舉動獲得印證。

第三次訪金包里萬事俱備

一九一五年初，筆者與另外兩位本地牧師再度拜訪金包里，並在這裡停留三天。這一次我們租了一間房子，同時作為佈道所和傳道師的住處。而那位日本官員也藉著這次「提供我們這些訪客在停留期間給予舒適的居所」作為表達他對這件事情重視的程度。當時已經有多人表達對基督教有極大的興趣，當他們得知將有傳道師派駐在這裡時，都顯得極為欣喜。當屋子必要的整修工作告一段落之後，一位熱心的傳道師被派遣來金包里，負責本地的事工。六個月之內，已經有四十位聽眾固定來參加禮拜並接受基督教教導，也已經開始學習閱讀羅馬字。教會頭一年找婦女或女孩來教會聚會有困難，但是後來她們對基督教的偏見逐漸消失，最後甚至有一些婦女進入淡水女學堂就讀。相信在這個基礎上，金包里教會的目標能夠有豐碩的成果。

金包里教會一百位基督徒固定聚會

第一次的洗禮禮拜約有十五位男人和婦女參加受洗，教會如今有超過五十位已經受洗的會

員。筆者上次拜訪金包里時，已有超過一百位基督徒以及慕道友參加早上的禮拜。這些基督徒自由的使用他們自己的方式，在他們的鄰居面前為上帝作見證，有一些年輕人希望將來能夠擔任牧師，當中有兩到三位希望將來回到他們自己的城鎮為當地居民傳福音。

「說謊的神明」差點拆散一個美滿的家庭

由於篇幅的限制，無法將金包里教會迅速發展到市鎮角落當中所發生的有趣事件一一說明，但是筆者願意在此介紹最近幾年歸信的一個基督教家庭的故事。

一對夫妻住在金包里鎮約五公里外的村莊，丈夫是一位農夫，離開家裡幾個禮拜的時間去城外做生意。當他回到家之後，他控訴他的妻子不貞，而她堅決否認這個指控。丈夫在狂怒之下去請示神明。在經過一連串處理這種問題的儀式之後，他獲得自己想要得到的答案。這些啞巴神明「如何被勸說並依照信徒的期望說話」是一件值得我們關注的事情。那個丈夫從神明那裡，得到妻子犯罪的確據之後決定懲罰妻子，且威脅要殺死她。

在上帝良善的旨意之下，這個丈夫聽見佈道者所傳的福音，當時佈道內容提到「神明有說謊的傾向」。這個大膽的指控引起了他的注意。不過在經過深思之後，他決定要學習更多基督新的道理。結果就是他得知自己的愚蠢、惡待妻子以及自己罪惡的一生。他的妻子也熱切希望自己能學習這個改變她丈夫心靈和意志的信仰。結果，這對夫妻後來成為熱心又快樂的基督徒。一九二〇年，筆者要回去加拿大的前一天早上受邀到他們家裡作客，要離開的時候，他們站在一起交給我一尊神像，說：「牧師，請將它拿去你的國家，為了這個神明，我幾乎葬送我

的一生。」如今他們兩個人都已經受洗，過著快樂的基督徒生活。

宜蘭的歸信消除種族偏見

宜蘭平原平埔族的信仰被歧視

宜蘭地區是台灣東岸一個美麗的平原，走山路要一天的路程，或由基隆港搭乘汽船六個小時的航程。這個平原的海岸是由約廿四公里連綿不絕的沙灘所形成的。沿著海岸線走，有廿個小漁村。山脈雄踞三角形平原的兩邊，由海岸到山邊的距離約十六公里。宜蘭的平原土地肥沃、水量豐沛，有十萬個漢人居住其中，幾乎所有人都是農民。早年有數千位平埔族人在這個地區居住，但是這樣的數字急遽減少，如今平埔族人不超過一、兩千人。

最初幾年，宜蘭平原上所有的教會都坐落於平埔族的村莊當中，那些高傲的漢人排斥平埔族人和他們的宗教，特別是當他們看見平埔族人的宗教是從外國人這邊得到的，讓歧視更加明顯，因此在宗教的事務上，兩個民族沒有接觸的必要。由於宜蘭與島嶼其他地區相隔絕，所以居住於此的漢人非常保守、極端的迷信，因此不願意接受耶穌的教義。

「扭轉歧視」觀念的宣教措施

一九〇八年，筆者第一次拜訪宜蘭，當時由嚴清華牧師擔任助手以及嚮導。筆者發現十六間教會當中，只有兩間位於漢人聚落的中心，亦即宜蘭以及羅東，羅東也是一個重要的市鎮。

在那個時候，整個宜蘭平原沒有任何一個漢人家庭跟基督教教會有關，次年，為了指導平原上的教會事務，筆者在當地停留一個月，在那裡主理聖餐，查驗主日學課程並且每天晚上與傳道師在宜蘭街上舉行佈道會，這種工作的方法持續了三到四年。在最初的時候，筆者就已經知道，假如能夠有漢人接受基督教的信仰，那麼基督教會就會由平埔族的村落轉往漢人的城鎮。因此在平原的首府宜蘭的街上租一間房子，並邀請一位本地的牧師駐在羅東——然而漢人仍然與這些「平埔仔」保持遠離，這是一個嚴重「族群歧視」的例子，顯示漢人有著非常顯著的民族優越感。

一位漢人被喚醒，耶穌福音進入漢人家庭

一九一四年，當筆者休假回來之後，再度利用一個月的時間留在宜蘭平原，與佈道者每晚在街上佈道。在這些聚會當中，有一次，一位漢人穿過群眾，走到台前，肩膀倚在門柱邊，仔細聆聽了兩場演講。聚會結束之後，他極為熱切的詢問筆者，剛剛說的耶穌，是不是真的？祂是否如我們所說的，為人行那些事；我們告訴他，那是真的。隔日傍晚，那個人再度來到。第三天，他帶著他的兩個小孩，讓他們坐在靠近台前的地方。由於他非常專注的聽講道，以致於忘記他身處於平埔族人當中。禮拜天時，他帶兩個小孩來參加主日崇拜，當天傍晚，他的妻子

— 167 —

也溜進來坐在基督徒婦女當中。很明顯的，這個人已經被喚醒，而他的內心也已經被所聽到的真理感動。

禮拜一的時候，這個人離開市區到約五公里外的地方工作。他的妻子聽說傳道師的母親過世，於是購買一副輓聯贈給傳道師，作為她接受這個新宗教的象徵。這一件事被她的婆婆知曉，因此毫不留情的毆打媳婦。當她的丈夫回來之後，丈夫走向侍奉祖先牌位與家族神明的地方，將中央的一尊神像拿下來，嚴肅的告訴他的母親，他已經厭倦過去的迷信以及拜偶像的行為，因此他決定要成為基督徒；並且也為了要表達其追隨新宗教的決心，將神像投擲在母親的腳前。他持續的參加聚會，不久之後，他能夠自己閱讀《新約全書》。隔年受洗，兩年之後，他的妻子也採取相同的作為，如今全家都在基督教會聚會。

建築讓安・韓達紀念禮拜堂

先前提到，漢人對於基督教的偏見逐漸消失，於是開始有許多人敢進入教會，願意拿取信徒傳予他們的聖經、聖詩；有些人更進一步願意購買福音書小冊。一段時間以後，有人為宜蘭市內的教會捐獻了一筆數千元的金錢，這件事情廣為人知，因此宜蘭教會建築的準備工作引起了很大的注目，如今已經購買土地，但是要將地上的草厝移走卻面臨很大的問題。當那間草厝的所有人得知，筆者打算向他們購買房舍時，他們立刻提出一個高得離譜的價格。然而在官員的協助之下，土地就被整平，教堂坐落於孔廟前的大馬路邊，「讓安・韓達紀念禮拜堂」就被興建起來。一位年老的平埔族寡婦捐獻一座

（Jane Hunter Memorial Church，今宜蘭教會）

掛鐘，每次在聚會之前就敲擊，不管是在主日或是平常日子大家「都通告將要傳講福音的信息了」，並且邀請人來聽耶穌的教義。傳道師住在教會裡面，另外還有四間房間作為宣教師巡迴時的居所，這是宜蘭這座城市最好的房舍之一。

禮拜堂興建完成後不久，陳其祥受聘前來宜蘭協助佈道的工作，他最大的兒子從神學院畢業，也被派來宜蘭服事。因此在這間新教會裡面有一位天賦優異的傳道師和他的父親，以及他盡責的妻子和信心堅強的母親，使得他們的工作極富趣味和熱情。在新的禮拜堂設立幾個月之後，舉行了為期五週的特別聚會。筆者藉著這個機會，與傳道師一起服事一位旅館老闆，使他歸信後，後來他成為教會最有天分的佈道家。

旅館老闆劉天來的歸信從內到外煥然一新

劉天來是他的名字，在多年以前他曾經是台中一位年輕的旅館老闆。他吸食鴉片，也是賭徒，揮霍無度，也是香菸的愛好者。他在日本度過好幾年混亂的生活之後，帶著風霜回到台灣。他前往各個寺廟，祈求神明幫助醫治他有病的身體，但是一切都枉然。最後，他前往彰化，在基督教醫院接受醫術熟練的英國宣教師蘭大衛醫生的細心醫療後，身體得到康復。在治病那段時間，他聽到福音，並與毫無幫助的神明和愚蠢的迷信相比後，他的內心瞬時明白開朗。他承認自己的罪以及先前愚蠢的生活。之後，他的改變極為顯著，他是由內到外完全的歸信。從那個時候開始，他不再觸碰鴉片或是香菸，然後開始宣揚主耶穌福音的力量和自由。當他出院治癒後回到家，就把他旅館當中「一切與福音不合」的東西清除掉，並且讓入住的旅客

知道福音奇妙的故事。他歸信的事蹟就成為他先前同伴、台中的賭徒們聊天的話題。有一天，有一位從沒聽過他歸信的賭徒老朋友來找他，六個月以後，朋友幾乎認不出他來。有一位從沒聽過他歸信的賭徒老朋友來找他，到了旅館的門口。那人問他，劉天來是否在裡面？他回答是。於是那人進去裡面，大聲喊他的名字，但沒能找到人。於是那人到門口，指責他說謊，大聲說：「劉天來沒有在裡面！」這時，劉天來露出往日的笑容，看著那個人，說：「你要找哪一個劉天來？去年的或是今年的？」那人認出他來，立刻窘促不安地問道：「你到底是吃什麼東西？怎麼改變這麼大！」他回答：「我吃耶穌的教義，坐下來，我要讓你知道這些故事。」

劉天來如今已經成為一位熱心的傳道者，同時仍是旅館的主人。他在台中時，擔任兩年執事，回到宜蘭之後成為長老。

日本官員上田熊喜「一個大有幫助」的歸信

在新教堂，聚會參加的人數很多。數日之後，有一位婦女被引導前來聽福音，她顯得格外有興趣。她是一位日本地方官員的妻子，那位日本官員因醉酒和賭博揮霍了很多金錢，這個妻子本身也是一位賭徒，很快地，他們就陷入經濟困窘的局面。那位官員決定將妻子和年幼的女兒趕出家門，只留下兒子，因此這位個婦女就此流落街頭、沒有居所。後來有基督徒邀請她到教會來聽福音，告訴她，「一定會獲得平安。」第一個晚上，她倚在後門邊聽，由於她長得比其他漢人婦女還高大，因此彎下腰來，眼光盯住台上的講者。第二天晚上，她再來聽。第三個

晚上，她邀請她的丈夫一起來聽。最初這位日本官員只是一笑置之，但是最後出於好奇，於是前來，但只是站在門邊聽講。但是人們將他引到台前，講台上的經文內容引起了他的注意。隔夜，他再回來，第三天傍晚，他帶著一條日本的彩色布巾，裡面裝滿拜神的物品——那是一包屬於他和妻子的東西，也有威士忌酒瓶、也有香菸。他藉著這次的行動與過去道別，而將未來交託在上帝的手中。這位日本官員是上田熊喜先生，自此他開始不再喝酒與吸菸，並且帶著異常熱切的心進入基督教會。他在帽帶之上寫著「基督徒」的字樣，別人因此知道他的生命已死而復生，所以改變服事的對象，就是基督。他瞭解福音，遵行耶穌的教導，並且將整個生命奉獻給上帝以及擴張國度的工作。

隔年，筆者榮幸的為他全家以及另外九位本地基督徒舉行洗禮。不久之後，上田熊喜先生勸服另外一位日本官員歸信——這位官員經常酗酒，並且在酒精的影響之下毆打妻子。他和妻子聽了上田熱心的見證之後，於隔週的聖禮典當中在漢人的教會裡接受洗禮。後來他的官位獲得晉升，前往台北市，並且在那裡加入日本人的公理堂。

日本地方官員和他全家受洗的事蹟，讓基督徒大受鼓舞，從那時開始，基督教發展極為快速，並且舊有的偏見見也逐漸消失。在歸信兩年之後，上田熊喜先生獲選擔任教會長老，他忠實的在自己的職位上努力工作，奉獻時間與能力給上帝。他知道基督教文字作品的影響力，於是購買了一百五十元價值的基督教書籍，然後把書分送給他認為會好好閱讀的人。他也在教會開辦日本兒童的主日學，在每個主日負責教導學生。上田熊喜先生是上帝恩典的鮮明例證。

福音在硬土羅東的勝利

在這個擁有三千位漢人、距離宜蘭約八公里外的城鎮羅東，實在是一個「考驗對上帝信心和耐心」的地方。多年以來，羅東這裡對基督教教會的偏見極為強烈，直到目前，這裡仍沒有任何一位漢人基督徒。十年前，在城鎮附近的村社有六間平埔族人的教會，因此在羅東鎮內必須加強努力，希望能夠建立漢人的教會。雖然有一位漢人的牧師在城內，是一位能力很強、個性開朗的人，在那裡也已經有一、兩年的時間，但以此判斷，他的服事並沒有在鎮民心裡留下什麼印象。

最排斥基督教會的辦事員張阿富歸信

在羅東鎮內的漢人當中，沒有一個人比張阿富更排斥基督教會。他是城鎮官府裡的辦事員，外表強壯、舉止粗俗、脾氣暴躁、話語尖酸刻薄。張阿富是漢人信仰當中最虔誠的信徒。他

一九一四年，他與另外三位進香客前往中國福州，希望在那裡尋得快樂、庇護和富裕之方。他在那次徒勞的旅行當中花費了五百元，到所有著名的廟宇去拈香敬拜，最後他們決定要從當地最有名的一間神廟當中「求取聖火，帶回自己的故鄉」。這不是一件簡單的事情，因為他們

「無論如何都不能讓這個聖火熄滅」才行。在橫渡台灣海峽的時候，所有人都暈船得非常嚴重。到達基隆時，他們發現誤了回鄉的船期。這意味著他必須在暴風雨的季節當中，攀登數座山脈。但是因為他是一位強壯的人，最後張阿富圓滿地將聖火帶回故鄉羅東。他先在自己的祖先牌位面前燒香，之後，他非常驕傲的以聖火點燃地方廟宇的香燭。

然而，由福州帶回來的聖火，卻無法將張阿富家庭裡所遭遇的厄運改變或趕走。在那之前，他的家人從來沒有染上那麼多的疫病。每個月，他都必須要請乩童來趕走家中的惡靈。不過大約同一段時期，在他家附近開設了一間佈道所，張阿富的小女兒就開始到教會去上主日學，很快的，她在教會裡學會一些聖詩以及羅馬字的書寫。不久之後，孩子的母親也開始對基督教產生興趣，她與傳道師的妻子熟識之後，也開始參加聚會。她的興趣隨著所聽的道理漸漸增加，但是卻讓她的丈夫開始警覺。由於小女兒在主日學的成績優異，因此傳道夫婦建議她應該前往淡水女學校接受進一步的教育——母親希望她去讀，但是父親張阿富卻頑強的反對。

當這個提議還在拉扯的時候，羅東教會舉行一場特別的佈道會，而陳其祥和兒子、旅館主人劉天來，以及其他傳道師受邀請前來協助，這位羅東鎮的辦事員張阿富也被說服前來參加。

這是他第一次聽見福音，這與先前他的口裡所說的以及對信徒完全排斥的情況截然不同。第一個晚上他表達了「對於佈道會當中所說的良好教導」讓他感到訝異，而後在佈道會期間，也每天晚上都來聽講，結果就是他的小女兒得以前往淡水就學。事實上是父親張阿富自己帶著她，爬過兩年前從福州廟宇帶聖火回來所踏過的山嶺而前往淡水。一年之後，他的妻子接受洗禮，而他自己也成為固定參加禮拜的慕道友，並且開始學習閱讀羅馬字的《新約全書》。他在相信

真道後不久後，就成為上帝恩典福音忠實的見證者。

有某次機會，張阿富來台北拜訪筆者，他告訴筆者，一次偶然的事件讓他的心裡留下了深刻的印象，喚起他發自內心對上帝的感恩，因為上帝的良善，讓他從迷信和偶像崇拜的力量當中獲得拯救。那天，他來台北處理兩、三年前曾與他一起前往福州，並從事「無益的進香之旅」的朋友的埋葬事宜。原來，在三天前，這個朋友前往中台灣北港著名的廟宇，但就在媽祖面前點香的時候，突然倒地不起。他的遺體被送到台北，那裡的警察僱請苦力將他朋友的遺體帶到郊外的墓園埋葬。但是苦力挖出一個裝滿水的地洞之後就棄置不顧。有人將這個消息告訴張阿富，他立刻前去，並為他的朋友尋找一個適合的埋葬地點。

張阿富不是一位信仰猶疑的人，甚至在他受洗之前就已經在家裡舉行過家庭禮拜。而他的慷慨可以從一件事看得出來——他將所購置的一大片位於城鎮中心的土地，贈送給教會蓋禮拜堂。現在羅東已經有幾個漢人基督教家庭了，他們與附近鄉下的平埔族人融合在一起，在城鎮當中建立一間教會。由此可以看到上帝在羅東的作為。

宜蘭市需要一間教士會所

— 174 —

有關在宜蘭建立漢人教會的事情還有許多事件，值得記錄下來，但是因為篇幅所限，無法一一訴說，另外在整個平原上也需要很多宣教師在此地指導。教士會期待在宜蘭市內建立一間教士會所，當中希望可以容納一位封立的宣教師以及兩位女宣道婦的派駐。在宜蘭設立這個教士會所，就可以更完整指導到花蓮港平原的教會——該地位於東台灣距離宜蘭有約一百公里的路程。

大浪翻滾的花蓮港

花蓮港是位於平原北邊的市鎮，人口約有兩萬名日本人及相當人數的台灣人。港灣內可以停泊日本的汽船，是一個開闊的海岸，那裡有著大浪翻滾、造成了無止盡的浪花景象。就算遇見最輕微的逆風，海浪也會變得極為激烈，使得沒有一艘船隻膽敢出海[1]。

登陸的困難與驚險

在這種海港登陸，有時候必須極為小心，因此在海岸上站立著約一百位原住民男女，並協助往來於離岸數百碼外的船隻和海岸間小舟人員的貨物裝卸工作，這些原住民當中，有些是精

湛的泳者。他們巧妙的穿梭於比他們高出幾公尺的大浪之間並進到小舟處。那些小舟在浪花後面等待泳者將輕繩索綁在大索之上，然後騎到大浪頂端衝上沙岸的機會，一等到粗繩到岸邊後，原住民立刻抓住粗繩，然後不耐煩的等候進一步的指示。在此同時，小舟也盡量開到浪花後，在船長的指揮之下，下令將小舟轉彎並將船尾面對海岸。岸上的原住民立刻發出一種非常特別的呼喊聲，將小舟自浪花頂端拉往岸上。此時乘客可能覺得「想像比體驗來得更好」——就在登陸過程的震撼聲中，原住民全部都蹲伏在船底。筆者曾經看見小船直立起來，然後摔向岸上，船身隨即裂成兩半。幸好乘客立刻跳船並獲救，但是小舟上的郵件四散在憤怒的海面之上，當天也不再有船隻登陸花蓮港，而汽船也必須另外尋找較安全的下錨之處。

鳳林簿記員的歸信大有鼓舞效應

　　從花蓮港往南約一百公里的某個地方已經興建了輕便鐵路，而五十公里處是鳳林的所在地。這裡是加拿大長老教會在台灣建立最為偏遠的教會。幾年前，有一些基督徒遷居來此處開墾，有些人從事農耕，有些人則是採集樟腦，而另外有些人住在城鎮當中。當筆者到北方花蓮港指導新教堂興建的時候，也乘機與傳道師一同前往鳳林，拜訪那裡的基督徒。他們非常熱

心，希望有傳道師能夠派往該處，這個要求於隔年就實現了。

一九一五年，在這個地方舉行過成功的佈道會，當時有三位傳道師以及宣教師在這裡停留三個禮拜之久。白天時去拜訪村落，傍晚又在城鎮舉行佈道會，也曾遭到極有影響力的本地人的反對。

在那裡，有一位在樟腦公司工作的簿記員未曾聽過福音，他告訴城鎮的長輩想要聽耶穌的福音，這位長輩勸告他不要去，並且講一些「關於這個新宗教的貶抑的話語」，想要讓年輕人失望以打消這個念頭。然而他並沒有因此而退卻，反倒在第一場佈道會中出現。這讓他產生極大的興趣。第二天傍晚禮拜開始以前，他就已經出現在街上的教會裡面，尋找與宣教師對話的機會。第三個晚上，他在一場演講當中站立起來，並且請求是否可以詢問問題？然後轉身對著群眾說：「我已經聽了三晚他們的演講，雖然我還不是完全清楚裡面的內容，不過我相信，由我所聽到的內容來看，這些人所講的話是真的。我不相信這些外國的宣教師大老遠跑來這裡，就是要對我們說虛假的事情。」然後他轉向宣教師並問：「對於耶穌赦免罪，你有什麼確據沒有？我的生活不是很好，我要知道更多關於赦免罪的事情。」在城鎮裡的異教徒當中，沒有任何人的名聲比這位簿記員來得更好，而且他的內心在那天晚上深受感動，進入真理並且找到好的依託。

在他歸信不久後，他想知道雙親若知道兒子成為基督徒的消息之後，會有何反應？因為他們也不曾聽過基督教的教義。然而，事實上，不久之後，他的父母也追隨他的腳步成為信徒。

幾個月之後，他寫一封信表達了他的內心的想法：「對於能夠聽到福音是一件多麼值得感謝的

事情。」一年之後，他接受洗禮。如今，我們聽說他已經到南部教會成為執事的消息。

鳳林的基督徒受了這位簿記員歸信的事後有極大的鼓舞。有部分的異教徒丟棄他們的神像、有些人的名字已經登錄進慕道友的名單當中。他們接下來的步驟就是建立教堂。日本官員在城鎮裡提供大片的土地作為建堂之用，而先前勸告簿記員不要去教會的地方長輩，也捐獻廿五元作為教堂的興建基金。基督徒們自己也募集了大約七百元，加上他們自己獻工擔任建築工人。一九二一年，教堂興建完成，如今大約有一百位成員，包括受洗會員以及慕道友。先前的偏見逐漸的消失，將來的發展實在可期。

上帝的忠僕陳其祥安息主懷

筆者最近聽到陳其祥長老安息的消息，認為這個章節不應該在沒有介紹這位傑出人物的生平情況下就結束。

一九一八年，他和當時在宜蘭擔任傳道的大兒子遷往南台灣，他的兒子受聘前往當時台灣最大間的教會擔任傳道師，他的第二個兒子在日本京都大學就讀，準備進入基督教的傳教工作，第三個兒子在中台灣擔任傳道師。第四個孩子，是一位年輕人，正在日本就學中。

陳其祥自從離開宜蘭到他安息為止，他巡迴了整個南台灣的教會。此外，他也協助他兒子在台南的工作——雖然他的身體狀況不是很理想，但是他不斷計畫如何擴充上帝的國度——當中最受歡迎的計畫，也是他花費許多精神推動的，就是結合一群平信徒，奉獻他們的時間和各樣方式為台灣傳福音工作的努力。他成為基督徒整整十四年的時間，專注於個人的傳道工作：

鼓勵軟弱的信徒、對異教徒傳福音，並且在別人有需要的時候，慷慨地提供一切。

從他歸信開始，他強烈地期望每一個兒子都能夠獻身，這已經在前面提到過。他的家族非常敬愛他，的確，我們實在很少看到過如此順服的上帝子民——而這些愛是相對的。也是因為他如此付出，所以他的兒子能夠受到這麼好的教育，並且為他的主提供適切的服務。

在台灣的基督徒當中，很少有人像他這樣有毫不動搖的信心、如此獻出心靈和生命、如此聖潔的方法，如此熱心地將福音傳給同胞以及如此尊重和愛護不同種族的人。如同陳其祥長老一般，他真可稱為是一位歸信的學者。失去他之後的台灣無法保持原貌，他已經得到賞賜，他的影響增廣，而他的工作也將由後人持續不絕完成。在那榮耀之處，恩典的冠冕，他已經得到。使徒約翰在異象中，看見的人群裡，有一個適合他的位置了——「此後，我觀看，看見有許多人，沒有人能計算，是從各邦國、各支派、各民族、各語言來的，站在寶座和羔羊面前，身穿白衣，手拿棕樹枝。」（啟示錄七章九節）

—— 179 ——

禱告詞

噢！全人類的大牧者，我們感謝祢，因為祢關心、愛我們以及其他所有的人群，因為祢看見世人如同沒有牧者的羊群，四散在草地及山邊，祢就憐憫我們。我們也為那些前往艱困遙遠之地去分享祢的憐憫及去尋找失喪的人們，來感謝祢。

特別是為離開我們國家、前往遙遠的福爾摩沙的人來感謝祢，請祢不斷鼓舞他們的心靈，直到他們看見祢勝利的十字架建立在島嶼的城市和鄉村。願他們與台灣同工獲得健康和保守，日日得到聖靈的更新，因此可以多結果實。讓那些新信徒的信仰被建立、過著屬靈的生活，而年輕的教會能在熱情與屬靈活力中成長，在團契連結中得到歡欣。

噢！上帝我們要向祢懇求，讓我們那些在自己家鄉的人，能夠關心不在他們圈欄裡面的羊群，讓我們每個人都熱切的追尋救贖，並且能夠彼此代禱，直到所有的人都得到接納、在上帝與天使的面前歡喜為止。以好牧者的心以及為了上帝的緣故禱告。阿們。

卷
三

第九章 ◆ 婦女宣道會在台的豐碩貢獻

為台灣失學婦女設立女學機構

北部台灣教會第一次清楚提到的婦女事工，出現在一八七九年的報告書中。加拿大婦女宣道會在過去幾年當中曾轉交馬偕牧師一筆固定的金額，作為教育基督徒婦女之用途。一八七九年，閨虔益夫人協助馬偕夫婦教導多名歸信的婦女。一八八一年，馬偕寫信回母會，要求一筆三千元的金錢，作為興建女學校舍之用。他的要求獲得母會的允諾，並於一八八二年完成校舍的興建工作並開始使用。當時有四十五位學生，大多來自宜蘭平原。

草創時期的女學校「草地堡壘」

由於台灣社會風俗，極難讓漢人信徒的女兒前來學校就讀，因此學校的學生最初是女孩與年長婦女合班上課。草創的女學校與牛津學堂坐落在同樣美麗的地點，但由於中間沒有用高牆隔開，以致漢人不願意將女兒送到這種未受保護的機構就讀，因為這會與「女孩不拋頭露面」的風俗相牴觸。由於當時急需教育婦女，所以學校內部就由傳道師夫人、傳道師寡婦以及部分的女孩組成一個在「草地堡壘」的歡樂大家庭。馬偕綜理校務，馬偕夫人、葉夫人（Mrs. Iap）以及其他同工擔任教育婦女的工作，而敬虔的陳火牧師（一位能力強且信仰虔誠的人）指導她們研習聖經，每天早上與傍晚，整個主內大家庭在牛津學堂集會，當年的情景如今已成為許多人快樂的回憶。

與婦女宣道會合作

然而，一般人都認為「應當要有更多北台灣的女孩與婦女來學校就讀」才行，婦女宣道會於一八九四年的報告書裡提到有關台灣的事工部分，協會內部一開始就已經準備好要提供一切所需，來協助台灣婦女的宣教工作。

首批女宣教師來台協助教育婦女事工

一九〇〇年，首度返國述職的吳威廉夫人在婦女宣道會舉辦的研討會與中會例會的每一場演講，都特別強調「北台灣急需女宣教師」。她回來台灣之後寫信給婦女宣道會，督促她們趕快派遣女宣教師前來。一九〇二年，這個請求被轉到海外宣道委員會，內容當中請求希望盡速

派遣兩位未婚的姑娘前來籌辦女子學校。為了回應上述的請求，一九○五年秋天，有兩位女教師受任派來台灣，她們是金仁理姑娘與高哈拿姑娘。

透過學校教育改變生命

這兩位認真的姑娘經過兩年的努力，並學會本地語言之後，她們開始計畫女學校的籌備工作，而台灣政府對於「設立各個教育機構抱著極深的興趣」就是這個時期的重要因素。為了要達到學校最大的效益，兩位女宣教師在學校開學以前，就先去拜訪了南台灣以及中國內陸的姊妹教會，並非常仔細地研究他們的政策與方法。

女學校（Girls' School）受人信賴

一九○七年十月，這間新的女學校開學，這是北部台灣婦女極為重要的歷史事件，而且兩位外國女宣教師來到台灣這麼短的時間之內就得以實現。而且當時她們尚未完成兩年的語言學習課程，這要歸功於她們忠實而有效率的工作。我們可以想像，最初有廿四位膽小的女生初到淡水，她們懷著恐懼不安的心情。但她們到達時才發現，這所學校不僅有近兩公尺高的牆圍繞

於四周，事實上是將校園封閉起來以保護她們的安全。儘管父母將自己交托給外國宣教師照顧，但這麼安全的環境卻讓那些女學生們得到相當大的安慰。不久之後，這些女學生將她們原先的不安已消失得無影無蹤，師生間的情誼快速的增長。很快地，這些台灣女學生不願將她們「在草地堡壘的住家和島上居民和地方的住所交換」。隔年，女孩們的雙親受邀來到學校探視，父母都非常驚異地發現學校的舒適、房間的整潔、照料者的道德高尚以及女兒身體的健康。當父母們看到這麼高的圍牆時，不僅先前的疑慮完全消失，也覺得自己的女兒住的是這麼安全的環境和交到令人值得信賴的人手中。父母們很快發現到淡水女學校是道德上最安全、最受到大眾歡迎、最有宗教指導和教育情操的教育機構，同時也是一所在北部台灣經濟效益上極佳的學校。

新校舍建築完成吸引更多人就讀

當年建築於一八八三年的舊校舍，如今已經破舊不堪，於同一個地點再建造一棟更大空間的建築，並於一九一六年五月正式啟用。值得注意的是，不僅吸引更多人聚集於此，更重要的是教育界的領導者以及台灣總督的出席，並且他們在典禮當中還以教育為專題並發表演講。

增加女子中學教育的課程

藉著這個機會，淡水女學校增加中學生的一般類課程，這個新增加的內容與日本女子中學的課程類似，再加上基督教的教育。這些課程都是以日語講授，因此當學生想要前往日本內地

深造時，能夠適應更高等學府的教育。

台灣唯一的女醫生

在這裡必須要提及一位亮眼的基督徒女孩，她在淡水中學畢業之後，前往東京學習多年的醫學。一九二○年畢業後回來台灣，她是本島第一位也是唯一的女醫生。她是一位認真且吸引人的年輕婦女，筆者希望她用生命來幫助自己的同胞。如今，教會因為醫館關門了，無法提供她發揮所學的機會，因此她目前在台北市的公立醫館服務。

富家千金的願望

淡水鎮郊有一間宮殿般的住家，房屋的主人是一位非常富有的漢人。根據當時漢人的傳統風俗習慣來說，男人是可以娶三位妻子的。這個主人受過很好的教育，雖然他不是一位基督徒，但他對基督教的教育帶來的益處很感興趣，因此他將女兒送往女學校就讀。最初他的那些異教徒的妻子們都不贊成這件事，但逐漸地，基督教福音在他的女兒心裡占有一席之地，最後這個女孩也成為一位真正的信徒。在此同時，女兒也關心自己家人的信仰問題，一點一點的，透過女兒的影響力，三位妻子逐漸對基督教產生好感，並且歡迎每天到訪的聖經宣道婦，不久之後三位都進入教會，學會讀寫台語的羅馬字，如今她們都已經成為受洗的基督徒。這個主人目前還沒有成為基督徒的跡象，但是我們可以大膽預期，不久之後，他將成為上帝國度的一員。這個女兒在女學校畢業之後，前往日本深造，期望將來回來可以協助自己的同胞。本來我

們可以想像她的將來是這般的狀況──以她家世的富裕與豪華，定然會及時結婚，嫁入一個富裕但異教的家庭。但卻跟如今她那大有用處、快樂以及樂於助人的情況相反，所以我們仍然為女學校感謝上帝。

由於學校的事務極為繁忙，使得兩位宣教師姑娘除了關心學校的學生之外，實在沒有多餘的心力去照顧這個地區的異教婦女。在暑假期間，她們也安排下鄉訪視活動，但是大部分都被訪視學生的家庭和她們的朋友所占滿了，訪視目的是嘗試去引發其他女孩們去學校學習的興趣，以便增加學生的人數。

婦學校（Women's School）訓練更多聰慧的女性

很快的，大家都知道女性十分需要聖經宣道學校（Bible School），因為婦女可以在聖經學校接受教育，然後再出去教育自己的姊妹。一九一〇年，聖經學校成立了，由高哈拿姑娘負責校務，裡面的學生來自信徒和非信徒、貧窮或富裕的家庭。從那時開始，有許多傳道師的妻子來到這裡，得益於學校的教育，並接受短期或長期的訓練。有些人接受兩年完整的教育，畢業後成為聖經宣道婦。在經過短期的訓練之後，有些人回家不僅成為更好的妻子，也變成更為聰慧的母親，參與自己社區的基督教工作。聖經學校也成為傳福音的機構，許多學生初入學時是異教徒，但是在畢業時已經成為決志的基督徒。

— 187 —

優雅的聖經宣道婦

許多被聖經學校影響的事例當中，有兩位學生的經驗特別有趣。兵仔嬸是一位有錢人的太太，也是鴉片煙癮者，家住大甲。有一次，她因為身體不舒服而前往距離不遠的彰化基督教醫館治療。在那裡，她獲得基督教的福音而成為熱心的信徒。讓她感到欣喜的是，當她出院回家之後，發現附近成立一間基督教會，有許多人去作禮拜。於是她開始參加聚會，但是受到丈夫極力的阻擋，有時候甚至會打她。然而她仍然堅持到教會去。經過一段時間之後，她的丈夫不再反對，雖然他不願意成為基督徒，但卻允許她前往婦學校受教育。在學校中，她的進展極為快速。在完成學業之後，她的能力也足以適任基督教工作，因此受到任命成為聖經宣道婦。由於丈夫已經娶別的女人為妻，兵仔嬸得以自由從事基督教工作。八年來，她不眠不休的在醫館、教堂認真的服務，也與女宣教師一起巡迴各地佈道。由於她的舉止優雅又有吸引力，因此能夠進入富裕人家去宣教，而她謙卑的態度和對自己同胞的關心，也讓她成為窮人家歡迎的訪客。

小妾「安心」的故事

另外一位婦學校的畢業生「安心」也是一個有意思的故事。當安心還是小女孩的時候，信奉異教的母親就以微薄的價錢把她賣給別人。等她年齡稍長之後又被轉賣別人，最後成為一位富有農民的小妾，住在台灣中部的台中市郊。於此同時，她的母親成為基督徒，並且不斷想念這位失去的女兒。那天終於來到，那位富有的農夫過世，而安心也知道從今之後的日子將是令人無法忍受的困難，因此決心前往佛教寺廟出家度過餘生。她身上穿著僅有的服裝，偷偷離

開那裡，在前往山上寺廟的途中經過了故鄉，而她的母親也聽說女兒的事情，就邀她回家過夜。在上帝奇妙的帶領下，恰巧那天筆者前往台中去，與前述歸信的旅館主人劉天來見面。當天傍晚，劉天來邀請一些基督徒在家中舉行祈禱會，當中一位就是這位帶著女兒安心的母親。

當時安心已經廿二歲，從被賣的時候算起已經十六年之久。筆者並不知道這些背景故事，但是羅馬書十二章一到三節，對於那一位打算前往山上佛寺出家的女孩來講卻極為合適。安心以前從來沒有聽過福音，信息內容讓她立刻有所回應，結果就是數日之後，她沒有前往山上寺廟修行，反倒是前往婦學校就讀。她在學校裡非常熱忱的學習，也非常認同基督教的真理，其他宣教師在談到她時，認為她是所有唸過書的學生當中最有潛力的婦女之一。安心在一九二二年畢業，就立刻出去宣揚基督教平安和拯救的福音。如今加拿大曼尼托巴的青年協會提供她擔任聖經宣道婦的經費支持。

兩位忠心的婦女工作者

在此應當介紹兩位非常忠心的婦女工作者，如今她們還是持續努力地工作。葉夫人，她是馬偕博士時代舊婦學的教師，婦女宣道會重組學校之後，她仍然繼續在學校教書多年。最近幾年她在城內擔任聖經宣道婦，陪伴宣教師們巡視鄉下的教會。她對於聖經的熟習以及多年基督徒的經驗，使她成為最寶貴的工人。她合宜的外表和謙卑的舉止，使她得以毫無困難地進入異教徒家中，而她傳講的信息總是適切且對別人有幫助。她的女兒曾經是我們宣教師們的老師，而她的兒子在醫館擔任數年的藥劑師工作。

過去四年當中，羅夫人用特別的方式吸引人進入基督教，她原本是非常保守的人，成為基督徒以前很少見識到家庭以外的世界，甚至成為信徒之後，她也怯於與基督徒婦女之外的人相處。丈夫過世之後，她前往婦學校就讀，顯示出她適合擔任服務教會的一面，不僅透徹瞭解基督教真理，並且能夠很快地將她所瞭解的部分傳達給別人，將基督福音的信息用溫和而真摯的方式傳達到人的內心。

女宣教師再添兩位生力軍

一九一〇年，黎媽美（Miss Mabel G. Clazie）姑娘到達台灣，而安義理姑娘（Miss Lily Adair）於一九一一年來到這裡；由於女學校與婦學校兩間學校以及醫館對人才的殷切需求，因此沒有足夠的人手去進行對本地婦女的傳教工作。這些機構都需要她們的協助，這實在是因為缺乏宣教人手的緣故，這個問題持續到一九一四年，才正式擬定對婦女傳教的工作計畫。

醫療體系的關顧與照管

病患的關懷者

在醫館當中的婦女工作實在進行得非常順利。當宋雅各醫生重組淡水醫館，第一位受到醫療照護的人是貧窮的寡婦安夫人。她的名聲很廣，在過去十五年來，她的名字傳遍醫館以及北部教會。安夫人到醫館的時候，年紀已經很大，並且得的病症幾乎無藥可治。吳威廉夫人因為會講台灣話，所以協助照顧她。在醫館外圍的一個小角落就充當她的病床，經由醫生的醫術、耐心及不辭辛勞的照顧下，她終於痊癒，也自修學會台語羅馬字之後，開始教導其餘的病患，很快她就成為病患的關懷者。她照顧的患者當中有一位名叫「木仔」的人，一位年輕眼盲的異教徒。他來到淡水醫館，安夫人照顧他並且教他福音、《聖詩》，後來他也成為基督徒。身體康復之後，他前往台南盲人學校訓瞽堂讀書，畢業之後擔任按摩師，得以養活自己。他現在住在宜蘭，而他的妻子、父母都是教會的成員。

在此可以再介紹一點安夫人所做的工作：一九二一年婦女事工報告書當中，用以下的文字介紹安夫人：「安夫人的外表並不吸引人，穿著也儉樸。她唯一的期望就是為基督贏得靈魂，也因為帶領了許多人信主而歡喜。在領人信主的這些人當中，有一位七十二歲的婦女，她之前是素食的佛教徒，也已經有五十年的時間。當她信主後，一看到安夫人，心裡就浮出保羅說的這句話：『上帝也揀選了世上卑賤的，被人厭惡的，以及那一無所有的，為要廢掉那樣樣都有的。』（哥林多前書一章廿八節）」

開朗而快樂的見證

因為婦女醫療工作而改宗的果實之一，就是如聖徒般的萬興夫人的歸信。大約十二年前，

她來到淡水偕醫館，在這裡聽到耶穌的愛，因此她的生命完全改觀。不久之後她學會閱讀，並且參與每週的婦女聚會，並且與宣教師一起拜訪婦女。但是不久之後，她的體力逐漸不濟，最後只能躺在床上。她的居所是黑暗骯髒的小房間，房內的泥地板高低不平，面對著一間小的起居室。進入房中的唯一亮光是由大門（牆上的小洞）照射進去的，還有屋頂上的幾片鑲嵌的玻璃而已。她躺在一個簡陋的架子上，其他的傢俱就是一張桌子和長凳。牆壁上貼著從《聖經》拿下來的圖畫，她就這樣在床上躺了六年。她非常希望能夠引領丈夫歸主，也曾有一段時間好像有這個可能性，但是後來於他對生病的妻子逐漸厭倦，因此娶了小老婆入門，這些事並沒有為她帶來盼望和安慰。曾經有許多人拜訪過她，包括宣教師們。所有人都一致認為對她來說，救主至為寶貴，而肉體的病痛與不便根本不算什麼，她總是耐心十足又充滿開朗，隨時準備好將對人分享耶穌的愛。在她生病的那期時間當中，鄰居都由她口中聽到福音的信息，甚至在她的幫助下能夠閱讀和背誦聖詩。

在她受困於病床上的那段時間，她尚未受洗，但當她知道自己可以在小房間內受洗並領取聖餐時極為高興，因為她多年來的盼望就是如此，但是抑制自己不敢向教會提出這種要求。有一天傍晚，在舉行過聖餐之後，長老們、宣教師和他的妻子，以及高哈拿姑娘前去拜訪萬興夫人的家。那次拜訪的經驗是，只要在場的人都難以忘懷——那個簡單的洗禮與聖餐典禮有聖靈同在，她的快樂無法以筆墨加以形容。她感覺自己順服並遵從主的命令，並且已經準備好隨時可以離開這個世界。從那時候開始，淡水教會只要舉行過聖餐典禮之後，就會有一小群人（三或四位）與牧師一同前往她家，在病床邊舉行簡單的聖禮，紀念救主的愛為她帶來的平安。

當她感覺自己的身體比較健康之後，她期望能夠前往台北馬偕紀念醫院，她不只是希望在那裡得到幫助，更希望在那裡有機會可以對同樣在患病中的人講話。宋雅各醫師安排了搭乘火車的一切細節事務，並且陪伴她前往。她在馬偕醫院停留數個月，也能在院區內活動，也可以對其他女病患說話，為許多人帶來祝福與奇蹟，以及為救主所作的開朗而快樂的見證。

然而她在地上的使命也接近尾聲，回到淡水不久之後就蒙主恩召。她為救主贏得鑲滿珠寶的冠冕。所有認識她的人，沒有人會忘記她生命馨香之氣帶來的影響──「她雖然已經離世，但是她的話語卻仍在述說不已。」

烈以利姑娘監督護理部門

馬偕紀念醫院在台北開院之時，婦女宣道會負責的是護理部門，一九一二年秋天，烈以利姑娘被任命為監督，在此之前，既沒有外國人、也沒有台灣婦女擔任護士的工作，所以家屬來了之後還要等男督導和醫院苦力到達，才可以進行下一步的工作。新的醫院開張之後，這一切舊習完全改觀。但是，外國的護士很快便發現她們的工作需要很大的耐心，因為要求漢人去遵守外國機構的衛生規定，並不是一件容易的事情。由於烈以利姑娘在學會本地的語言之前就得開始工作，因此她需要一位翻譯人員，於是柯夫人（偕以利，馬偕的次女）擔任這個職務。有幾位年輕婦女（她們曾經就讀女學校或是婦學）接受過訓練，又在適當的時機畢了業，且通過宋雅各醫生的醫事服務流程，並獲得了政府的證書。

具有發展性的醫療事工中斷

在這幾年當中，醫院對婦女的醫療照顧有很大的進展。有許多人的肉體與心靈獲得極好的治療，不只教導《聖詩》吟唱，也教導患者背誦《聖經》經節，更有許多患者學會用羅馬字閱讀《聖經》。醫院在一九一九年關閉，因為母會沒有醫療宣教師可以派遣來台灣所致，因此這個必要且極具發展的事工就被迫終止了。在那之後，烈以利姑娘前往鄉下進行婦女工作。醫院和優良設備的關閉對母會實在是一大挑戰，因為是母會的協助，才讓海外宣道委員會有實現上帝國的最大可能性。

....

穩住地方教會結實纍纍

....

女宣教師的益處

教會在婦女工作的推展上，沒有比「發展地方教會」更有成效。宣教初期，要讓婦女或女孩來聽基督教信息是一件非常困難的事情。當一位男性宣教師或台灣的傳道人進入一個異教徒的家庭的時候，家中的婦女都會消失，她們經由半開的門縫、竹簾或隱密的角落，聽宣教師或傳道師的談話內容。而女傳道師以及聖經宣道婦卻能自在的於大廳中與女眷講話。

台北婦女開展新頁

　　最近幾年，社會上對婦女的態度有極大的轉變，由於婦女不再裹小腳，因此有更多婦女可以外出，如今她們也對家務以外的事情感到興趣，準備好要聆聽各樣的信息了。

透過閱讀大開智識之門

　　無論去到哪裡，女宣教師都會引起人們的好奇心，但是當她們在一個地方待了一到三個禮拜之後，人們對她們的好奇變成對她有興趣——但不是對她個人，而是對她所帶來的信息有興趣。她們事工的部分內容是將女基督徒組織起來，教導她們《聖經》和羅馬字。這些課程通常會在早上舉行，下午是挨家挨戶的探訪工作，傍晚就在教會舉行佈道會。因此，婦女當中能夠閱讀《聖經》的人數穩定的增加中，基督徒婦女的信仰更為堅固，並影響未信的婦女能聽到福音。在鄉下工作中，最讓人感到快樂的就是「遇見那些曾經讀過女學或婦學，但如今成為傳道娘或其他工作並盡責的服務教會的人」。她們當中，有些人是在遙遠偏鄉服務，因此當女宣教師到達她們的所在地並去拜訪時，帶給她們的歡喜和鼓舞是無法以筆墨形容的。特別是學生時期的友誼更因此更新並強化，她們也商量要如何為自己的社區奉獻心力。這些早期的學生無一例外，都願意陪伴宣教師們，將自己的腳步踏入異教徒以及所有需要的家庭當中。最大的遺憾是沒有足夠的女宣教師有空閒前往鄉下巡視，這種訪問只能偶一為之。

教會開辦固定成長課程

大甲鎮的婦女工作，在數年當中有長足的進展。已婚或未婚的女宣教師曾經數度拜訪這個城鎮，為婦女舉辦一些「能在一段時間內，一週舉行兩到四次的課程」。參加的婦女都顯示出對閱讀和背誦《聖經》經文的喜愛，她們對於基督教真理的回應也令人激賞。九年前，每週一次的《聖經》課程開課，直到如今，課程不曾間斷過。曾經參加這個課程的牧師娘，如今已是八個孩子盡責的母親，這個課程的成功大部分應該歸功於她。這些婦女也安排週六去挨家挨戶探訪，目的是要邀請那些未信主的姊妹前來教會，這些事工的成果展示在「主日禮拜的婦女人數多於男性」上。

我們可以想像，這些本地教會的同工看到這些成果之後，用充滿歡欣以及信心的態度去展望未來。如今在大甲教會當中，可以找到的基督徒同工比其他的地方更多，不只是牧師娘、還有醫生娘（醫生本人是教會長老）、一位執事娘、一位傳道娘以及一位聖經宣道婦，這些在大甲教會忠心服事的人，都是畢業於女學校或婦學校。不過或許其他地方的發展也有值得鼓勵的地方。

大甲這種情況讓那兩位女宣教師準備下鄉佈道時，心裡非常高興。其中一位還特別被任命去關注客家地區的宣教工作。

為家庭開辦幼齡教育機構

婦女工作的最後一個部門是幼稚園，這與大稻埕教會有關。大稻埕教會在兩年前成立一間主日學幼稚園，這個事件引起社會大眾的興趣與熱情。幼稚園有三個中心地：台北，新竹和宜蘭。幼稚園的開設可以為教會工作帶來極大的助益。雖然宣教師夫人並沒有如同其他同工一般受到宣道會的任命，但是她們卻是教士會當中最活躍的力量來源。作為宣教師夫人的多重任務之外，她們也貢獻自己生命的大部分時間在教會的事工上：有些夫人教音樂，部分夫人在中學校或婦學校教導一般的課程，有些人在淡水、台北或其他地點主持《聖經》課程，或陪伴她們的先生前往鄉下巡迴佈道。

多年以前，有一位宣教師娘每週在北投庄（Hokuto，今北投）舉行《聖經》課程。那裡有一位貧窮的寡婦，她靠著前往山邊撿拾柴火，賣給村莊的人當作她維生的來源。每天賺取十五分錢，唯一的女兒是一位九到十歲的小女生，也不間斷的陪伴母親上《聖經》課。宣教師娘從一開始就注意到這個小女生，因為她的個性開朗、有吸引力，並且對《聖經》很有興趣。由於她是一位極有潛力的學生，因此宣教師娘提供一個機會讓她進入女學校就讀，也安排學校一些工作機會，讓她可以在學校打工來賺取自己的生活費。畢業之後，她成為一位教導新進女宣師的教師。如今她是婦學校的老師，忠心且值得信賴，她心中最主要的期望是幫助自己的同胞歸信。

第九章 ◆ 婦女宣道會在台的豐碩貢獻

現今需求的女性宣教呼召

多年以來，我們不斷向加拿大母會提出女性宣教師、教師、佈道家以及護士的需求，如今這個訓練年輕女性以及為台灣婦女的生命帶來光明和快樂的機會，再度向您提出，並且發出挑戰。誰願意回應？如今我們急需下列的婦女加入我們的行列：

- 一位受過大學師範教育的女性
- 一位家庭管理學的教師
- 一位女學校的音樂教師
- 七位前往鄉下工作的女佈道家
- 五位前往客庄工作的女佈道家
- 兩位福佬地區工作的佈道家
- 兩位在馬偕紀念醫院工作的護士

「我可以差遣誰呢？誰肯為我們去呢？」

禱告詞

噢！祢是光，在祢沒有黑暗，我們承認祢是世界上對付一切陰暗罪惡、愁煩以及死亡的答案。我們謙卑又誠摯的感謝祢，因為耶穌基督祢將光明照進婦女們面臨的黑暗命運裡，我們稱頌祢，馬利亞之子，祢在人類的關係中獲勝，祢提升婦女由被漠視變成愛的關懷，由受限到幸運，由受貶抑到光榮的階層。

我們懇求祢的祝福臨到台灣的婦女，讓她們接觸解放與啟蒙的福音，打開心門接觸真理，與那些在婦女當中服事的女宣教師們同在，當她們在家裡、在路邊、在教堂中、在學校與醫院中，能宣揚祢的名。將祢的祝福與豐富賞賜聖經宣道婦，讓她們透過學習和歷練得到豐富的裝備，好叫她們能夠在聖靈和上帝的大能下作見證。

願祢的恩典與婦女宣道會同在，因為她們將祢愛的信息帶往福爾摩沙和其他國家，也願國內的基督徒婦女都能與全世界的姊妹快樂地宣揚和分享上帝的信息，超乎萬名之上的聖名，以榮耀的主禱告。阿們。

第十章 ◆ 未來的展望

在過去五十年當中，不管台灣南部或北部教會的教勢都有極大的進展。然而，這個工作只能算是剛剛起步，因為在台灣島上每有一位基督徒，就有一百廿二位非基督徒；在三百五十萬人口當中只有一百五十間佈道所，這種不適當的情況——如果我們知道全島有四千五百個「三百到五百人」的村莊、九百個「五百到一千人」的村莊、一千個「一千到三千人」的鎮、八十二個「三千到五千人」的鎮、廿個「五千到一萬人」的鎮、十一個「一萬到六萬人」的城市——就更為明顯了。上述統計還不包括數千個分散在山上竹叢裡或全島小角落的村民，除非我們在過去五十年的努力成果上加緊腳步，否則台灣的住民歸信以前，這些信主的世代就都將消失不見。

我們必須記住，以台灣這島嶼的地域性以及人口的規模來說，就算我們要努力推動大規模的事工，對於上述這兩者都不會有壓倒性的聲勢：目前在台灣只有一個聯合的教會（是指聯合南部和北部長老教會而成立的「台灣大會」而言），而沒有其他宗派的分化而形成發展的障礙。在此地進行工作的兩個教士會，屬於英國長老教會以及加拿大長老教會，在許多年以前，他們就已經在這個地方合作傳福音了。瞭解這些以後，就會知道增加具有獻身精神的本地傳道

人、適當的宣教師——教師、醫生以及佈道家，加上更重要的是全能上帝大能的作為——是必須的要素，在「這個世代之內讓台灣人成為基督徒」這個目標才不會被當成是空泛的口號，而是一個具有挑戰性的目標，而我們也能帶著信心去努力達成。

台灣的經濟社會以及宗教生活的快速轉變，使得基督教會必須嚴肅的探討並且採取快速的行動。沒有一個國家比日本改變得更激烈：在政治上面臨危機，而宗教也正面臨嚴酷的考驗，然而，基督教卻在這個帝國當中快速的發展，敵對基督教的態度逐年遞減。在台灣，有許多基督徒官員在政府當中占有重要的地位，並且隨著官員人數的增加，影響台灣那些受過教育的人更加地喜愛基督教信仰。

阻擋台灣社會進步的諸多原因

台灣教育環境崇尚「不可知」論

過去，阻礙台灣社會進步的舊思維有祖先崇拜、迷信、保守主義以及文盲等四個問題，如今已經被新阻礙取代了。台灣由於缺乏儒教經典，因此祖先崇拜已經逐漸式微，在台灣的儒教系統已經四分五裂。快速發展的日本已經藉著教育這個過程，讓台灣人的新世代看見舊

有宗教信仰的許多空虛之處。大部分日本或台灣的教師對宗教上的態度是屬於「不可知」（agnostic）論者，因此有許多在舊有迷信環境成長的年輕人就學之後，原先的信仰都會動搖，然而學校也沒有提供可以取代的東西。

偶像崇拜日漸衰微

偶像崇拜仍然頑固的生存於大眾的思想當中，他們相信惡靈的作弄以及過去在道德上的賢人偶像其良好影響仍然存在。一般群眾仍然相信，如果忽視偶像的崇拜，一定會招惹牠們的怒氣而帶來厄運，但若敬拜牠們就會帶來好運、農作物豐收及萬事亨通。然而，年輕的一代已經不像他們祖先那樣容易受騙，因此許多廟宇都已經廢棄，只有少部分的廟宇被人整理、也只有少數廟宇受到熱心信徒的捐獻。另外，宗教節期當中，浪費金錢的行為並不受日本政府的鼓勵。日本統治打破了中國傳統保守主義的基礎，在此同時，日本所引進西方各樣的事物，快速的改變台灣整個民族對於外面世界的態度，這一切都對台灣人產生極大的影響，使得偶像崇拜快速的式微。

文盲漸漸消失

真正發展最大的阻礙之一是來自於台灣人「不識字」——或許在現代社會當中，沒有一個國家像日本那樣盡一切的努力，要將「文盲」這個阻礙從民眾的生活中消除掉。如今在日本，只有百分之五的人不識字，而先前在台灣，每一千人只有六個人識字，這種水準下形成的社

會，無知的程度是相當駭人的。日本藉著在台灣普設公立學校，讓這一切完全改觀，也為提供了快速傳揚基督教信仰相當良好的基礎。這件事可以由許多方面得到證實：基督教書刊的販售、索取福音單張和《聖經》單卷本的數量穩定成長當中。在台灣，有兩位《聖經》的書籍販售者，還有一位宣教師的工作是專責將基督教文學書籍翻譯成台灣本地語。所有到政府、學校就學辦事的台灣人，都是雙語使用者——當他們無法念讀出中文漢字時，可以用日文的讀法瞭解其含意，而年輕的基督徒可以讀得懂羅馬字的台語，所閱讀的報紙有日文和中文欄，因此本地的文盲就此被消除，同時也消除了國家和宗教進步的最主要障礙。

但是，雖然舊有的阻擋及障礙已經慢慢的消除，但是如今仍有一些非常嚴重的問題危及台灣社會真正的進步。

娼妓、飲酒及賭博三大惡文化值得警惕

台灣教會必須要去對付的最主要障礙，跟其他國家面對的阻礙是相同的。人們會期待日本統治台灣最顯著的效果就是對台灣社會進行的大改革。雖然本地的犯罪率已經下降到一定的程度：這要歸功於日本政府的作為，但各種惡習，如吸食鴉片、賭博、酗酒以及娼妓業仍然存在，這些對當地人的生活都帶來很壞的影響，不過我們必須指出的是，台灣賭博和吸食鴉片的情況已在減少當中。另一方面，許多國家正在對酗酒習俗進行改革的同時，台灣的啤酒廠卻快速的增加當中。日本人喜歡喝烈酒，當中許多人因為酗酒而毀了一生；除非這些可惡的烈酒從台灣國民的生活習慣當中移除，否則將來只有走向毀滅的道路。台灣人也開始模仿日本人對

酗酒的喜好。在台灣，對於飲酒，也沒有任何的政策可以限制，大家可以隨心所欲的購買、販售酒精飲料或是宴客，也可以自由收藏任何數量的烈酒（美國於一九二〇至一九三三年間頒布「禁酒令」）。不過平心而論，目前沒有很多台灣人受到烈酒文化的影響。基督教會對於這個事件的立場是很清楚的，大家可以參考先前第六章提到「大會對於烈酒和麻醉藥品的決議」。

知識分子崇尚虛假學說不容忽視

引進日本現代教育，同時也所帶來了所謂「知識階層對福音的阻擋」。這是不能忽視的部分。西方非基督教文學助長了對精神信仰的破壞力，學生們閱讀「敵對基督教」哲學的虛假學說以及科學證據，而在日本大學的學術圈裡，認為基督教和科學互相衝突，因此有數百位台灣學生去日本的大學進修之後，這種說法也逐漸在台灣風行起來。

「阻擋」就是挑戰

以上這些阻擋並不單獨出現於東方社會，所以不要因為這樣而洩氣。雖然他們對我們千百年來矗立於壓迫和風暴當中的福音信仰是一個新的挑戰，但我們堅信，基督終將獲得勝利，愛與真理將會成功。因為基督掌權，所以不管是在西方或東方，都不會有什麼限制與阻擋是耶穌基督無法克服的問題。假若祂在跟隨者的生命中顯現、假若福音也被完全的傳揚出去，而祂的法則在所有的道德和宗教環境當中就被忠實地執行了，那麼我們就毋須懼怕或質疑最終的結果，所以這是對我們的挑戰。

台灣社會令人振奮的七大轉變

但是我們也必須提到，台灣現在有一些「令人鼓舞的現況與振奮的發展…

人民追求獨立的思考

法律與秩序的出現，宗教完全的自由，在在鼓舞人們去進行獨立的思考，個人隨意依照自己的良心而行，而不會遭到父祖輩、社會或政治當局的威脅。基督教被認為是對社會有益的宗教，是能夠讓人的心靈獲得提升的力量。有許多人為了各種原因，不希望自己立刻成為基督徒，但卻樂於讓他們的後代接受基督教的教誨。一種自由的精神正在擴散當中。

基督徒的道德被本地人大大認同

除此之外，基督教教導裡所禁止的惡事，現在已經被一般人認為那些「惡事真的是邪惡、並且對公眾的生活是有害的」。不管在台灣什麼地方，基督教的牧師與傳道人都被一般人認為「是高於非基督教宗教的」宗教代表，而不像祭司、道士、算命仙、乩童這類人，都被認為他們不僅毫無用處、甚至對於社會的進步也帶來壞處的人。基督教的傳道人經常受到日本官員的邀

請，去對非基督教聽眾演說，說明有關道德改革的事宜，因此基督教會如今已經比較不會被認為是外國的宗教，而被當作是本地人的宗教以及個人、國家公義的推動力量。

社會大眾接納宣教師

五十年來，宣教師在北部台灣的作為，證明早期台灣人對宣教師的指控是虛假與愚蠢的。

如今他們可以與任何階層的人交往，而不會有任何的不便或遭到孤立的對待。人們感激宣教師，因為為了改善島上人而來到這個島嶼。一九二一年，筆者曾經在深夜搭乘特快火車時發生意外，火車的引擎被另一輛貨運火車撞擊，因為嚴重的擠壓而變形，伙伏因而喪生。次日清晨，火車上的乘客看見火車遺骸，他們對於沒有造成更大的傷亡感到驚訝，進而發現我也是乘客之後，當中的一位台灣人大聲叫出：「宣教師在車上，這就是我們沒有喪生的原因。」要是在五十年前或稍後，宣教師可能會被指責是「一切災禍的元兇」。

接受親友是基督徒的身分

早年的時候，台灣流傳一些有關外國宗教的荒誕傳說，例如：「他們離棄父母[1]，是『米基督徒』[2]，不崇敬鬼神和佛陀，放棄一切天賦的才能，並不優於豬或狗」，這些指控和其他的說法曾經廣泛流傳著，但是如今一切都已經改變。若聽到他們談論基督徒，話語內容定然會令人感到驚訝，「他們不怕惡靈，在每個禮拜天敬拜上帝，他們比較快樂，每個人只有一位妻子，他們的家中比較少爭吵」，這些對於基督徒特別的標記，普遍受到一般非基督徒的認同。

當中最為有趣的說法是，基督徒比較不容易生病。許多基督徒生病，但又奇妙的獲得痊癒的故事為一般人所熟知。事實上，就算基督徒是用一般的治療方式得到了痊癒，但仍然不會減損一般人認為「那是因為基督徒的上帝治療」的結果。基督徒在流行病期間，染病的比例真的要比一般人來得低，統計的數字可以證實這個說法。一九一九年，馬偕醫院被政府醫療部門徵用三個月，作為當時霍亂流行極危急時的治療醫院。醫院兼收日本人和台灣人，每一天有數起死亡病例，在醫院周圍的基督徒被允許每個禮拜天可以在禮拜堂聚會，然而當時，一般人卻被禁止集會，甚至學校都因傳染病而休學。

這個流行病期間有數百人死亡。根據牧師和傳道師對於他們駐在當地的瞭解，並沒有任何一位基督徒死亡，因為那些基督徒嚴格的遵守衛生當局的指示，而一般人卻忽視那些指導。流行病期間，基督徒的生活比較愉快，截然有別於一般人「焦躁、沮喪和憂慮」的樣貌。每個禮拜天早晨，基督徒舉行禮拜，他們是一群從無知和迷信的捆索中得到釋放並快樂的人們，他們讚美上帝，因為祂保護他們免受流行性致命的疫病攻擊。要是在五十年前，基督徒會被認為是疫病的起因。

葬禮文化明顯差異

台灣一切的變化當中，沒有一項比「社會風俗的改變」更為明顯可見。在這當中，有許多可以歸類於令人鼓舞的改善部分，而其他則是會讓真正的改革遭遇到困難的。台灣社會上提供的「方便」成為時間和金錢花費的最主要原因。台灣的青年如果有能力的話，他會花費大量的

金錢和朋友消磨在茶屋或更令人厭惡的所在。西式的生活、西式的食物和服裝，雖然極為昂貴，但是仍然被他們模仿。至於他們的葬禮進行、婚禮的風俗都比數年前花費更多的金錢。台灣人模仿了比較簡單而不矯飾的日本人的生活方式。基督教對社會風俗習慣的影響，可以由葬禮的行為當中看出來，基督教葬禮的特色是安靜、秩序良好以及嚴肅。行走在葬禮隊伍最前面的是主日學的孩童，他們手裡舉著書寫合適的聖經章節的旗幟，這截然有別於異教徒隊伍以及秩序混亂的葬禮隊伍，更特殊的是異教徒隊伍當中有鑼鼓的敲擊聲，令人煩躁的誦經音樂以及隊伍後面披麻帶孝哭泣的家屬。這樣的對比吸引了一些比較有判斷力的非基督徒。或許基督教和異教的明顯差異在於基督徒對過世的人的態度、葬禮的行進隊伍與埋葬逝者的方式。基督教對於一般人社會生活與習慣的影響也逐漸增加中。

對婦女地位的影響

近年來，台灣的婦女獲得比較好的地位，是最重要的社會事實。關於裹腳的問題，日本政府曾經對台灣的婦女極為寬容，他們從來不會去強迫已經裹腳的婦女放開綁腳。然而對年輕的一代，則是嚴厲禁止這種風俗。而這種帶有身體傷害性風俗的消失，只是時間的問題。如今大家普遍穿著布鞋和皮鞋，因此戒除這個風俗，對於台灣的婦女來說，意義深遠。對台灣婦女來說，舊有的生涯規劃已經成為過去，進入公立學校就讀的少女人數也逐漸增加中，她們在教室和遊戲場與男孩一起活動。年輕的女性擁有完全的自由，可以去搭乘火車去旅行，也經常在特別舉辦的佈道會時，和她們的朋友前往教會。經由這種方式，非基督徒的婦女與基督教的婦女

有較多的接觸，因此是基督徒發揮影響力的很好機會。

注重工作與休閒均衡

另外一個鼓舞人心的狀況，是台灣人民的勤奮。台灣超過三百萬人口，居住在約一萬平方公里的土地當中，其他地方是布滿原始森林的高山。然而，未曾聽聞島上有失業的問題。所有的人都擁有工作。日本行政當局非常強烈反對社會上有「寄生」的行為，要求每一個人竭盡所能去賺取生活的費用。當年輕人有能力工作時，就必須負擔家計，與這相連必須一提的就是，除了高等學校學生以外，有益健康的運動並沒有在台灣島上得到發展的機會。這種西方人家庭生活當中最主要的活動，及大部分西方人會利用許多時間從事的娛樂，對於台灣人或是東方人來說並沒有什麼吸引力。但是，東方社會已逐漸體認到休閒活動以及體育發展的重要性。

台灣本土教會五十年的挑戰

台灣社會未來的挑戰

儘管台灣有明顯的進步，以及前述鼓舞人心的轉變，令人無法不去思想：「台灣在現代亞

洲的展望為何？」並且對此表達最深的關切。在最近這幾年當中，在物質和人力資源上，這個地方有快速的發展，這些巨大的發展將同時為世界各國帶來幸與不幸，而這也將成為西方世界無法忽視的挑戰。這個挑戰就是東方人必須要知道（不能有一絲的懷疑），「上帝的拯救和重生的力量是這個世界的救贖，和平和世人和諧關係的掌管者」。

台灣五十週年宣教歷史回頭挑戰加拿大教會

在台灣五十年來的宣教和事工發展的歷史上，如今已經回過頭來挑戰加拿大的教會。先鋒者馬偕的獻身、成效、英勇作為和成功結果，也讓隨後的宣教師都承接了這個光榮的任務。台灣信徒定然會轉身要求母會和海外宣教師們必須有相同的獻身精神。在過去的五十年當中，上帝的恩典讓台灣教會成長，如今要面臨更大的信心和努力。當初，從單獨的那一位被稱為「番仔鬼」的宣教師馬偕開始，如今已經有廿位加拿大宣教師以及五十六位本地協助教會的建立。當九位也已經受封立成為牧師。如今到處都是機會，期待大家能夠前來此地協助教會的建立。當初，開創者馬偕經過極大的努力才獲得第一位信徒，如今已經有二千二百六十四位正式的會員和一千五百六十三位小兒會員，另外還有二千九百四十二位尚未洗禮的慕道友。一九一二年，台灣的教會自立奉獻七千一百五十四元（將近三千六百美元），一九二一年，金額已經增加到二萬六千零二十元（近一萬三千多美元）。台灣初期沒有學校或醫院，如今有一間神學院、婦女聖經學堂、男子中學、女子高中以及馬偕紀念醫院。在過去的五十年間，加拿大教會慷慨的投資金錢支持這些事工，而保護這些投資、增加紅利的唯一方法，就是教會投注更大的投資和

適當的支持。

加拿大母會必須持續協助

有些人或許會問：「為何還要求更多的宣教師？為什麼不靠本地的傳教者去對他們同胞傳福音？」或許，假如將宣教師召回，本島也會逐漸的福音化，但是達成這個目標的時間將會被推往更未知和更遙遠的將來。台灣現在和未來許多年都需要宣教師，需要宣教師的帶領和指導本地人，訓練傳教人員，計畫去推動各樣的機構（是那些具有達到成功機構所必備的進取、強有力的動力），這是本地傳教者尚未具備的條件。如果有人建議宣教師退出本地，首先會遭遇來自本地的傳教者一致的反對。因為任何在各種程度上削減人員的舉動，會讓本地傳教人失去得到基督教真理更高深知識的機會，失去對自己同胞福祉關注的使命感，為台灣教會帶來毀滅性的影響，也會讓「加速本島福音化」的目標遭到嚴重的阻礙。

對上帝子民開放大門

馬偕紀念醫院是一間建築優美、設備優良的醫院，過去五年裡它關閉不只是因為欠缺醫

— 211 —

生，也是因為海外宣道會欠缺經費以致無法派遣醫生——難道醫院的關閉不也代表著「對有需要的人關閉上帝的大門」嗎？這也意味著對上帝國度關起大門——如今，這不是個必須回應的挑戰嗎？

留住台灣本土菁英

在過去五十年的對台宣教史當中，北台灣的神學院從不曾有過數量充足的同工，宣教師從來無法將他所有的時間都投注在教學的工作上，他總是必須兼顧其他的職責，結果神學院也遭到很大的損失。無疑的，如果這種政策再繼續下去，將來很難再吸引學生到這裡就讀。那些具有英文能力的中學畢業生，已經開始將他們的目光投注到日本更高等的教育機構上——讓那些有獻身志願的青年前往海外接受神學教育，這實在是一個嚴重的錯誤。對那些年輕人來說，台灣的宣教師和教師一來足以擔任這個任務、二來也對台灣的情況熟習，和日本的學校相比，這樣的教育環境能夠提供更好的訓練。

福音傳揚的工作

在宣教工作上，需要的宣教師有多少人？宣教政策擬定者對於「每一位宣教師要負責的人數」其看法各不相同，有些人說一個宣教師要負責二萬五千人，有些人說五萬人。就算是以五萬人來看，在北台灣也需要至少卅名以上的宣教師。事實上，從來不曾有一位宣教師可以將他的精力完全投注在牧養或佈道工作之上，並且如果有任何受封立的宣教師返國休假，他的工作

就會陷入停頓。

儘管展從未不是那麼樂觀，需求卻從來不曾像現在這樣殷切，宜蘭目前擁有十萬人口，每三平方公里住一千人，除了短暫的拜訪之外，沒有常駐的宣教師。如今有七位本地傳道師計畫提供本地人心靈的需求。因此目前急需一位受封立的宣教師以及兩位女佈道家來進行傳道福音的工作。另一個有力的大門已經開啟，台北平原上有超過十萬人住在城市當中，另外十萬人住在周圍的城鎮與鄉村當中，一位宣教師駐在市內，另外一位宣教師駐在城鎮和鄉村裡，這可說是最低的要求。

原住民的工作

到目前為止，台灣宣教區域尚未被接觸到的地區是原住民的區域，他們以「獵頭族」的名聲著稱於世，關於他們的情況在本書第二章已經有所說明，那些尚未馴服的原住民住在台灣中部，除了交換他們沒辦法生產的物品以外，很少跟外面的世界接觸。日本政府在一九二○年的統計，原住民的人口是十三萬人，如今政府進行一項迫切的計畫，希望說服他們接受文明，放棄野蠻的風俗習慣。如今在原住民的地區興建有廿五間學校、一百零五名教師、三千六百九十三位學生，但是他們還欠缺一項最重要的事情，那就是有關耶穌基督的知識。如今是對他們進行傳福音的機會。他們傳統的束縛已經逐漸被打破，新時代的曙光已經向他們發出第一道亮光並照亮他們，這個光明的遠景將會帶來什麼呢？

客家與福佬的宣教

先前已經提過，鐵路南邊的新竹地區住有廿五萬客家人，當中有十一間佈道所，從來沒有一位外國宣教師可以使用他們的語言佈道，這個地方至少需要一位受封立的宣教師與兩位女佈道者。新竹平原城市裡的人口數是兩萬人，周圍村莊的人口是這個數字的三倍。城市裡面已經購買一塊很好的土地，最近將會有一間佈道所設在那裡，因此必須要有多位宣教師駐在當地，在這個廣闊的地區進行福佬與客家的佈教工作。

台灣的婦女事工

經由學校、醫院、婦女的課程以及其他機構的努力，許多台灣的婦女已經聽過福音的信息，也有不少人見識到祂的力量與自由。這個工作持續進行，但是這對於加拿大教會的婦女來講，這是一個又大又具挑戰性的責任。

過去十八年來，婦女宣道會派遣九位女宣教師來台，但是這並不代表真正在教會實際工作的主要力量，在這個人數當中，如今有一個空缺尚未補足，再加上總是會有一些宣教師休假返國。九位同工而已！他們要負擔北部台灣那麼多成年和未成年的女性，特別是最近以來一些舊的風俗解體，對婦女的歧視也消失，許多的婦女與女孩希望獲得教育的機會，她們的精神和心靈已前所未有為基督教真理開放！

需求實在非常巨大，教士會請求十四位新的工作者前來協助婦女工作。這的確是個謙卑的請求。因為眼見現今的同工都過勞得可怕，加上面對現今這個排山倒海的機會來臨，同工的狀

況也不太適合再加重工作，因此請求再增加人手。

台灣兒童事工

我們敢忘記台灣的兒童嗎？影響非基督教家庭子女的機會已穩定的增加中，基督教的孩童在公立學校與他們一起上學，與他們建立比前述更為親密的友誼。為了這個大好展望的事工，過去兩年來，我們提出急迫的請求，希望能夠派遣受過這種特別訓練的宣教師來台協助。

等待收成的莊稼

田地已經成熟、等待收成，不再有政治的阻擋與社會的障礙，宗教的歧視逐漸消失，成千的村落等待基督教機構、教師工人的到來，而病人等待那些以其專業的技術和愛心關懷的醫療宣教師。台灣的人民友善、好客以及善體人意，隨時感激他們自己受到的恩惠，以愛心與友善來回報。他們仍在古老的廟宇當中祭拜神明，無力去除他們舊有的風俗。福音對他們而言，是唯一能帶給他們滿足且了解內心需要的信仰，必須廣傳。如果我們延遲，或者無法用適當的回應去面對台灣緊急的呼聲，那我們將會發現數世紀以來，宣教師的努力將無法把握住如今這個稍縱即逝的機會。如果加拿大教會勇於任事，在上帝的幫助下，這個任務將不會失敗。體會到現在情況及對於將來發展的重要性，讓我們以新的信心、新的勇氣、新的獻身精神來面對主，並回應祂的呼召，直到祂的名字在整個「美麗之島」都為人所知，而上帝的國度也得以建立為止。

祂吹響永遠不會退縮的號角，

祂在審判寶座前去篩選人心，

我的靈魂，趕快回應祂，

我的雙腳將要雀躍，我的上帝正在行進。

◆　◆　◆　················

禱告詞

我們在天上的父，願人都尊祢的名為聖，願祢的國降臨。赦免我們，沒有像祢所教導的真誠的祈禱，並且在祢的眼前阻擋自己的方法與才能，我們的代禱與生命，以致於直到今天，萬國對祢的愛仍然所知有限，海島仍在企求祢的律法，請提醒我們，儘管先前的失敗、自私以及不忠，祢仍然信賴我們，讓我們將祢的信息傳揚給全人類。

當我們意識到，在我們面前有多少困難橫阻於前時，幫助我們信心堅定；有多少誘惑讓我們放棄初衷時，阻止它。祢的子民無論在何種情況下，都應當宣揚祢是世上唯一的拯救者，願祢所揀選服事的宣教師，都能快樂的回應祢的呼召，不要讓我們當中有任何一人在祢掌權時失敗。

我們的感恩加深，因為祢的福音在北部台灣的勝利，也請賜予我們勇氣與信心來面對島上尚未完竣的事工，將祢的祝福傾倒於那裡的宣教師身上，因為他們是代表祢和我們，也傾倒在台灣教會領袖的身上。願上帝慈愛的大好消息迅速的傳揚於全地以及萬國，直到萬民以雙膝跪拜，每一張口都承認耶穌基督是主，將榮耀歸與聖父上帝。阿們。

附錄 ◆ 統計數據

我們教區的人口（台灣北部）

- 漢人 　　　　　　　　　　　一、二七八、五〇〇
- 日本人 　　　　　　　　　　七六、〇〇〇
- 原住民 　　　　　　　　　　一七、五〇〇
- 總人數 　　　　　　　　　　一、三七二、〇〇〇

教士會成員

- 加拿大宣教師 　　　　　　　二〇
- 封立牧師的台灣人 　　　　　九
- 尚未封立牧師的台灣人 　　　四七

- 成人會員 　　　　　　　　　二、二六四
- 受洗孩童 　　　　　　　　　一、五六三
- 未受洗慕道友 　　　　　　　二、九四二

學校與醫院

- 神學院 　　　　　　　　　　一所
- 婦女聖經學校 　　　　　　　一所
- 男子中學 　　　　　　　　　一所

- 女子中學　一所
- 馬偕紀念醫院　一間（因為欠缺醫生，已經關閉四年）

自養
- 一九一二年為北台教會奉獻　七、一五四日圓
- 一九二一年為北台教會奉獻　二六、○二○日圓（一日圓等於五十美分）

需求的教師數量：

男性

封立的佈道家	八位
醫生	三位
中學教員	三位
化學家	一位
宗教教育指導者	一位
事工經理	一位

女性

佈道家	五位
醫生	一位
護士	三位
女學校音樂教師	一位
家政教師	一位

註釋 ◆ 譯者補充之珍貴史料

推薦序　鄭仰恩牧師

1　這是原本的書名，Duncan MacLeod, The Island Beautiful: The Story of Fifty Years in North Formosa (Toronto: Presbyterian Church in Canada, 1923).

2　本序文部分內容引自鄭仰恩，〈論加拿大教會聯合運動及其對台灣教會的影響〉，《定根本土的台灣基督教：台灣基督教史研究論集》（台南：人光，2005），頁125-127。

3　吳清鎰，〈我們印象最深的宣教師們〉，《台灣基督長老教會北部教會九十週年簡史》，鄭連德・吳清鎰・徐謙信・鄭連明編著（台北，1962），頁26。

4　鄭連明，〈自教士會成立至吳威廉牧師逝世（1905-1923）〉，《台灣基督長老教會百年史》，鄭連明主編（台北：台灣基督長老教會，一九六五年六月），頁154-156。

5　吳清鎰，〈我們印象最深的宣教師們〉，頁26。

6　約美但於一九〇七至一九一六年間擔任台北神學校校長，任內曾到芝加哥大學進修，跟隨著名的自由神學家學習，回台後將聖經批判學（Biblical criticism）介紹給學生，並教導學生第一、第二、第三以賽亞的區別，也主張約翰福音的作者是「長老約翰」而非「使徒約翰」，這導致後輩同工劉忠

堅為之困擾不已。徐謙信，《台灣北部教會暨神學院簡史》（台北：台灣神學院出版部，1972），頁50-52。

7 徐謙信，《台灣北部教會暨神學院簡史》，頁52-55。

8 有關北部教會的「新人運動」，參廖安惠，《北部台灣基督長老教會『新人運動』之研究》（台南：國立成功大學歷史研究所碩士論文，1997）

9 〈第三十一屆北部中會議事錄〉，刊於《台灣基督長老教會北部教會大觀——北部設教百週年紀念刊》，黃六點主編（台北，1972），頁101。

10 鄭連明，〈自設教五十週年至設教六十週年（1923-1932）〉，《台灣基督長老教會百年史》，頁201。

11 徐謙信，《台灣北部教會暨神學院簡史》，頁54。

12 引自筆者於二〇〇〇年十月三十一日於加拿大彼得堡（Peterborough）蘇若蘭牧師自宅所作訪談資料。

第一章

1 甘治士牧師（Georgius Candidius）是第一位來台的荷蘭改革宗教會（Dutch Gereformeerd Kerk）宣教師，主要傳教的對象是西拉雅原住民。他在與原住民短暫接觸之後寫出《台灣略記》（Cort Verhael van de Eyland Formosa），是目前瞭解十七世紀初葉台灣原住民最重要的民族誌。

2 颱風的肆虐也讓馬偕印象十分深刻，因為他在旅行中幾度遭遇颱風面臨極大的危險，他在From Far Formosa記錄幾次遭遇颱風的經驗：「我第一次遇見颱風是在一八七四年，那年颱風肆虐整個島嶼，當時我正由雞籠趕路前往艋舺，我來到一個水深的溪邊，搭上一艘木板船渡河，還沒有到達對岸之

前，颱風已經抵達。在黑暗當中，船隻被吹翻，我摔落底下爛泥的水中，我已經忘記當時是如何拉著被風吹倒在岸邊的竹叢並並到達滑溜的岸邊，但是我到達艋舺的時候已經是半夜，很幸運的立刻與學生在那裡找到棲身的所在。當天有一艘前往淡水的汽船在雞籠港遇到颱風的襲擊，天亮之後整艘船只能看到部分的殘骸，船員幾乎全部罹難，如今在岩石之上豎立起一個白色的十字架紀念這個事件。

數年之後，有一次與我的學生葉順一起前往雞籠，當我們到達可以俯瞰矮雞籠港的最後一座山頂之時，我們看見海港後的海中，出現一個黑暗的水牆，矗立在咆哮的海浪與低矮雲層之間，數千隻海鷗急速的往內陸飛去，大聲吵雜的鳴叫著，我們知道這些景象的意義，於是立刻加速我們的腳步。正當我們進入城鎮之時，一陣無法形容的怒吼聲響起，暴風雨就此開始，開始幾滴雨水，然後狂風暴雨接踵而至。每一個人立刻尋找躲藏的地方，而我們立刻躲到完成一半的小寮裡面，當中有數隻黑豬為伴。我們整晚躲在小寮當中，屋外是颱風可怕的怒吼以及巨浪的聲響。天亮之後整個街道浸泡在及膝深的水中，菜園和稻田都泡在水裡，隨時可見颱風破壞所造成的損失。」

作者劉忠堅牧師在此所提到的地震是發生在一九〇六年三月十七日的梅山地震，該次地震為芮氏規模七點一，造成六千七百六十九間房屋倒塌，以及一千二百五十八人的死亡。至於同年夏天北台灣的地震，未見記錄相關資料。相關資料請參考中央氣象局網站。

瘧疾是十九世紀來台宣教師與旅行者的夢魘，馬偕牧師來台第二年首度苗栗之行後就染上瘧疾，這個疾病讓他在後來的年歲中受到高燒與疔瘡的苦惱，由於當時對於瘧疾的病因認為是地氣所造成，因此馬偕平常並沒有住在牛津學堂邊西班牙式的平房中，而是住在屋後的二樓小房間，目的是防止地氣的傷害。

樟腦是台灣物產當中最受矚目的產品，十九世紀台灣的樟腦產量為世界第一。由於利潤豐厚，因此一八六八年，滿清與英國政府為了專賣問題爆發「樟腦戰爭」，南部的天主和基督教會因為戰爭產

生的民族主義，而同時受到暴民的攻擊。

作者劉忠堅不是第一位提到原住民身體的外國人，馬偕的 *From Far Formosa* 以及甘為霖

6 （William Campbell）的 *Sketches of Formosa* 書中都有類似的描述。

7 日本時代的台灣農村流傳一句俗語：「第一憨，種甘蔗予會社磅」，表達出當時農民對於日本財團壟斷甘蔗收購的不滿。由於農民對於收購價格沒有置喙餘地，只能接受日本財團剝削，後來隨著社會運動的勃興，不滿的農民果然爆發「二林蔗農事件」。

8 羅伯特·郇和（Robert Swinhoe, 1836-1877）誕生於英屬印度加爾各答，是動物學與東方學家，也曾在台南與淡水擔任領事官，一八五六年搭戎克船拜訪台灣，一八五八年以英國戰艦不曲號（Inflexible）翻譯官的身分繞巡台灣尋找遇難的歐洲船員，一八六一年受命擔任台南的副領事官，一八六五年成為淡水領事官，隔年轉往廈門繼續擔任領事職位。他在台灣期間對島上的動物進行調查研究，撰寫台灣物種研究論文，也曾以台灣植物參加一八六二年倫敦世界博覽會（The Great International Exhibition），由於他對於台灣動物學的研究，有些台灣的動物以他的姓氏命名，如：斯文豪氏赤蛙（Odorana swinhoana）、斯文豪氏攀蜥（Diploderma swinhonis）、藍腹鷴（Lophura swinhoii）等。

第二章

1 荷蘭宣教師為原住民編著的教理問答，有甘治士牧師的ＡＢＣ問答（已經遺失），尤羅伯牧師編著的大、小教理問答（以上為西拉雅語）。花德列牧師（Jacobus Vertrecht）編著的基督教信仰要項（以上為法波蘭語），這些教理問答內容切合當時原住民的風俗習慣，如今已成為瞭解當時原住民宗教文化的重要資料。

2 這些學會利用羅馬字書寫西拉雅語的學生，被漢人稱為「教冊仔」，他們在荷蘭人離開台灣之後，仍然繼續教育子弟書寫的方法，直到十九世紀初期母語失落為止，總共有一五〇年，這些以西拉雅語書寫的文件被稱為「新港文書」，也是土地買賣的契約書。

荷蘭統治期間，原住民族較大的反抗事件如「迪加事件」（亦稱濱田彌兵衛事件）或「麻豆事件」，都是統治初期發生的事情，經過一六三五年荷軍征伐之後，原住民基本上都已經順服荷蘭殖民當局的統治，而尤羅伯牧師在一六四三年離開台灣，因此作者劉忠堅牧師所說的與歷史事實有些出入。

3 關於荷蘭改革宗宣教師殉教的事蹟，記載在荷蘭末代總督揆一（Fredric Coyett）所編寫的《被貽誤的台灣》書中的增補之中，甘為霖牧師在翻譯該書做為 Formosa under the Dutch（中文版書名為《荷據下的福爾摩莎》）的附錄時，並沒有收錄本章，因為本章內容對於宣教師有讚揚也有批評。

4 這裡所說的首位宣教師是指馬雅各醫生（James Maxwell）。一八六五年台南佈教失利之後，他曾經與必麒麟（Pickering）前往內山原住民區域拜訪，希望能夠在那裡設立教會，他們的訪問紀錄收錄於必麒麟的《台灣開發史》（Pioneering in Formosa）書中：

5 一八六五年秋天，我還在海關任職時，曾經拜訪位於台灣府北方十哩處的新港社，在此我看見了一個古老的平埔族部落，它存在的時間可以追溯至荷蘭統治的時代，新港曾經被哪些仁慈的開拓者當成主要的宣教據點，如今的村落也住有當時原住民的子孫，然而這些平埔番的穿戴與中國人相同，並已忘記他們的古老語言了。本村落的頭人是平埔族人，也是我的好友，他曾經在言談中告訴我，他的族人大部分移往內山，散居各處，甚至最遠可達遙遠的東部海岸。

英國長老教會的醫療宣教師馬雅各醫生是我的朋友，他們剛被無知且懷有偏見的居民趕出台灣府，且被限制只能在打狗港區傳教，當他聽到我的旅行計畫後，表達希望能和我同行的想法，因為

他想，心思較為單純的原住民比那些自滿驕傲的漢人更容易接受福音。馬雅各醫生不僅人品高超，同時在解熱和眼科方面的醫術卓著——顯然這種醫療能力會在單純的平埔番和生番之間，被看成是非常神奇的能力。

6 岡仔林住民們自信的稱他們自己為「番」，而老人們仍然保留他們祖先留下來的語言，他們讚美早期的荷蘭移民者，對所有的白人有好感，宣稱兩者之間有親戚關係，聽他們說話實在令人動容，特別是當我聽到一位老婦對著我們說：「你們白人是我們的親戚，你們不像那些剃頭的壞中國人，你們稱呼自己是什麼人呢？唉！數百年來，你們遠離我們，而如今當我的眼目昏花，接近死期之日，我們將因為見到紅毛親戚而得到祝福。」

7 阿爾弗雷德·華萊士（1823-1913）是十九世紀英國博物學家，他巡迴於荷屬東印度群島，一方面尋找天堂鳥，一方面進行動物物種的研究，他最著名的作品是《馬來群島科學考察記》（The Malay Archipelago），以及和達爾文聯名發表的論文〈自然天擇的進化論〉，建立生物學進化理論的基礎。本文所引用的資料出於馬來群島一書。

8 在這裡所稱的「教師」，是荷蘭改革宗教會當中的「學校教師」（Schoolmeester）一詞，台灣的學校教師大都由識字的士兵充任，尤羅伯曾訓練五十名原住民擔任學校教師，但是前者因為酗酒或私生活不檢點而遭到懲罰，後者則是因為要維持生計而經常曠職，造成學校教育的困擾。本文宣教師受難故事當中，最受荷蘭人懷念的是威廉·韓布魯克牧師（Rev. Guillem Hambroek），他在死亡脅迫之下，仍然鼓勵荷蘭人要奮戰到底，後來因此殉職。他的兩位女兒在城破之後被抓，成了鄭成功妾女，這一段遭遇在後來被寫成史詩紀念，而荷蘭鹿特丹火車站附近的教會也設有韓布魯克牧師的紀念碑。

9 所謂的分類械鬥是指漢族移民分為漳、泉與客籍三股勢力，彼此互相仇視不斷械鬥，再加上滿清派

駐島上官員貪汙情況普遍，引發人民不滿而爆發民變，滿清官吏則是利用台民間矛盾，而鎮壓弭平民變。曾經發生影響巨大的民變有朱一貴事件、林爽文事件等。

10 牛皮換土地的故事除了台灣外，在東南亞與美洲大陸上也都有類似的故事，故事的內容大同小異，同樣都是表達對殖民者欺騙原住民的批評。至於台灣南部，首先與西方人接觸的不是日本人，而是新港社的平埔族群，因為他們當時居住熱蘭遮城附近的土地上。雖然有部分日本人與原住民進行鹿皮交易，但是是否形成聚落？需要進一步研究。

11 此處所描述的就是一八九六年的「芝山巖事件」。台灣總督府任命伊則修二為首任學務部長，他招募了六位老師前往台灣教授國語（日語）：楫取道明、關口長太郎、中島長吉、桂金太郎、井原順之助和平井數馬。一月一日，這六位在台北士林芝山巖學堂任教的日籍老師被抗日分子殺害，史稱「芝山巖事件」。事後，日本人在芝山巖設立神社，以紀念罹難教師，神社前，日本首相伊藤博文並親書「學務官僚遭難之碑」。

第三章

1 事實上，北台灣教會的肇建者並不是十九世紀的馬偕，而是十七世紀的西班牙人，如果以改革宗的傳統來看，第一位到達北台灣的牧師是荷蘭改革宗教會的馬可·瑪修士牧師（Pre. Marcus Masius, 1655-1662），他在台灣北部的雞籠、淡水和三貂角三個地點設立教會和學校。關於當時教會和學校的情況，請參考林昌華〈十七世紀中葉改革宗教會對北部台灣原住民的教化：以Macus Masius牧師（1655-1662）的淡水與雞籠教務報告書為中心而述〉（西班牙時期台灣相關文獻與圖像國際研討會），國立台灣歷史博物館籌備處，二〇〇三年十月廿七至廿八日。

2 關於馬偕的父親：在馬偕過世廿五年後出現的一篇文章裡有簡單的描述，喬治·馬偕（George

Mackay），外號「戈帝」（Gordie），他並不是一位好脾氣的人或毫無瑕疵而可以讓母親教導孩子學習的模範父親，他有時候會滔滔不絕講著「最好不要出口的話」，他那敏感和批判性強烈的個性，到他離開人世前都沒有改變。請參考For the Presbyterian Witness, George Leslie Mackay of Formosa.

3 馬偕的祖父亞歷山大‧馬偕（Alexander Mackay, 1799-1884）所參加的滑鐵盧戰役，發生於一八一五年六月十八日，當時他是十七歲的少年。在馬偕的相關文獻當中，並沒有提起他的父親從蘇格蘭移民到加拿大的時候，他的祖父是否也同行。

4 一八四三年，蘇格蘭發生了教會的分裂。由於蘇格蘭長老教會，教職的任免全部掌握在貴族和大地主的手中，有許多牧師認為，這種權利應該歸屬於教會全體會員的選舉，因此在前一年的蘇格蘭總會開會時，有將近五百位牧師和眾多的長老，在著名的牧師查麥士（Rev. Thomas Chalmers）領導之下離席，抗議教會制度不合乎加爾文信仰的精神。牧師們放棄了政府支付的謝禮、教會和牧師宿舍，他們憑藉著對上帝的信心，雙手空空的離開，這些牧師和長老成立另一個教會，稱為蘇格蘭自由教會（Scotland Free Church），並召開第一屆總會。第二年，馬偕所屬的左拉村蘇格蘭長老教會也加入蘇格蘭自由教會，而該教會在一八六一年改稱為加拿大長老會，一八七五年和其他三個長老會合併成為加拿大長老教會（Presbyterian church in Canada）。請參考林昌華，〈馬偕牧師與淡水--日記與書信的考察〉（淡水學學術研討會--過去‧現在‧未來），台北：國史館，一九九九年，第七七頁。

5 在這裡所謂的問答，應該是指長老教會所使用的《衛斯敏斯德小教理問答》（Westminster shorter catechism）。這個教理問答的內容從「人生主要目的」到「主禱文的教導」，共有一〇七個問答。

6 馬偕沒有正式接受醫學訓練，但是他在英國長老教會教區參觀之後，知道「醫療工作」對減緩一般人對外國人的疑懼有很大的幫助，因此到台灣不久之後，就請求母會派遣具有醫學背景的宣教師前

來協助他。然而第一位醫療宣教師華雅各醫生因為妻子的過世而離台，使得原本可由兩位宣教師在台醫療與傳道的分工機會提前結束，因此馬偕就不再向母會申請醫療宣教師，反而利用先前所研習的醫學常識，在外國醫生的協助之下，進行臨床的醫療。他所進行的醫療，除了內外科的工作以外，也正式開刀，擔任起麻醉師的角色，在開刀之前為施打稱為歌羅芳的麻醉藥劑。他所進行的醫療工作，在日本領台之後，曾經遇到資格不符的問題，但是馬偕並沒有因此放棄行醫的機會，他最後的醫療行為是為英國領事館的一位警官開刀，取出手臂當中的子彈並且加以清創換藥，當時他已經因為喉癌而接受過數次的手術。一八八八年偕醫館的〈年度報告書〉當中，馬偕除了報告前一年中醫館所治療患者的疾病類型以外，也用一半的篇幅向西方人介紹中醫治療的原則、過程、病症以及處方。綜觀馬偕在傳教的醫療工作，實在是他在台灣服務的三個支柱之一（其他兩個支柱為傳教和教育）。

7 賓威廉（William C. Burn）是一位蘇格蘭牧師的兒子，從他的父親開始，就對海外宣教和教會復興非常有心，但當時的教會對此事並不熱衷，他十七歲時選擇修習法律，同年在愛丁堡也決定要成為一名傳道人，之後進入格拉斯哥神學院（Glasgow），在神學院時加入海外宣教師協會（missionaries association），畢業時就已經決定要成為一位海外宣教師。在賓威廉的日記中曾記載，他在神學院畢業後，在敦第（Dundee）的聖彼得教會牧會，牧會時曾有一次前往市場佈道，那一次的佈道會讓他經歷一次靈性極大的震撼，使他發現對異教徒宣教的重要性。筆者認為他在加拿大的培靈會中所說的，大概不出靈性的復興和宣教的重要性。請參閱：Rev. Jas Johnson, *China and Formosa: The story of the mission of the Presbyterian church of England*, New York:Flemin H Revell Co. 1888。

8 馬偕從普林斯敦神學院畢業之後，並不是直接前往蘇格蘭，而是向加拿大長老會的海外宣道委員會申請，希望能夠成為加拿大長老會第一位派往海外的宣教師，但是委員會以「教會尚未準備好」為

由，婉拒了他的申請。因此一八七〇年九月九日馬偕寫一封信給麥拉蘭，對於他所屬的教會尚未準備好海外的宣教工作表達內心的遺憾，之後他才前往蘇格蘭的愛丁堡大學，在退休的印度宣教師杜夫博士的教導下，學習印度相關的課程。請參考林昌華，〈馬偕牧師與淡水：日記與書信的考察〉（淡水學術研討會——過去·現在·未來）台北：國史館，一九九九年。

9　根據馬偕日記的紀錄，他並沒有在廈門拜訪當地的教會，而是在那裡轉搭前往台灣的「金陵號」（Kin-lîng）縱桅帆船前往打狗。

10　關於嚴清華的禱告，馬偕在一八七二年五月廿五日的日記當中有詳細的紀錄，內容如下：「噢！祢是真實的上帝，數個月前我還不認識祢。請祢幫助我讓我能夠更加的瞭解祢，因為我一般人所服事的偶像不能拯救他們的靈魂，我由心靈的最深處誠摯的感謝祢，我感謝因為祢帶領馬偕牧師來到台灣，請祢幫助我，也藉著聖靈讓許多人能夠認識耶穌。因為我們智慧有限，請祢幫助我們有更多的智慧來瞭解祢的話。我們期待也希望能夠有另一位年輕人來到我們中間，然後有更多更多的年輕人前來，這是我們內心真實的渴望。（心所願）」

11　陳火原名陳榮輝，是北台灣第一批接受封立的牧師，他的兒子陳清義成為馬偕大女兒媽蓮的丈夫，在馬偕過世後那一年擔任淡水教會的牧師，一九二三年，為了慶祝北部教會設教五十週年，陳清義編著 *Pak-pō Tâi-oân Ki-tok Tiʉ-lô Kàu-hōe ê Lek-sú* 與本書英文版劉忠堅牧師的 *The Island Beautiful* 同時成為北部教會歷史的第一本出版著作。

12　吳寬裕原名吳益裕，馬偕的日記當中，對於他的信主過程有簡單的描述：「吳益裕，油漆匠，三十歲，他好幾次惱怒、譏笑阿華。他進來，並且承認他錯了。他習慣站在門口，對我們投擲小石塊。之後他安靜從小洞中（如果門關著）望進來裡面，來看、來聽裡面是怎麼回事。然後他會等著在他的老同伴阿華回家的路上，如果有別人在場，他就會扯他的辮子、打他耳光、在街上阻擋住他的道

路、發出噓聲或者是以所有的方式攻擊他。現在他來到我的面前，說他對自己的行為非常的懊悔。

他確信偶像都是沒有益處的，並且熱切的希望能多認識上帝。他的臉孔狹窄，看起來有傑出的能力。」他受洗之後，母親非常惱怒，有好幾次險些傷害了他。直到吳益裕的妹妹生病，得到馬偕的醫治之後，他的母親敵視基督教的情況才完全改觀。

13

根據馬偕日記的紀錄，北部教會的第一次洗禮在一八七三年二月九日舉行，當日記錄如下：「當唱詩歌的聲音盈滿整個房間和附近街道後，五個人走向台前。我向他們詢問幾個問題，他們以宏亮且堅定的語氣應答。我立刻為他們施洗以避免任何攪擾。受洗後，他們站起來面對群眾，向他們作見證。

嚴清華，廿二歲，已婚。

吳益裕，油漆匠，卅一歲，未婚。

王長水，代書，廿四歲，已婚。

林孽，木匠，廿六歲，未婚。

林杯，工人，四十二歲，妻亡。

第四章

1
《記錄》全名是《加拿大長老教會記錄》（Presbyterian Record）（亦為了方便起見，統稱《加拿大長老會會誌》），是加拿大長老會的機關刊物，創刊於一八六三年，發行到現在。《記錄》在十九世紀時，經常會以全文照登的方式刊載當時宣教師的報告書，成為研究宣教師書信一份非常重要的史料集。台灣神學院的史料中心收藏有關於台灣的部分內容影印。

2
作者劉忠堅牧師所提的時間有誤，一八八五年六月時，法軍就已經撤銷封鎖。法軍是在一八八四年

八月五日開始砲擊雞籠港，而軍艦繞過來攻擊淡水的時間是在十月二日。馬偕於十月廿五日在葉順陪同下前往香港，羈留在那裡，直到隔年四月十九日，才再度回到淡水。

3 黎約翰牧師過世的時間是在一八九一年四月廿三日清晨一點廿五分。請參考馬偕日記當天的紀錄。

4 吳威廉在馬偕離開台灣兩個月之後，寫信回母會，書信當中表達他對於目前的生活與工作滿意的態度，書信內容節譯如下：

5 「我們的生活並不單調，我太太比起我來更是如此，我常常都在鄉間旅行，六天前的週六，我前往廿四公里遠的南崁教會，在上下台地時我們有時坐轎、有時步行，台地大約兩百公尺高，再上面是寬廣的茶園，而台地下的峽谷則是疏落的稻田，在無數險陡的山谷下則是各種的菜園，這種景致讓我回想起所聽過馬偕博士在上次休假返鄉演講中對台灣的讚嘆，『福爾摩沙！福爾摩沙！美麗的福爾摩沙！』我們全家身體狀況都非常良好，一年前的上個禮拜天傍晚，我們剛抵達淡水港，這一年來，我們過得很快樂，如果今天再給我一次選擇的機會，我們仍然會決定留在這裡。」

雖然馬偕返國休假時，吳威廉牧師夫婦才來台不久，但是藉著他們夫婦的努力以及嚴清華的協助，北部教會在平靜當中度過，這可以由吳威廉所寫的報告書看出梗概：

吳威廉、宣教師　淡水，福爾摩沙，一八九三年十月廿九日

馬偕博士離開這裡已經超過兩個月了，他離開後開設有四間教會，第一間在苗栗、第二間是大湖口、第三間為社後、第四間位於竹塹市內。而這四間禮拜堂的開設是在馬偕博士離開台灣之前就已經安排妥當的，現在這裡總共有六十間教會，毋庸置疑的，在異教環境的六十間教會中工作，困難是常常會發生的而且需要處理和解決的。一如往常，他們告訴我教會所發生的事，但是自從馬偕牧師離開以後，這些問題都由漢人們自己圓滿解決的。而大部分都是由嚴清華牧師介入處理的，唯一尚未解決的是有關領事權的案件，是早在馬偕博士離台前，就已發生的。上週阿華前去錫口，協助處

理我們的人和天主教徒的糾紛，問題很快就獲致解決，他從錫口轉往台北府，與地區的清國官員交涉有關要釋放一位在一年前，遭誣告謀殺而被收押的新店教會信徒。因他長時間遭到幽囚，使得新店教會的會友沮喪，但如今陳火牧師與全教會都因他的獲釋而大大的歡喜。

這篇報告書也刊登在一八九四年的《記錄》當中，這裡節譯部分內容。

6 馬偕是在一九〇一年五月一日承認自己的病是無法治癒的事實，當天，偕以利在她的看護日記當中記載這個轉變的過程：「五月一日，兩位醫生前來檢查他的喉嚨後，說喉內的腫瘤變得更大了，當他們告訴他，情況轉趨惡劣之後，父親哭了，幾乎無法進食。」

7 「聖經宣道婦」是指曾經在淡水女學接受過教育的婦女，大部分人是來自東台灣的噶瑪蘭族婦女，這些受過女學教育的婦女是馬偕在台灣進行宣教工作重要的一個環節，在他的手稿「台北的紀錄」當中，馬偕比較這些「女工」和「姑娘」（外國女宣教師）的差異，認為如果想要在北部台灣有好的宣教成果，那麼應該多訓練本地的婦女來推展婦女的傳教工作。請參考，馬偕手稿，林昌華譯〈台北的紀錄：姑娘與女工〉，《台灣教會公報》台南：教會公報社，二〇〇一年。

8 關於噶瑪蘭族地區所設立的教會數目，就目前所留存的文獻紀錄，有徐謙信牧師所主張的廿八間，郭和烈牧師主張的四十二間，郭水龍的廿三間，這些主張何者比較接近真實？譯者主張，教會數目的計算應該根據馬偕日記當中，有設立長執的教會才能算是一間獨立的教會，因此只有十六間教會而已；而其他的地區，只能算是舉行佈道會的所在。而這些地方參與的人數，極有可能大部分是來自別的教會的信徒。請參考林昌華〈馬偕日記當中的噶瑪蘭族〉，「中央研究院：平埔族群與台灣社會國際研討會論文」，台北：中央研究院民族學研究所、台灣史研究所籌備處，二〇〇〇年。

第五章

1　南部中會是在一八九六年二月廿四日成立，而北部中會遲至一九〇四年才成立。當南部教會成立中會之後，馬偕感受到不小的壓力，為了化解北部教會信徒的疑慮，因此設立了有中會形式卻不具「中會」權力的「中會」體制，郭水龍牧師在他的手稿〈北部教會史實〉當中，稱呼這個時期的中會為「假中會」。因為每次開會雖然有牧師、長老與宣教師出席，但是每次開會都是由馬偕或嚴清華牧師發言，會議成員只能接受他們的提議。並且每次的開會並不做任何記錄。因此不能算是正式的中會機構。

第八章

1　這裡所謂的「花蓮港」，並不是指如今的花蓮港口（在劉忠堅牧師撰寫此書之時，本港尚未興建），而是花蓮南濱的海邊，因此只能算是一個海灣而已，而不能稱為「港」。在花蓮興築新港以前，來到花蓮的船隻無法靠岸，必須藉由小舟接駁，而居住在東昌村附近的阿美族人就成為協助接運旅客和貨物的工人。

第十章

1　基督徒被控離棄父母，最主要原因是指基督徒並不接受祖先崇拜這個習俗，在父母的葬禮上也不願意拿香崇拜父母所致。但並不是指真正的放棄奉養在世父母的責任。

2　所謂的「米基督徒」的說法與戰後本地人說基督教是「麵粉教」的說法相類似，意思是那些到教會的基督徒是為了現實的利益，例如為了米或麵粉而去，並不是因為真正的宗教情操。

— 233 —

Rev. George Leslie MacKay was extracting teeth for locals in 1893.
馬偕在宜蘭武暖（噶瑪蘭）平埔教會為信徒拔牙看病。

Bu-loân Chapel. A.L.M. extracting teeth.
武鸣
1893.

NOTES

The Island Beautiful
The Story of Fifty Years in North Formosa

BY
Duncan
MacLeod

BOARD OF FOREIGN MISSIONS OF THE PRESBYTERIAN CHURCH IN CANADA
CONFEDERATION LIFE BUILDING, TORONTO 1923

VANCOUVER TAIWANESE PRESBYTERIAN CHURCH 35TH ANNIVERSARY (est. 1985)

CONTENTS

ACKNOWLEDGEMENTS

Geneneral Assembly of Canada Presbyterian Church (PCC's name before 1875) met at Chalmers Church, Quebec City in June 7-14, 1871 approved to send George Leslie Mackay as an oversea missionary. On the night of Tuesday, September 19, 1871 Mackay was commissioned to be the oversea missionary at Gould Street Presbyterian Church in Toronto. Mackay said goodbye to his family and friends in Woodstock train station on the morning of October 19, 1871 and headed to his mission field. He arrived in Northern Formosa on March 9 of the following year. He had planted the seeds of the Gospel in many villages and nurtured the first group of Christians in Northern Taiwan. They loved the Lord, were His faithful servants, and established the foundation and development of the church in Northern Taiwan. When Mackay passed away on June 2, 1901, it was a crisis in the mission field of Northern Taiwan. Many Christians were wondering and worrying, someone even asked: "Is there tomorrow for the church" ? However, history proved that the church belongs to God, not

Mackay. God's church continues even without a leader. Due to Mackay's unselfish service to the Lord, many more people were inspired and called and followed in his footsteps to carry on the torch of the mission to spread the Gospel. As Paul said "Be imitators of me, as I am of Christ."(1 Cor 11:1)

Churches in Northern Taiwan celebrated their 50th anniversary in 1922. Both missionary and local minister published important materials the next year. One such text was Ching-Yi Chen's "Northern Taiwanese Presbyterian Church History" in Romanized Taiwanese which was later translated into Chinese and published in 1997. Another one was written by missionary-scholar, Duncan MacLeod's " The Island Beautiful, The Story of Fifty Years in Northern Formosa", was published by the Board of Foreign Missions (now the Life and Mission Agency) of The Presbyterian Church in Canada in 1923. The content of his book is abundant and is the most important history of the first 50 years of churches in Northern Taiwan. Unfortunately, there has not been a Taiwanese translation published.

Vancouver Taiwanese Presbyterian Church celebrated its 35th anniversary in 2020. In response to the love of God, we decided to publish this book bilingually as a bridge between Taiwan and Canada. We hope that both PCC and TPC will remember God's amazing presence in this historical achievement. We would also to thank the Presbyterian Church in Canada for sending a missionary to Northern Taiwan 150 years ago.

We would also like to thank the following people for their help in publishing this book. They are: Rev. Ian Ross-McDonald, General Secretary of The Life and Mission Agency, PCC who

gave us permission to translate it into Chinese and republish it in English; Rev. Dr. Yang-En Cheng of Taiwan Theological College and Seminary to make arrangements with the translator and help with editing; Rev. Dr. Chang-Hua Lin of Yu-Shang Theological Seminary for his translation and many footnotes to help readers to have a better understanding; Team of Chu-Lou Publication Company.

Ta-Li Hsieh, M. Div. / Ph. D.
Minister, Vancouver Taiwanese Presbyterian Church
Presbytery of Westminster, PCC
March 9, 2021

FOREWORD

THE last message from George Leslie Mackay to the Canadian Church was "Will Formosa be won for Christ? No matter what may come in the way, the final victory is as sure as the existence of God. With that thought firmly fixed there will be but one shout 'Blessed be His glorious name for ever, and let the whole earth be filled with His glory. Amen and Amen.'"

The end is not yet, but the jubilee of the North Formosa Mission has come. Enough has come to pass in these fifty years to give the assurance that Dr. Mackay's confidence will not be put to shame. Beautiful Formosa will some day be "all glorious within." In this redeemed and glorified world Formosa will shine as a star in the firmament. One needs but to compare conditions as they then existed with conditions as they now are in order to recognize the rising tide. Some day righteousness will cover the earth as waters cover the deep.

When Mackay landed, he was alone, without home or friends and amongst an unfriendly people. Christianity was regarded as an

evil cult, and the missionary was called a "foreign devil." Finding entrance was like besieging a city. The taking of Bangkah in "From Far Formosa" is a graphic description and typical of the general attitude and peril. Hatred expressed itself in violent persecution when opportunity offered as, for example, during the French invasion in 1884. To-day all is changed. Persecution has ceased; officials are friendly, and many not themselves Christian recognize the social value of Christianity and cooperate in promoting the Church of Christ.

Amongst the impressive stories of striking conversions given in this book is one in which an official invited the missionary to open a mission because he found himself unable to suppress the vice that prevailed. The mission was opened, and the Gospel did what the law could not do.

Whilst there have been persistent appeals during the years for more foreign workers, and unquestionably larger results would have appeared had the staff been strengthened, yet there are at the present time twenty foreign missionaries with educational and medical institutions that have grown out of the one seed sown fifty years ago. It was a fruitful seed and has multiplied many fold. There is hope in the future. Staff and equipment and popular favour are full of promise. Even the heathen recognize the superiority of Christianity over other religions they have known.

When a cholera epidemic raged in 1919, the Mackay Memorial Hospital was used by the Japanese, and Christians and non-Christians were treated without discrimination. Many were dying daily, but it was noted that no Christians died who obeyed instructions, which they usually did. Christians were allowed to assemble, whilst heathen assemblies were forbidden. In the presence of death Christians were

cheerful, confident, hopeful, whilst the heathen were fretful, fearful, superstitious and thereby the more exposed to danger. The heathen acknowledge that Christians are happier in their homes, not given to opium or gambling, more cleanly in their habits and more sanitary in their surroundings. Upon such foundations what may not the harvest be when the centenary celebration comes! In the last analysis, however, notwithstanding all these advantages, all will depend upon the maintenance of that consecration of life characteristic of the founder of the Mission and of his successors.

To the Rev. Duncan MacLeod the preparation of this volume was a labour of love. Mr. MacLeod's national characteristics enabled him to understand and appreciate Dr. G. L. Mackay and his fellow missionaries as few others could. Furloughs are supposed to be for rest and recuperation for future work, but missionary furloughs are sadly invaded by invitations difficult to refuse, but to which the missionaries cheerfully respond.

The series of prayers, which so fittingly closes each chapter, has been prepared by Rev. J. Lovell Murray, D.D., Director of the Canadian School of Missions. Thanks are due to him for the valuable addition he has thus made to the book.

The editing and publication of this interesting story was placed in the hands of the Rev. H. C. Priest, than whom few are more capable. Mr. Priest's services in behalf of the missionary education of the young people of all our Churches is generally known, but his large share in the publication of missionary literature for young people is not so well known. By his careful and accurate editing of this volume he has placed the Church under further obligation.

R. P. MacKay

CHAPTER I

"ILHA FORMOSA"

CHINESE geographers inform us that once upon a time some fierce dragons, which had dwelt for ages near Foochow, China, bestirred themselves into activity and, for a day's frolic, glided out unseen through the depths of the ocean. Arriving in the vicinity of the present island of Formosa, they became exceedingly playful, and after ploughing through the earth itself, they made their ascent, throwing up the bluff at Keelung head, and then, writhing their way towards the South, with violent contortions heaved up a regular series of hills and mountains, until at last, with a flap of their formidable tails, they threw up the three cliffs which now mark the extreme south of the Island.

Physical Features

Description and Location

The island of Formosa, called "Ilha Formosa" (Beautiful Isle) by the Portuguese mariners, who were the first Europeans to visit it towards the close of the sixteenth century, may be compared to an illshaped pear with a somewhat elongated stem at the south. Its position would indicate that the restless wave, the persistent ocean current, the frequent earthquake and the raging typhoon, through millenniums of activity, had gradually separated it from the rest of the islands in the Bashee channel to the south.

The island lies lengthwise, almost north and south, off the south-east coast of China, separated from the mainland by a channel about ninety miles wide at the north and two hundred miles in width at the south. From Amoy, China, the boat trip occupies twenty-four hours, from Hong-Kong three days, and from Moji, Japan, three days.

Formosa, in early days, was numbered among the Loochu Islands, and was once known by that name. For several generations the Chinese have called it Taiwan, or "Terraced Bay," — a word that is thought by some to have been derived from "Tonghoan," meaning "Eastern Savages." It was probably on this account the Dutch always referred to the aborigines of Formosa as "East Indian Savages."

Off the west coast some sixty miles, lies a group of sixty-

three islands called the Pescadores. To the east likewise are to be found a number of islands, two of which are peopled by Chinese colonists, and a third by a very primitive race, lower in the scale of intelligence and paganism than even the savages on the mainland of Formosa.

Formosa is about 264 miles long and 80 miles in width, with a coast line of 710 miles, and an area of approximately 14,000 square miles. It is half the size of Scotland, somewhat larger than Vancouver Island, and about twice the size of Lake Ontario.

Two-thirds of the island is made up of mountain ranges of striking beauty, forming a majestic, unbroken ridge from the north to the extreme south. This mountainous territory has been associated, from earliest history, with the name of the Formosan head-hunters. The other third of the island consists of a strip of rolling arable land from twenty to thirty miles wide, occupied, for the last two or three hundred years, by Chinese colonists. This narrow strip of alluvial soil, starting in the foothills, drops gradually down till it disappears in the low-level plains that skirt the western sea-coast.

The interior and eastern section rises very abruptly from the western foothills, range after range vieing with one another in their mad, upward climb, till they reach, in places, a height of over thirteen thousand feet; then, as if their ambition for supremacy had suddenly subsided, they drop precipitously, deep down where the waters of the Pacific lap the solitary crags beneath.

Many a traveller has tried to describe the wonderful sight of these famous "cliffs." Professor Chamberlain in his book, "Things Japanese," pictures them thus:

"The cliffs on the east coast of Formosa are the highest and most precipitous in the world, towering in places sheer six thousand feet from the water's edge.

"The scenery is of rare beauty. From the water's edge to the very tips of these mountains may be seen trees, large and small, shrubs and grasses of all sorts, growing in a most luxuriant manner. In some places there are marks of large landslides, but there are few places where the wild savage cannot find a path or at least a foothold, when chasing the deer and wild boar from out their mountain lairs."

Mountains

Directly inland beyond these lofty peaks, near Central Formosa and under the Tropic of Cancer, and rising to a height of 14,000 feet above sea-level, stands Mount Niitaka, also called Mount Morrison, the pride of Formosa. Few have ever reached its highest point, not only on account of the danger due to the presence of savages in the neighborhood, but also because of the expense of the trip, which cannot be undertaken without a large party of Japanese guards. These mountain tops are snow-capped for a good part of the year.

Lofty mountains are associated with deep valleys and turbulent rivers. To this, Formosa is no exception. As the traveller stands on a mountain top, there stretches out before him one unbroken panorama of beautiful minarets, deftly carved by Mother Nature, foaming cascades, deep gorges, and a strange mixture of evergreen meadows, nestling in the restful lap of the lower hills and surrounded by young groves or primeval forests.

Lakes

Formosa can boast of but few lakes, the most famous being Lake Candidius, named after the first Dutch missionary. This lake, situated in one of the most picturesque spots among the mountains of Central Formosa, at an elevation of over two thousand feet, has become, in recent years, a centre of great interest. With a view to centralizing at this point all the electric plants of the island, the Formosan Government has undertaken operations on a large scale. Several hundred feet higher, a tunnel has been opened through which a mountain stream is to be turned for the purpose of raising the lake sixty feet higher than its original level. Between the lake and the valley below there is a drop of probably a thousand feet in the first two miles. Here a huge power house is to be erected that will supply the whole island with light and power. At the present time a railway is being opened which passes within a mile or two of the lake, and extends some distance beyond, into the heart of the savage territory.

Typhoons

Formosa is famous for its periodical typhoons. Indeed, there are those who credit Formosa with creating these destructive agents. On the contrary, the lofty ranges of the island, two hundred miles long, often check the onward rush of the typhoon toward the Chinese coast, turning it from the north to the west and south, and thus causing it to pass away in a strange and mystic stillness, while the fear-stricken onlooker gazes at the mass of wreckage, the mad mountain torrents and flooded plains, which it leaves in its path. Following a typhoon, the Taihoku plain generally becomes

a veritable inland sea, with Taihoku city a floating island in the centre. The rushing mountain streams overflow their banks, at times carrying away bridges and acres of paddy fields. Great efforts are constantly being made by the Formosan Government and large sums expended to protect life and property and counteract the damaging effect of these typhoons.

In 1920 Taihoku experienced the highest flood for forty years. The whole plain and city, including the mission compound, were several feet under water. Houses were flooded, and the Chinese, on rafts, scoured the district for lost property. As the Japanese policemen were engaged in their work of rescuing the people and bringing them to places of safety, they discovered the hospital caretaker, up to his waist in water, holding high in his protecting arms his precious pig. Not until his much prized possession had been safely locked in one of the upstair bathrooms of the hospital, where it was kept until the flood had passed, did he respond to the call to assist in rescue work. Such treatment to this animal, so much despised in some other lands, is by no means uncommon in Formosa.

Earthquakes

Formosa is the centre of the Japanese and Philippine Archipelago, and is near the centre of the earthquake zone. Consequently earthquakes are quite frequent occurrences. They seldom, however, create much excitement or result in serious disaster, though a few months before the writer reached Formosa a very heavy earthquake in Kagi, a city in Central Formosa, destroyed many houses and lives; and the summer after his arrival

a still more severe earthquake did considerable damage in North Formosa.

It is not generally known that the study of seismology was started in Japan. Leading European scientists were invited by the Government to come and study the phenomena of earthquakes on their own native soil. The result has meant much to architects and builders throughout Japan, while our own mission has reaped no small benefit, since more effective measures are now used to make secure the foundations of all our mission buildings. While this involves a heavier initial outlay, it ultimately effects greater economy and relieves any fear of actual danger from ordinary earthquakes.

Climate

The climate of Formosa varies from wet, bleak cold to extreme heat, with no frost or snow except upon the mountains. Generally speaking it is humid and hot the most of the year. The climate In the north differs considerably from that in the south. In North Formosa, January, February and March are the cool winter months, whilst in the south this period is one of ideal, sunny weather. June, July, August and September are the hottest months throughout the island, while in October, November and December the heat moderates and the weather is enjoyable. The average temperature ranges from fifty degrees Fahrenheit in winter to eighty-five degrees in summer, but, owing to excessive humidity, the heat is more trying than in countries with a drier climate. The fact, however, that of the missionaries and business men belonging to the foreign community in the island, some have been living

in Formosa from thirty to forty years, is evidence that to many foreigners, at least, the climate is not too unfriendly.

To escape the extreme heat of summer, most of the missionaries go to their mountain cottages, which are located about two thousand feet above sea-level, and are distant only two or three hours' journey from either Tamsui or Taihoku, where the two mission compounds of Canadian Presbyterians are situated. This summer resort is a great boon to the missionaries, and particularly to their wives and children.

Diseases

Among the various diseases that frequently become epidemic, malaria has been the most troublesome to the foreigner. The anopheles mosquito, however, which is the malaria fever carrier, is no respecter of persons, except in the measure in which it seems to love fresh diet. Among the great services rendered by the Japanese has been that of reducing the mortahty from malaria. At the present time, except in a very few swampy districts, this disease is not considered a serious hindrance to life or work in Formosa.

White Ants

White ants are not creatures that the missionary may overlook. Why does he waste time on them? Just because they waste his time and property more effectively than any other creature. They are the most destructive, yet the most fascinating, creatures we know. They carry on their work of destruction in silence and in obscurity, through day and night, in the earth beneath and on the earth above, and are not afraid to aspire to the most exalted elevations or the

finest mansions.

The instinct of this pale, soft, and innocent looking little creature is amazing. He seems to find out, in some mysterious way, that a certain desirable article has been placed in some particular spot. A leader starts to discover a track, which may be through a small hole in a concrete foundation. He will bore through wood, or even lime plaster, with perfect ease. Once he has opened a small passage the size of his body, the whole army of his followers silently and in an apparently endless procession march on toward the object of attack. With wonderful precision they cut a hole through the floor and enter a box, a desk, the leg of a table or a bureau. The leader of the gang evidently has no difficulty whatever in directing operations at the precise spot. Their work is accomplished so skilfully that, after the whole army has deserted the place, the destruction they have wrought will be known only by the hollowness of the articles they attacked. The Government of Formosa has for years made a careful study of this industrious little insect, and has been endeavoring to discover chemicals and oils that will effectively prevent its destructive operations. The white ant creates a serious and perplexing problem for the missionary architect, though experience is beginning to teach how it may be at least partially met.

The Mission Boards at home will have to bear in mind that these natural destructive agencies — white ants, earthquakes and typhoons — can never be completely overcome and that, therefore, to build solidly at first is the only wise policy.

Natural Resources

Agricultural Products

Formosa is rich in agricultural products. The land yields two full crops of rice a year, of which several million bushels annually are exported to Japan. Since Japanese occupation, the work of irrigation has been largely developed. Among the important products are camphor, sugar-cane, tea, millet, maize, barley, potatoes of all descriptions, indigo, pease, beans, peanuts, hemp, jute, and other kinds of fibrous grasses. The principal fruits are oranges, bananas, pumalos, persimmons, pineapples, plums, peaches, mangoes, and other varieties for which only the natives have cultivated a taste.

Camphor

Camphor production in Formosa goes back two hundred years, and at the present time is one of its most valuable industries, well over ninety per cent, of the world's camphor being produced in that island. The Chinese immigrants of earlier days, whose ancestors had already discovered the art of distilling camphor, as soon as their curious eyes caught sight of the primeval camphor forests of Formosa, gave themselves to its production. Later on, the more warlike Highlanders, the Hakkas, who were immigrants from South China, came. From the first they chose the strip of uncultivated foothills bordering on the territory of the wild head-

hunters, and began to turn the hillsides into tea and sugar-cane plantations, potato patches, and paddy fields. The more aggressive of this sturdy and daring people took to camphor distilling.

For generations many deadly feuds took place between the Hakkas and their savage neighbors, who gradually were driven farther into the mountain fastnesses. Many of the Chinese were killed by these head-hunters. The savages would stalk among the lower hills for days until they got their game. Little time was lost in severing, with the knife which always hung from their belt, the head of their unfortunate victim. With pride they would carry back to camp the trophy of their success and valor.

The Hakkas themselves became experts at the same game. They, too, would stalk for their prey on the outskirts of the foothills, and in turn snipe the savage, taking, not the head alone, but the whole carcass, and feasting on it with satisfaction and relish. The current belief among them was that savage flesh was the choicest. There are many Hakkas, some of whom are now evangelists, who can recall such experiences.

The Hakkas constantly gained ground, until today they have the perpetual leasehold of a large tract of territory, once the lawful possession of the aborigines. Because of the unscrupulous way the camphor forests were being cut down by these colonists, the Japanese authorities have made the camphor industry a Government monopoly.

The process by which the camphor is extracted from the tree is simple, but interesting. The machinery is inexpensive. With the axe and saw the distiller first fells the tree. Then, taking a gouge-shaped hatchet, he cuts out of the tree small chips cross-wise. These

chips are placed in stills which are heated by a fire underneath. The camphor vapor which rises is made to pass through iron pipes into boxes, where it is cooled by running water. There it condenses into crystals resembling hoar frost. This crude camphor is placed in vats, where, as it settles, the camphor oil sinks to the bottom and is thus extracted. The camphor then is put into bags and the oil into coal-oil tins, and sent to the factory at Taihoku.

The Japanese, with their keen sense of national development, are carrying on the work of camphortree afforestation on a large scale. Formosa is consequently likely to continue for generations to lead the world in the production of camphor.

Sugar

The sugar industry of Formosa was begun by the first Chinese colonists in the sixteenth century. It was considerably developed by the Dutch and later, as the records show, was much encouraged by the family of Koxinga, the first Chinese Governor. Under Japanese experts this has become one of the most thriving industries of the island. Japanese sugar companies have increased rapidly, and much territory has been secured for sugar-cane production. It is to the credit of the Formosan Government that of recent years laws have been enacted for the protection of private Formosan farmers against the injustice and coercion of these private companies.

There are now many large sugar factories, operated with up-to-date British machinery, where the services of all foreign experts have been dispensed with and where a most lucrative business is being conducted. In the mountains there may still be found a few mills of the old, crude type, operated by Hakkas, in which

the cane is crushed by iron rollers, propelled by the water-buffalo. The change from the crude Chinese method to that of the modern Japanese mills is a striking illustration of the enterprising spirit of the Japanese people.

Tea

The Chinese immigrants were the original cultivators of Formosan tea, the most popular blend of which is Oolong. The first European to discover the value of this special blend was Mr. Robert Swinhoe, the British consul at Tamsui. About 1867, the first shipment was sent to America. The export trade from the first has been largely in the hands of British, American and Chinese merchants, but, of recent years, the Japanese have entered the field. They tried, but without success, to develop green tea trade. Now they have several firms, the largest of which is the Mitsui Company, carrying on black tea trade.

Of late years the Formosan farmers have not shown much enthusiasm in tea plantations. They are finding other ways of making a livelihood and more profit from other agricultural products. Moreover, they are discovering that, whilst they cannot make tea-growing pay, the Chinese tea-brokers and middlemen are reaping huge profits. In this connection, it is gratifying to know that the British and American firms, which have been carrying on trade in Formosa for about sixty years, have always maintained a reputation for fairness and business integrity. The writer has often heard the farmers state that if Chinese middlemen were as fair and as honorable as Western merchants they would have no complaints to make.

Opium

In the ninth century opium was brought to China by travelling Arabs, and in the twelfth century was imported from India in sailing vessels to the mainland of China. At a much later date, China was actually forced to open her ports and her markets to the opium trade. When the Chinese colonists came to Formosa they brought with them the opium and the smoking habit. At the time Japan took possession of the island about seven per cent, of the people were opium users.

After much deliberation as to the future treatment of these drug addicts, the policy adopted was a system of licenses in order to bring about the gradual suppression of the use of opium. The licenses had to be secured within a certain time, after which no more would be issued. Thus, as the old users pass away, the number is being reduced. In spite, however, of the fact that any who use it without a license are imprisoned or heavily fined, there are still many of this class in the island.

The opium industry is carried on in Formosa as a profit-making Government monopoly. It is hoped that as the moral enlightenment of the nation advances, public opinion will become so strong that the Government will find this policy untenable and will effect the total prohibition of the trade. In China, although the opium trade has been illegal since 1917, the Chinese Government has been unable to enforce the law. Poppy fields have again begun to appear in many sections of that vast Republic, although there are encouraging instances of recent attempts at effective suppression. Unfortunately, the menace has appeared in another form, particularly in China. Opium in the form of morphia is being

manufactured in large quantities in Britain and the United States, sold to Japanese firms and by them smuggled into China.

The suppression of opium in every form has become a problem of international significance. It has been under discussion at the Hague and recently at the Washington Conference. At present strenuous efforts are being put forth to secure the suppression of the opium traffic by the passage of the Miller Bill through the United States Congress. The League of Nations, through its Advisory Committee on Traffic in Opium, is endeavoring to secure that countries where the poppy is grown shall guarantee to restrict its cultivation to a quantity sufficient to supply only medicinal requirements. Many would rejoice to see the Formosan Government remove this blot from her good name and put the drug beyond the reach of her people.

Tobacco

The tobacco industry in Formosa has already become a Government monopoly. Probably more money is spent on tobacco in its various forms than on opium in its worst period. Men and women, young and old of every class, both Japanese and Formosan, are addicted to this habit, some of whom are cigarette fiends as incurable as opium smokers. Western nations, however, while living in glass houses, dare not cast stones at Japan. Western tobacco and cigarette companies are exerting themselves to the utmost in seeking to develop their trade in China. In Formosa the barrier of an effective Government monopoly shuts them out. Nevertheless the process of moral and physical injury goes on without let or hindrance.

Mineral Resources

In addition to her agricultural products Formosa can boast of valuable mineral resources.

Coal

Coal in large quantities is to be found on the island. It is a new formation, and though generally used for household purposes, is more suitable for steamships, general manufacturing plants, and electric power houses. This abundance of coal makes possible many electric plants throughout the island. When the territory of the aborigines is explored, it is possible that in those unknown mountains large quantities will be discovered.

Koxinga, the famous Chinese pirate, knew the value of coal, but the superstitious Chinese opposed the idea of digging into the earth and thus disturbing the multitudes of demons who might be offended and molest the defenceless inhabitants. No wonder they opposed the first coal-miners in the neighborhood of Keelung! Was it not here that, centuries ago, those sport-loving dragons glided in a frolicsome manner out of Foochow harbor, and, skimming the surface of the Formosan channel, stuck their horny heads under the northern hills, bored their way in a wild and tortuous fashion and tossed up in their onward march the majestic mountains which to-day form the backbone of this picturesque island?

It was left to the Japanese, who have never shown much respect for the foolish superstitions of the Formosan people, to develop this industry. To-day, however, the majority of the mine-owners are Formosans. During the recent "Great War" Formosan coal was exported to all the seaports in the East.

Gas and Petroleum

Natural gas and petroleum also have been found, but, as yet, have not been developed to any great extent. Three years ago, near the city of Taihoku, a group of men, when digging for water, struck a vein of gas. A superstitious old lady, fearing they had let loose the fumes from the nether world, took a bundle of josspaper to the spot, and set fire to it, at the same time imploring the gods for mercy. Her appeal must have been unheard by the gods, for suddenly her hair caught fire, and but for these same well-diggers she would have perished.

Petroleum was first discovered near Byoritsu, in mid-Formosa, by an American. Several wells are now operated in that district by a Japanese Company. Natural gas, which is available in the same district, is used for operating the oil-wells. The oil is inferior to Western oil, but this is probably due to the need of a better refinery.

Sulphur

In the neighborhood of the Daiton range, in North Formosa, are found many hot sulphur springs. Half an hour by train from Taihoku brings one to the popular resort of Hokuto, where hundreds daily enjoy the hot sulphur baths.

Gold

The presence of the treacherous headhunters in the region of the Karenko plain, makes gold-mining in that section a dangerous enterprise, though it is carried on to some extent. The chief gold mines are near Keelung. A few years ago there was a great rush

to this Formosan Klondyke. While the rush has subsided, these mines are still in operation, and produce a fair amount of gold. As in other lands, the gold mines have brought physical, financial, and moral ruin to many. Stories of the wreckage of human life in this district are many and varied among both Japanese and Chinese youth.

Trade and Industry

The trade and industry of Formosa have been rapidly increasing in recent years. Keelung harbor is becoming a centre of considerable importance because of the amount of valuable export trade that passes through this seaport.

A Prophecy and a Challenge

Thus briefly have we reviewed the marvellous beauty, the main physical features and the natural resources of Formosa. Interesting as those are, in these studies we are concerned with them mainly in their relation to the extension of Christ's Kingdom. Formosa is yet one of the "isles that wait for His law."

As those brave voyagers of early days, sailing along the coast of the island and catching a glimpse of its mountain peaks, its glimmering cascades and its terraced plains, exclaimed with glad surprise, "Ilha formosa! ilha formosa!" — (Beautiful isle! beautiful isle!) shall not we of later days take these same words

as a prophecy of the time when Formosa's people, as followers of Him who is the "Fairest among ten thousand," shall know the beauty of the Lord, and when, in a vastly wider, deeper sense, the island shall indeed be Ilha Formosa.

◆ ◆ ◆ ·············

𝔇raper

O GOD, our bountiful Creator, accept our gratitude for this world of beauty in which Thou hast placed us and for the sense of beauty through which Thou canst speak to us of Thyself. All of Thy works praise Thee; and we whose eyes have been gladdened by the wonder and loveliness of the things which Thy fingers have fashioned would also offer Thee our loving praise.

MAY all who remain in ignorance of Thee throughout the world and especially those who dwell in the Island of Formosa be brought to know that Thou hast made them for Thyself and that only through Thy redeeming work can the ugliness and disorder of sin be removed and the radiance of the divine image come into their possession. May the beauty of holiness enter into their lives as they open their eyes and their hearts to the light of the knowledge of the glory of God in the face of Jesus Christ.

A ND wilt Thou grant, O fairest Lord Jesus, that Thy message may be conveyed more and more widely throughout Formosa, that Thy spirit may be communicated rapidly from life to life, until all of the Island Beautiful shall be radiant in the beauty of holiness and shall blossom with Thine own fairness as a garden of the Lord. Grant this for Thine own Name's sake. AMEN.

CHAPTER II

THE PEOPLE, THEIR RULERS AND RELIGIONS

W HO are the people living in the Island Beautiful? What is their history, and what do they believe? These are questions that at once arise, and to which we must have some answer before discussing mission work there. Naturally we think first of the early inhabitants.

The Aborigines

Various Groups

The aborigines of Formosa may be classified into three main groups. First, the Chhi-hoans, or "green savages," who have become famous on account of their head-hunting propensities, and

who may be divided into nine distinct tribes, all of which differ, to some extent, in customs and dialects. The second group is made up of the Ami and Lam-si-hoan tribes, who inhabit the Karenko and Pinan plains along the east coast of the island. These are semi-civilized, and, since the arrival of the Japanese, have engaged in farming.

The third group consists of the Pepohoans, or "savages of the plain," and the Sekhoans, or "cooked savages," who, of recent years, have become quite civilized. Some of them were brought into contact with Christianity during the Dutch occupation, while most of them throughout the island have been influenced by the mission work of modern times. It was among the Pepohoans and Sekhoans that the English Presbyterian Mission, in South Formosa, to a large extent, had its first entrance, while in the north these tribes were brought under the influence of the gospel during Dr. George Leslie Mackay's lifetime. They are, however, fast passing away, and the survivors are being rapidly assimilated, through intermarriage, with the more virile and progressive Chinese race.

Their Origin

The origin of these aborigines is clouded in mystery. There are no records to inform us who the immigrants were that first set foot on Formosan soil. Some claim that they were Negritos from the Philippine Islands. There are traditions to the effect that their ancestors came from the south, being driven north in the typhoons. The existence of so many tribes, differing in customs, folk-lore, and dialects, has so far proved a knotty problem for the students of ethnology. It may be safely assumed that the aborigines of Formosa

have a mixture of Mongol (Proto-Malayan) and Indonesian blood. The island, doubtless, was originally inhabited by some of the same people who moved northward on the general wave of migration and occupied the Philippine Islands as well as the southern part of Japan. There are evidences of some distant blood relationship between them and the inhabitants of the southern islands of Japan. At all events Japan, without doubt, had some intercourse with Formosa even in prehistoric days. Very early in historic times, Japanese pirates scoured the Pacific coast as far south as Macao. How they could miss this large island it would be difficult to surmise.

Their Isolation and Cruelty

Though we have no accurate record of their earliest intercourse with the outside world, there is abundant evidence that for generations these tribes were accustomed to carry on warfare with one another. The only policy on which they agreed was their stubborn resistance to all outside political interference. Japanese, Chinese, British and American ships came to grief on the stormy coast of Formosa, but scarcely any of their unfortunate crews ever survived, owing either to the cruel waves, or to the more cruel savages.

So far no Christian work has been done among the savages. For years the two missions. South and North, have been keeping this most urgent call before the home churches in England and Canada. Surely the evangelization of a hundred thousand savages is a problem to challenge the heroic young people of our land.

The Dutch Regime

In 1624, the Dutch East India Company took possession of Formosa. The policy of the Dutch in regard to their colonies was to send out, not only governors to take charge of civil and political affairs, but also missionaries to look after the religious welfare of the natives. Accordingly, three years later, in 1627, the Rev. George Candidius arrived, the first missionary to make known the Christian faith in the island. During the first half of the seventeenth century, Spanish and Portuguese priests had tried in vain to gain an entrance. The Dutch East India Company, the special purpose of which was to create trade in the East for the Dutch Republic, soon found the influence of the missionaries very helpful, with the result that before long the Church and State policy of Holland became its policy in Formosa.

The Work of the Dutch Missionaries

Great credit is due these missionaries for the work they accomplished. During the thirty-seven years of the Dutch rule, over thirty missionaries, besides teachers, were sent to Formosa. Preaching and the teaching of catechisms specially prepared for these primitive people were the methods employed. They transcribed the language into Romanized script, and through this means taught some of the natives the art of reading and writing. Some of the young men, indeed, went so far as to learn the Dutch

language. It was required that on Sundays they should dress in Dutch fashion and conform to certain other external regulations.

Their Failure

The difficulty in bringing about any permanent moral reform was a cause of continual distress to the missionaries, though the Rev. Robert Junius received much praise for the great changes which were brought about in the people during his years of toil among them. It is interesting to notice, however, that the Dutch officials claimed that a short time after he had returned to the Fatherland, several villages rebelled against their authority.

A few months after Koxinga drove the Dutch out of the island, there was scarcely a trace of their work, in the shape of schools or chapels, to be seen. The natives, encouraged by the Chinese colonists and soldiers, removed every vestige of the Western religion. Several of the missionaries and teachers were cruelly treated and at least three of them were crucified. Two hundred years afterward, in 1865, when the first English missionaries arrived in Formosa, the only trace of the old Dutch Church they found was some books which fell into their hands.

Why They Failed

Some reasons may be advanced to explain, at least partially, the failure of the work of the Dutch Church in Formosa. First, the policy of transplanting a Western system of Church and State among these simple-minded people was a mistake. For the most part, it was the political rod with the name of the Church, rather than the moral persuasiveness of the Gospel, that brought about

the changes effected in the outward conduct of these subjugated people. Idolatry was punished by law and religion was a matter of state compulsion. The missionaries came, not merely as heralds of the Cross, but as officials of the Dutch Church, supervised by the state officials whose headquarters were at Batavia, in Java. It was the case of a political organization making use of the civilizing agency of the Christian Church, for the purpose of developing its own trade. The missionaries taught not only Christian truth, but also rice-planting and other crude industries, a policy which, no doubt, could have been an effective evangelizing agency, had no state authority been associated with it. Alfred Russell Wallace, the famous scientist, who, while on a tour in the Dutch Malay peninsula, wrote at length on this subject, was delightfully surprised at the work which the missionaries had accomplished among these backward races, but while giving great credit to them for their success, called the method of the Dutch government "parental despotism."

In the second place, some of the missionaries were led to become traders themselves. Their salaries were paid out of the revenue which passed through their hands. Liquor and tobacco allowances were sent them from Batavia. They were in charge of the hunting licenses which were granted annually to the Chinese hunters. Furthermore, the temptation to waste much precious time at the chase was naturally very strong. Each missionary was allowed three hunting dogs, and each teacher, two. It is quite conceivable that some of them spent more time in hunting than in mission work.

In the third place, there were several moral lapses among

the teachers sent out from Holland. Some of the offenders were imprisoned, while others were sent back to their homeland. There are certain sins among civilized races, which, under the traditional laws of these savage tribes, are followed with severe punishment. Japanese officials confess that some of the outrageous acts of the headhunters, as when they rose in one night and slew all the Japanese in the district, were due to the misconduct of their soldiers. All these unworthy incidents in missionary life among the natives would create doubts in their minds as to the motives of even their father-superior, and nullify in no small measure the spiritual impressions and atmosphere created.

In the fourth place, baptizing by villages, as well as on personal profession of faith, was common among the Dutch missionaries. Mass movements in any land carry with them possibilities of large and very serious dangers. Men are saved not collectively but individually. Those who have been too free with the water of baptism have oftentimes had to drink their own bitter tears of repentance.

The Dutch regime came to an end before the missionaries were able to extricate themselves from this bondage of state and church — a system which, in the Western world, has not contributed to spiritual freedom, much less did it do so among the primitive races of Formosa.

Formosan Chinese

The Formosan Chinese make up the large majority of the population. Their first connection with Formosa goes back several centuries. Before the Dutch arrived the more daring of the Chinese traders and hunters had had some intercourse with the semi-civilized savages on the west coast. The political relation, however, between China and Formosa dates from 1662, the year Koxinga drove the Dutch out of the island. Following the civilizing influence of the Dutch, they crossed the channel in thousands and began to establish colonies.

Coming of Koxinga

About the year 1661 conditions in China were marked by much unrest and disorder, on account of the Tartar invasion. The famous Chinese pirate, Koxinga, whose mother was Japanese and whose father was a great Chinese warrior, could never be reconciled to the ruling in China of the Manchu dynasty, on account of the shameful treatment his father had received at their hands. He was successful in several encounters, but at last, completely outnumbered, was defeated near Nanking. With his brave soldiers, he withdrew to the neighborhood of Amoy.

His position in China becoming too uncomfortable, he entered into negotiations with the Chinese colonists in Formosa, which resulted in his appearing, early one morning in 1662, under the Dutch Fort, Zeelandia, with three hundred Chinese ships manned by twenty-five thousand soldiers, and demanding its surrender. After nine months of the most heroic resistance by the Dutch officials and soldiers, as well as by missionaries and teachers, they were compelled to surrender. Few pages in history are more

heartrending than those which relate the story of the sufferings of these brave Hollanders. The missionaries seemed to have suffered most, even at the hands of the semicivilized savages whom they had sought in so many ways to help. Koxinga did not long enjoy his triumph, his death occurring in 1663.

The Hoklos and Hakkas

With the coming of Koxinga, the Chinese colonists swarmed into Formosa by the tens of thousands. This tide of immigration continued steadily for several generations during the Chinese regime. A large stream poured in first of all from the district around Amoy in South Fukien. These were called Hoklos, and spoke the Amoy dialect. A later influx was from the Swatow district in North Kwangtung Province. These were called Hakkas, and spoke the Hakka dialect. When the Japanese took possession in 1895, the Chinese population was reckoned at about 3,000,000.

From 1663, the year of Koxinga's death, till 1895, when the Japanese took possession, was one long period of sanguinary struggles with the savages and of ceaseless rebellion among the Chinese themselves, without order or safe government in the island. This was practically the condition when Dr. G. L. Mackay landed in North Formosa in 1872.

Japanese Occupation

The Coming of the Japanese

The Japanese now govern Formosa. The events that led up to their occupation of the island are interesting. It should be borne in mind that China had no legal claim to Formosa. Koxinga was a sea-pirate, and it was with no right and without compensation that he took possession of the island. With the annexation of the Loochu Islands by Japan, Formosa was brought into closer geographical relation with that country. Whatever intercourse the Japanese had before with the Formosans was of a casual nature. The incident is recorded that when the Dutch landed in Formosa, they found a group of Japanese settled in the south of the island, who claimed ownership. The Dutch requested as much land as could be covered by the hide of an ox. Struck by the modesty of the request, the Japanese agreed to it. The Dutch took a hide, no doubt that of a huge water-buffalo, and cutting it into narrow strips, tied these together, forming a line long enough to enclose a plot of ground on which they built Fort Zealandia. The story goes on to relate that the Japanese left Formosa in disgust, while the Dutch settled down to the task of establishing their colony. By this time the Japanese traders had become interested in Formosa, though no political issues had yet arisen between the two nations.

In December, 1871, the month in which Dr. G. L. Mackay landed in South Formosa, a large Japanese vessel from the Loochu Islands was wrecked on the south coast of Formosa. The majority of the crew were murdered by the savages. A few escaped. When the news of the disaster reached Japan they sought redress from the Chinese Government, but were told that China had no jurisdiction over the unsubjugated tribes in Formosa. In 1873 a similar

shipwreck incident occurred, but this time the Japanese took the matter of demanding penalty into their own hands, a course which nearly led to war between the two nations. It was averted by China agreeing to pay an indemnity to defray the expense of the Japanese punitive expedition to Formosa, and giving assurance of better jurisdiction over the savage tribes.

Annexing the Loochu Islands

An event took place in 1879 which further widened the breach between China and Japan. Previously the Loochu Islands had paid taxes to both these nations. On their failure to pay these taxes to Japan, the islands, by one political stroke, were annexed to the Japanese Empire, to the great chagrin of the Chinese Government. Through the good services of General Grant, exPresident of the United States, who happened to be in Japan at the time, the trouble was finally settled in favor of Japan, and China was forced to swallow another of the bitter pills that outside nations through the years have so frequently dealt out to her.

Formosa Ceded to Japan

The most important event in the political history of the island took place in 1895, when China and Japan came once again into collision, this time regarding the situation in Port Arthur and Wei-hai-wei. Japan prepared an expedition which was despatched south for the Pescadores, a group of islands off the west coast of Formosa, which were regarded as the military key to Formosa. The Chinese government, on hearing of the capture of these forts, opened negotiations for peace, which finally resulted in the Treaty

of Shimonoseki, by which Formosa and the Pescadores were ceded to Japan. The treaty was signed on the 18th of April, 1895, on board a Japanese vessel, in the outer harbor of Keelung.

Japan's victory, through her shrewd and selfassertive diplomacy, helped in her rapid rise to the rank of a leading world power. Since that event, by successive moves, she has added greatly to her political prestige, not only in the East, but in the far West.

Uprisings in the Island

The signing of a treaty was an easy matter, but the subjugation of the frantic Formosans, who were maddened by the cowardly act of the Chinese government, was not so easy a task. The Japanese, however, were not to be intimidated by the general uprising throughout the island. They effected a safe landing, and, in a very short time, took possession of the north, and moved southward till they reached Tainan, the old capital of the island. Within a year the whole Chinese population was practically subdued. Local uprisings, especially among the Hakkas, continued for some time. The last one, which occurred in 1913, resulted in nearly one hundred Hakkas being beheaded. According to the public statement of the Japanese officials, Formosan Christians took no part in any of these local uprisings.

Subjugating Savage Tribes

A tremendous task still faced the Japanese government — that of subjugating over a hundred thousand head-hunters who inhabited the mountain fastnesses. These wild, savage tribes, lords

of the soil for millenniums, were not found amenable to either moral or physical persuasion, but fiercely resisted all encroachment on their territory by the invaders. There were serious differences at headquarters as to the best method of suppression. Some of the Japanese thought these savages were not human beings. However, those with saner and more humane views won the day. The policy of gradual conquest by force and constant diplomatic negotiations has practically brought about the subjugation of these tribes. Many lives were lost, both Japanese and Formosan, and much money spent in the difficult task. The scaling of steep and lofty mountains covered with primeval forests, and the crossing of deep gorges with their turbulent streams, was an experience to which the Japanese soldiers, brave and fearless as they are, were unaccustomed. Their loss during the campaign amounted to about ten thousand. Often in the middle of the night, the savages would come down on an isolated patrol of soldiers and, murdering them all, take away, as trophies of their prowess, every head they could carry. For the purpose of protecting themselves, not for the extermination of the savages, as some reports have stated, wire fences, locally electrified, were constructed by the Japanese.

Japan's Treatment of Her Colony

Gradually these savage people were pacified. In groups of fifties and hundreds, they were brought to the chief centres and shown civilized life in the cities, towns and villages throughout the island. They are now being taught farming and other methods of making a livelihood. Many schools have been established among them. It is hoped that in a short time the privilege may be granted of

preaching to them, without restriction, the gospel of God's grace.

The limitation now existing will be referred to in a later chapter. The writer believes that the best policy would be to appeal to the Japanese Christian Churches to undertake this as their own Home Mission work.

When Formosa was ceded to Japan, the eyes of all the world were on the Japanese Government. The Western nations wondered how she would succeed in her new experiment of subjugating and colonizing alien races.

Shortly after her occupation of the island, a Governor-General was appointed with complete military control, as well as civil administrative powers. Many reports were scattered abroad about the treatment the Formosans received at the hands of the Japanese during this period. Doubtless there were instances of the most trying provocation, as when the massacre of Japanese men, women and children by the Formosan brigands was followed by cruel reprisals. The reports sent home by the missionaries regarding conditions at that time indicate that there were two sides to the situation. Rev. William Gauld, who was in charge of the Canadian Presbyterian work in 1895, wrote: "Formosa is now a part of the Mikado's domain, and with the restoration of peace, it will, we trust, share in the civilization of that Great Empire." Dr. Mackay, after his return from furlough the following year, wrote in his report: "Many Japanese soldiers and coolies have shown their hatred to the religion of Jesus, and many Japanese Christians have stepped to the front for Christ our King.... Personally, I have met with nothing save respect and kindness from Japanese coolies, soldiers and officials, civil and military. I am acquainted with a

few officers whose demeanor, during those dark days, has been worthy of the highest commendation."

There were, no doubt, isolated cases where the behavior of certain classes of Japanese was most aggravating to foreigners from the West, and intolerable to the better class of Formosan people. The presence of brigands, who carried on pillage and murder, and who created general excitement and confusion among the peaceable inhabitants, made it very difficult for the Japanese soldiers to distinguish between the innocent and the guilty. Those who hated the Christians took the opportunity afforded for venting that hatred by falsely implicating many of them, and in this way were the cause of many Christians being put to death. Whenever, however, it was reported to the officials that those arrested were Christians, they were released. The result was that many heathen feigned Christianity by carrying Bibles and hymn books on their persons. Following the turbulent state of affairs that marked the first few months, conditions soon began to settle down. Order was established and an era of progress inaugurated.

The worst feature, probably, of the whole code of criminal laws in Japan is the principle that the accused is reckoned guilty until he has proved himself innocent. This has often led to men and women, in order to escape torture, telling what they thought the policemen wished them to tell. The Japanese officials themselves, without doubt, have recognized the serious consequences that must inevitably grow out of a basic principle so utterly wrong.

Educational System

The Japanese were scarcely a year in Formosa when they

began the introduction of an educational system for the Formosan youth. It will always stand as a sad reflection on the backward state of the island at that time, that Mr. Katori, head of the educational department, and his five associates were murdered in their office by a group of misguided Formosans. Notwithstanding this unfortunate circumstance, a system of "National Education" was established that year.

This interest in education has ever since been maintained. To-day there are normal schools, middle schools, girls' schools, technical schools, an agricultural school, and schools for experimental farming and forestry. Complaints have been made that the Japanese have shown no desire to give an opportunity for higher education to the Formosan youth. It is true that some officials at the head of the Department of Education took the view that the Formosans, being a subject race, did not need such educational advantages. The civil administrators in Formosa to-day, however, are planning better things. A new educational policy is now being outlined by the government, which provides for additional middle schools for boys, a few of which will be opened to both Japanese and Formosans alike — a great advance on the old policy of racial separation. At the present time, hundreds of Formosan young men, and a considerable number of young women, are in attendance at the chief centres of learning in Japan.

Medical Advance

In no department has Formosa made more progress under Japanese rule than in that of medicine. Over twenty years ago a medical school was established in Taihoku. It was not long till

many Formosans were considering the medical profession. From this school forty to sixty students graduate every year. In Taihoku city are two large hospitals, one of which will compare favorably in size, staff and equipment with the hospitals of Western cities. In the larger centres throughout the island there are hospitals under the direction of Japanese and Formosan doctors, while most of the smaller towns boast of a government dispensary and a Formosan doctor. Among these native doctors are a few Christians, several of whom are office-bearers in the church.

Encouragement of Agriculture

One of the most important steps taken by the Formosan Government, for the encouragement of farming and industry in general, was that of handing over the land to the people as their perpetual possession. Under Chinese control, it was the property of land owners, and the tenant never knew when he might have to move. The opportunity was now given to all to put in their claim for the land which they were occupying, and to have it duly registered. The consequence was that as soon as these farmers realized that the land was their own and that under Japanese law their property was safe, they at once took a new interest and began improvements on the land. Complaints are sometimes made that in remote sections, where subordinates are in control, the Japanese citizen receives better treatment than the Formosan, but generally this difficulty is removed by more careful supervision on the part of higher officials.

Material Advance

Without fear of criticism, one has to admit that Formosa under Japanese rule during these twenty-eight years has made remarkable progress in things material. When one compares the present prosperity of the people and conditions in general with the past, one is compelled to give great credit to the Japanese for their genius as a colonizing nation, and for the singular success of the Formosan government in the development of the resources of the island. Post-office, telegraph and telephone systems have been successfully established. Railway and steamship facilities have enhanced trade, industry, and commerce, and have contributed to the general comfort of the people. Harbor improvements, irrigation on a large scale, the opening of sanitary wells, the establishment of water-supply for the larger centres, the construction of electric plants throughout the island, improvement in sanitary conditions, the opening of several thousand miles of public roads, and other features are evidences of the progressive policy of this prosperous nation.

Formosan Aspirations

It must not be overlooked that the Formosan people still regard themselves, with no little sorrow, as a subject race, and hitherto they have been treated as such. Though convinced that under Japanese rule they are much more prosperous, there is still left the painful feeling that they are governed by an alien power. This feeling has been asserting itself in recent years, not through rebellion, but through the expressed hope that the Formosans may be recognized as citizens with complete franchise entitling them

to share in the administration of affairs in their own native island. Steps are being taken to meet this general aspiration among the more educated and intelligent. The younger generation, however, is becoming so rapidly Japanese in manners, language and dress, through education and constant association with the Japanese, that one can readily conceive of the final merging of the two races in Formosa. The recent removal of hindrances to intermarriage will accelerate the process of assimilation.

Social and Moral Wrongs

While in material affairs there has been remarkable advance, in which the people have benefited exceedingly, in matters moral and spiritual, we fear there has been no progress, except in so far as Christian missions have affected the social and religious life of the people. Some features, new to Formosa, have been introduced that have not been for the moral uplift of the natives. Prostitution, which is legalized in Japan through a policy of segregation, has been introduced into the island, and has brought moral disaster to many, Japanese and Formosans. If we in the West were free from many of these social and moral evils, we could more readily criticize some of the objectionable features of the ethics of the Japanese government, but whilst living in glass houses ourselves, we may well hesitate before casting stones.

Religious Liberty

From the missionary point of view, there is the greatest religious liberty in Formosa. Christian work is conducted without any hindrance on the part of the government or its officials. It

is safe to say that never has there arisen during these years any misunderstanding between the missionaries and the government officials. Sometimes, where policemen did not know of the existence of this liberty for the propagation of the Christian faith, difficulties have occurred between them and the Christians, but in every case these difficulties have been settled by the higher officials in a satisfactory manner, on several occasions policemen having been removed to avoid further trouble. We question if any country enjoys a larger measure of religious liberty than do the Formosan people at the present time. Some years ago the Governor-General, on assuming office, gave instructions to have a religious census carefully taken in Formosa. As a result of the census, he publicly expressed his opinion that only the Christian faith was doing anything for the moral uplift of the people. Under the sane and able administration of the present Governor-General, Baron Den, it is expected that even greater progress will be made along every line.

Japanese Churches

To meet the spiritual needs of the Japanese citizens, the Presbyterian, the Congregational and the Episcopalian Churches of Japan have been organized, some of them for over twenty years. They are not, however, meeting the needs, to any extent, of the non-Christian community. They are self-supporting, but, having no outside financial support, they are not in a position to take up the task of the evangelization of their own people in Formosa. We fear the Christian Churches of Japan have not yet fully realized their responsibilities in this important matter. A visit from the Japan

Evangelistic Band, under the capable leadership of Mr. James Cuthbertson, gave striking evidence of what might be done along this line in the future. He and three able evangelists conducted a three months' campaign throughout the island, both among the Japanese and the Formosan people, with marked success.

The Religions of Formosa

Lack of Religious Genius in the People

The longer one lives in Formosa, the less he values the religious genius of the people. Unreality and indifference to the moral demands of any practical religion are manifest. Often the most ardent devotees of their religions are the most immoral men in the district. It would be difficult to find anywhere religion and morality more completely separated. The gambler goes up to the temple to pray, not as a publican, not even as the pharisee, but as a man who implores the gods to help him in robbing another of all he can, though he knows it may mean the ruin of that man's family. The young woman who lives a life of shame, with her gold necklace and anklets, her showy rings, and her hair bedecked with golden ornaments, goes up without a blush on her face and prays to the gods to give her prosperity. The tragedy of it all is that few even think of the flagrant incongruity.

As in China, the three main religions are Confucianism, Taoism and Buddhism. These are so completely merged, that

the follower of any of the three has a tinge of each in his or her religious life and practice. We must first of all, however, consider the religion of the aborigines.

Animism

A study of the religious beliefs of the aborigines reveals the fact that while there is a wide divergence among the different tribes as to the actual objects of worship, all are spirit worshippers. To some these spirits are resident in the sun or moon, while to others the spirits dwell in the mountains. A few worship idols, though idol worship is not general throughout the various tribes.

A peculiarity of the savage religion is found in the Ami tribe. They believe in the imperishability of spirit and in the existence of a heavenly place of rest, but they condition their entrance into heaven upon the acceptance of a certain rite or ceremony consisting of the sprinkling of water, coupled with prayer, by an official "Prayer Teacher." Once every year, in the month of September, the "Prayer Teacher" is called in and the service held. In this way they feel that they are assured of an entrance into the land of eternal happiness.

The exceeding ferocity of the aborigines, as exemplified in their head-hunting custom, which is common to nearly all tribes, is one reason why they have been left so long without Christian teaching. They regard this savage custom as an observance of ancestral teaching, and therefore of deep religious significance.

Confucianism

The longer one studies Confucianism the more deeply one is convinced of the difficulty of placing it among the classic religions

of the world. Except for the repeated mention of "heaven," which could not have had any personal significance for Confucius himself, one finds scarcely any trace of deep religious genius, such as is found, for example, in Buddhism.

Taoism

Taoism appears as a filthy, poisonous stream that has filtered down the wider current of China's superstitious life, gathering more filth on its downward course, till at last it has permeated and degraded the whole religious life of the people. The result is a conglomeration of spiritism, demonism, witchcraft, sorcery, fortunetelling and other elements which have brought bondage, blindness, ignorance and spiritual death. In fact, the Taoist priests are the most useless and degraded men in the island. They entertain the people at their religious performances, such as the rite of rescuing souls from purgatory, by repeating most degrading rhapsodies. Men and women, young and old, listen till all hours in the night, and regard it as pleasant entertainment.

Buddhism

Buddhism, on the other hand, entered China at a moment of dire spiritual need.

Confucianism had nothing on which men's souls could rest. No future hope was given and salvation was all from within. Buddhism came with many elements which seemed to meet the cravings of the human heart. It offered the forgiveness of sins and purification; it preached universal salvation and the ideas of mercy, pity and love; and promised release from pain and sorrow,

as well as the hope of the "Western Heaven." Its ethics were very much purer and higher than anything the Chinese had ever been taught, and indeed had a striking similarity to the moral law of the Ten Commandments. The priests gave evidences of a life of real self-sacrifice. If any elements are to be found in the religions of Formosa that may be regarded as preparatory for the entrance of Christianity, they will be found mostly in the Buddhist religion.

Many men and women who are seeking release from the burden of superstition, and whose hearts are hungering for the best that their own religions can offer, are among those who most readily respond to the Gospel with its gracious appeal, its glorious deliverance, and its triumphant hope.

The Population and Our Responsibility

What shall be said of the responsibility of the Canadian Church to give to these peoples, in obedience to the command of our risen Lord, the gospel of light, and love and liberty?

According to the government figures for 1920, Formosa has a total population of 3,714,899. Of these, 3,450,000 are Formosan Chinese, 85,000 are aborigines, while 153,000 are Japanese citizens. The rest are Chinese from the mainland and about

80 foreigners, consisting of Consuls, business men, teachers, Roman Catholic priests and British missionaries from England and Canada. Of the total population of the Island Beautiful, the Canadian Presbyterian Church has assumed the responsibility for the evangelization of upwards of one and one-half million. Is she adequately discharging her obligation?

Draper

O GOD, who hast made of one blood all nations of men, help us to recognize our kinship with all mankind and to count the men and women of Formosa our very brothers and sisters. May we, to whom in Thy mercy and wisdom the gospel of Thy Son has been made known and whose life has been enriched and uplifted thereby, think of them in love and humility.

DELIVER us from all racial self-esteem and from any depreciation of those who are less privileged than we. Touch our hearts with Thine own compassion for those whose heart and whose flesh cry out for Thee, the living God, but who can only grope in vain after Thee until they find Him who is the Way and also the Truth and the Life.

GIVE us to discern the priceless value and the unlimited possibilities of every child of Thine, however distant and different from ourselves. Help us to respect every human personality, to reverence the capacity for God in every soul and to share Thy yearning over every individual life to which Thou art longing to reveal Thyself. Grant this, O God, for the sake of Thy Son, Who is the Desire of Nations and the Light of the World. AMEN.

CHAPTER III

THE PATHFINDER OF NORTH FORMOSA

A S we have seen in the previous chapter, the Canadian Church was not the first to begin missionary work in the Island Beautiful. Two hundred years before its pioneer representative was sent, Dutch missionaries had been at work in the South and the island had been consecrated by their blood. In 1865, the English Presbyterian Church established its mission in the South. North Formosa, however, was virgin soil for missionary effort and into this field the Canadian Presbyterian Church was divinely led.

Early Years

The founder of the Canadian Presbyterian Mission in North Formosa, Rev. George Leslie Mackay, D.D., was born in the Township of Zorra, Oxford County, Ontario, on the 21st of March, 1844. His parents came to Canada from Sutherlandshire, Scotland, in 1830. His grandfather was a Highland soldier who had fought at Waterloo, a distinction that doubtless was not without its influence on the family of six children, of whom the future missionary was the youngest. At all events, George Leslie Mackay all his life carried with him, not only the bearing of a Highland soldier, but the authority of a Highland chieftain.

Those were stirring days in Presbyterian circles. The same year that Mackay was born, the Presbyterian Church in Canada passed through an experience similar to the memorable "Disruption" of the preceding year in Scotland. Many of the congregations withdrew from the "Auld Kirk" and formed the "Free Church." Among these was the Zorra congregation, to which Mackay 's parents belonged, and of which the minister was Rev. Donald MacKenzie, who, like many others, preached every Lord's Day in both Gaelic and English.

In those days there were few Sabbath schools or young people's societies. That did not mean, however, that the children of Zorra settlement received no religious instruction. It was indeed far otherwise. George's parents brought with them from the Highlands of Scotland their sacred traditions and strong religious convictions, and cherished them the more in their new log-cabin in the backwoods of Ontario. The books commonly found in the homes of the people in those days were the Holy Bible, the Confession of Faith, the Shorter Catechism, Boston's "Fourfold

State," "The Saint's Everlasting Rest," "The Anxious Enquirer," Guthrie's "Great Interest," Samuel Rutherford's "Letters," and "Memoirs of Robert Murray MacCheyne."

It was in such an atmosphere our Formosan hero was born, nurtured and partly equipped for his life work. From his earliest years George opened his heart to eternal realities. If you had asked him when he began to love his Saviour, he could not have told you. If you had asked him why he became a missionary he would have referred you to God's eternal purpose and counsel. From his childhood he was deeply impressed with things divine, and under the faithful ministry of Mr. MacKenzie, as well as the religious training of godly parents, he yielded his life fully to the service of the King of kings.

The godly, Highland home of those days produced strong, robust character. The altar of family worship was the chief corner-stone, and the atmosphere was wholesome and impressive. There the Sabbath of the Lord was a delight. The thoughtless might look upon the day as one of long, weary hours, but to George it was one of peculiar enjoyment. Then there was the memorable "Communion Season," when the Highland ministers, together with the "Men," spoke on the "Question." At such seasons, Rev. John Ross, of Brucefield, used often to assist Mr. MacKenzie, for it was through this man of God that Mr. Ross was led into a personal experience of Christ.

Guided by these religious teachers, George drank deeply at the fountain of religious truth. The Bible was to him a constantly open book. To him the ancient prophets were real. With his vivid imagination he saw them as giants standing on mountain peaks

of a great spiritual drama, and often longed to scale the heights from which they peered into the future and to see the expanding plains beneath. He was a great lover, too, of the Psalms, which, with many other passages, he learned by heart. Before reaching his teens, he had also committed to memory the Shorter Catechism.

After finishing, at an early age, his public school course, he followed his teacher, Mr. Shaw, an excellent school-master, to the high school in Omemee. Mackay never shared in the sports. He preferred a book and the quiet byways and green meadows to the playground.

Missionary Ambitions

At the age of sixteen, he secured a first-class teacher's certificate. He was, however, already hearing strange voices from unknown lands and having visions of regions beyond. Only the Eternal knew what was going on in Mackay's heart during those years of silent but persistent preparation. He was not an ordinary youth, and was not likely to follow the ordinary tracks of man. Two piercing eyes he had, but more piercing still were the eyes of his soul, with which he saw Him who is invisible and the life work that seemed to be mapped out for him by Providence.

Determination was written distinctly on his face, and having heard the divine call, he made up his mind that whatever talents God had given him were to be placed on the altar, without reserve,

for the service of his Lord and Master. Even in his youth there was much of the Highland mystic element fashioning his life. Few people knew what he was thinking about, and fewer still knew what his next move would be.

When a mere lad teaching school he used his spare hours in the study of theology and medicine. Few men, who, like Mackay, were not professionals in medicine, have had such a remarkable career in that sphere of service. Of special interest is his record in teeth extraction. As one reads of the number of teeth he extracted during his missionary career, in some years upwards of a thousand, one is tempted to imagine that his very presence among a group of Chinese produced a strange desire to get rid of their teeth.

As he grew to manhood his heart was stirred at the thought of the great needs of the heathen world. Had not the story of India, as told by that prince among missionaries, Dr. Alexander Duff, on his tour through Ontario in 1854, come to his ears when he was ten years of age? Had not the famous missionary to China, William Burns, passed through Zorra in his boyhood days and turned the young heart of the future Formosa missionary to that land of teeming millions? All these events were not mere accidents, but were of divine ordering, and they burned deep into his life. Dr. Duff he could never forget; Burns, of China, and China's millions were in his mind day and night.

At Princeton and Edinburgh

After a year at Knox College, Toronto, he left for Princeton Seminary. During his college course there he served two summers on a mission field at Mount Albert, north of Toronto. There are those who still remember the impression he made on that community.

In those days one could not be long in Princeton without hearing much of the great Scottish divines, Dr. Candlish and Dr. Guthrie. It was not strange, therefore, that as soon as Mackay graduated from Princeton he set out for Scotland, taking up his residence in Edinburgh, where he sat at the feet of those two Free Church worthies. That same winter he again came under the spell of Alexander Duff, then a veteran, with long, white, flowing beard, like a venerable prophet, who was touring Scotland, trying to kindle the missionary fires afresh in his fatherland. It was a difficult task. There was one heart, however, ready to respond to his fiery message. Young Mackay followed Duff up and down the land like a young Elisha in the shadow of Elijah.

His decision was reached. His life was to be devoted to service in a land in which Christ was not known. His next step was to return to Canada and offer himself for missionary service to his Church, although there were few in the home Church who knew anything of the youthful probationer.

Appointment and Ordination

His application for foreign mission work was in the hands of

the Committee and his speedy departure depended solely on the decision of the General Assembly, which met in Quebec city on the 2nd of June, 1871. The young probationer was invited to be present. The Assembly was agitated with questions of hymns and organs, Auld and Free Kirk problems, and the new Church Union movement. These questions, however, had little interest for young Mackay, whose thoughts were absorbed in the enterprise which had become the passion of his life, namely the evangelization of the world.

The Committee's report urged the Assembly "to favor mission work among the heathen," and stated that "a man has offered and the Church seems prepared to meet the liability. Mr. Mackay, a student of the Church, having passed the winter under Dr. Duff, is now in this city, ready to undertake the work which the Church may appoint." The Assembly accepted the Committee's report in the following minute:

"That the offer of Mr. George L. Mackay's services as a missionary to the heathen be cordially welcomed, and that he be, as he is hereby, called by this Assembly to go forth as a missionary of the Canada Presbyterian Church to the foreign field:

"That China be chosen as the field to which Mr. Mackay shall be sent;

"That the Presbytery of Toronto be authorized to ordain Mr. Mackay to the holy ministry, and to make arrangements, in accordance with the Foreign Mission Committee, for his designation to the work whereunto he has been called."

On the evening of September 19th, 1871, the ordination service took place in Gould Street Presbyterian Church, Toronto,

where Rev. John M. King, D.D., was pastor. That was a memorable evening, In addition to Mackay, there was ordained that evening a young probationer. Rev. George Bryce, who had been recommended by Dr. King to establish Manitoba College in Winnipeg. Both the Home Mission and Foreign Mission Committees were represented, the former to designate Rev. George Bryce to the work in the West, and the latter to designate Rev. George Leslie Mackay to that in the far East. These three men mentioned, each of whom afterwards gave such fruitful service to the Presbyterian Church, had, in turn, the honor of filling the Moderator's chair at the Assembly.

Mackay was now actually set apart for the work upon which his heart had been set so long. One month was left him for the visitation of the Canadian churches. He himself called this the "iceage" of the Presbyterian Church. Many of the ministers did not take him seriously, and consequently their congregations were by no means enthusiastic. But Mackay was not to be discouraged. In fact he struck out of his vocabulary the word "discouragement." He had seen a heavenly vision and to it he could not be disobedient. He had pledged himself faithfully to follow Jesus to a far distant land, and his Church had accepted him for that service.

Departure

Departure for his chosen field involved separation from home and loved ones. While in such natures as those of the Mackay

household sorrow may be buried out of sight, it is none the less keen, and Mackay shrank from this ordeal.

On the 19th of October, a month after his designation, he bade farewell to his people. His departure that morning was the talk of the district. "There goes George Leslie Mackay off to China. I wonder what will become of him?" one might be heard saying to another; while another, with a keener mind, uttered what was more significant: "You will never guess what the next report of Mackay will be; he has always been a mystery to us." Yes, off to China! Not quite a simple undertaking in those days. It was a grand venture, a great leap of faith in God's purpose and of trust in His infinite resources. His credentials were the "Great Commission," written large on the tables of his heart, and also on the fly-leaf of the Bible presented to him by the Foreign Mission Committee.

On the Voyage

On the first day of November, 1871, we find Mackay a passenger on board the America, in San Francisco harbor. As the ship moved out, and later as it left the mountain tips on the horizon, a sense of deep loneliness, such as he had never before experienced, swept over him. Behind him he left friends, many of whom, it is true, no doubt misunderstood him, ahead of him lay a new and strange land, with yet stranger people. Some of his feelings at that time he disclosed in his writings. "Sooner or later,"

he writes, "one enters Gethsemane; I found mine that day, and in the little cabin the soul was staggered for awhile."

It was doubtless cheering to him to look forward to landing in Hong-Kong, where the British Flag floated, and where he would be assured of British freedom and protection. A good deal of time on the voyage was spent in studying the map of China, in addition to several missionary books. Years before he had heard Rev. William Burns relate the story of the work in Swatow and Amoy, where the English Presbyterian Church had established promising mission centres. That story was still fresh in his mind. By the time he reached China, he had doubtless learned something also of Formosa, for many stories of adventure in that island had already spread throughout the East.

On his arrival in Hong-Kong he was met by Dr.Eitel, an English missionary, and the next day visited Canton, where he found two American missionaries, one of whom he had known at Princeton. A few days after reaching Hong-Kong, he was on his way to Swatow. The Swatow missionaries had been informed of his appointment to China, and had heard of his arrival. They had hoped that Mackay might co-operate with them in their mission work, but they did not know their man. He was soon convinced that this was not the field he was seeking, and so moved northward to visit the mission station at Amoy.

Echoes of Formosa had reached him, however, and he felt he could not settle anywhere till he had seen that island. So, drawn by the mystic cords of destiny, he is next to be found on board a small steamer making for Takow in the South of Formosa. He had strong conviction that, not China, but Formosa, was to be his

field of labor, and accordingly wrote home to the Foreign Mission Committee to that effect. The Committee at first questioned his wisdom, but his first report after landing removed their misgivings, and led them to the conclusion that divine leading had guided this choice of field by their first missionary to the far East.

The English Presbyterian Church had started work in the south of the island in 1865. Dr. James Maxwell, Rev. Hugh Ritchie, and others, had established a promising station at Takow and, at the time of Mackay's arrival, were opening a new station at the old capital, Tainan, from which place they had been driven a few years before. When Mackay landed in Takow, he learned that Mr. Ritchie and family were visiting chapels twentysix miles away. With a Chinese convert as a guide, he set out in search of the English missionary. That was in December, 1871. From then till the 7th of March, 1872, he was entertained in that missionary's home.

We have followed Mackay all the way from the home land to South Formosa. We see him now sitting in a corner of Mr. Ritchie's home, a Chinese teacher by his side. While studying Chinese colloquial, he makes a careful study of conditions throughout the island. He learns of the million Chinese in the North who have never heard the Gospel. He feels that the mystic touch of the hand that has hitherto led him is urging him to be up and enter the field in the North. At length he makes known his decision to Mr. Ritchie. "God bless you, Mackay," is his friend's glad response. So with the opening of spring, we find Mackay and Ritchie, with Dr. Dickson, who joins them at Anping, on board the Sea-Dragon, a small steamer north-bound, and on March 9th they reach the

harbor of Tamsui.

Beginning Work in North Formosa

No other spot in the north of Formosa is so beautiful, whether viewed from the land or from the sea, as Tamsui harbor. The charm of such a landscape touched the Canadian missionary, and Mr. Ritchie's exclamation, "Mackay, this is your parish, "found its echo in his heart. It was indeed his parish for twenty-nine years of arduous, zealous labors.

From the harbor could be seen the old Dutch Fort, the British Consulate, the lofty Daiton mountains, whose highest peak rose 3,600 feet above sea level; and across the river, more commanding still, towered to a height of 2,100 feet beautiful Koan-im. The little town of Tamsui, with a population of five thousand, nestled along the river-bank, and extended over the hill above. A feeling of adventure, mingled with a strange and compelling attractiveness, filled the mind of the young Canadian missionary, to whom the whole territory was handed over with the prayer and blessing of his fellow missionaries. A simpler way of transferring territory which belonged to the King of kings could not be imagined.

As Mackay stood looking at the whole panorama, the mountains, the river winding southward like a monster serpent, the villages on its banks and the green paddy-fields mounting the hillsides step by step, and as he thought of the multitudes there

who were without Christ, he felt his heart strangely warmed. The field which his Lord had entrusted to him, far exceeding in natural beauty his fondest expectations, actually stretched before him, awaitting the seed-sowing, the cultivation and the future harvest. It was an historic moment for George Leslie Mackay and for the Presbyterian Church in Canada.

In those days, Tamsui, for all its beauty of location, was a town of narrow lanes and endless din, of filth and smells, of rats, and, above all, of poisonous mosquitoes. It was Saturday when they arrived. Sunday was spent in the warehouse of a British merchant.

On Monday morning they started southward, on foot, to explore the land. No doubt the three missionaries enjoyed an abundance of merriment and pleasantry on their journey. They would not have exchanged their lot for all the comforts of a Western palace. From the absence of any reference to Mackay's sense of humor, one is led to conclude that he did not possess too much of this wholesome virtue. He always appeared serious, not only in the presence of foreigners, but also among the Chinese. He was extremely sensitive. There is every indication, however, that on this journey he was particularly happy in spirit, and now that his field of labor was settled and the consequent strain he had been under was relieved, he could enter into every innocent hilarity that might be going the rounds. From the records left of this trip, the experiences of the trio must have been intensely interesting and novel to the young missionary, as they endeavored to accomplish the impossible task of evading Chinese smells, of swallowing Chinese mince-meats, of defying Formosan mosquitoes, of teaching the pigs better manners, and of becoming reconciled

to the fellowship of the familiar guests of a Chinese inn. In the course of a few days, they reached the most northerly station of the South Mission, where the boundary line between that and the new mission was defined. After a few days spent among the converts in a Pepohoan village, Mackay, with one Chinese, started back to Tamsui, there to begin his work alone among those who hated and despised the "barbarian."

Early Experiences

Many of Mackay's experiences during the first few months are recorded in other volumes. That the arrival of the Canadian missionary, a Formosan preacher and a cook, should cause such commotion, and stir up so much animosity at the very beginning, may be a surprise to some. Before Mackay arrived, wild rumors were in circulation about the "Jesus Doctrine." It was reported that the foreign missionaries plucked out the eyes and hearts of all the converts after death to make medicine, that they sent men to the market-places to throw poisonous drugs on meat and vegetables. These, and other stories still wilder, were freely circulated. An idea that was prevalent, over which the people were much excited, was that foreigners came with the purpose of taking possession of the island. Some time before Mackay arrived in Tamsui, the Chinese in South Formosa, instigated by influential men, molested both Roman Catholic and English mission chapels. On receiving

the report, the British Consul, who was at the time in Hong-Kong, sent a British man-of-war direct to Anping. The Chinese were alarmed and pled with the English missionaries to continue their work, promising no further trouble.

First Fruits

While crossing the Pacific, Mackay had prayed that God would give him as his first convert a young man of such gifts and graces as would make him effective in preaching the gospel. The Lord seemed to be preparing the way for an answer to his prayer. One afternoon, after Mackay had settled in his little hut in Tamsui, a man of pleasing demeanor and above the average in intelligence, entered the room, desirous of talking with the missionary. He had travelled extensively in China and was therefore more ready to enter into conversation with a foreigner. On his second visit, Mackay gave the young man a hymn book. It was not long before the missionary became fully convinced that this was the one for whom he had prayed.

The story of Giam-a-hoa's conversion is related in "From Far Formosa." He developed into a man of singular ability in every line of Christian work. He was a good teacher, and preached with clearness of thought and language. The young missionaries could follow him, both in conversation and in the pulpit, much more easily than they could any other native. He acquired a remarkable

knowledge of Church law and order, and seemed to have minute acquaintance with all the affairs of mission work, Mackay put absolute confidence in A-hoa, and made him his lifelong companion.

Mackay tells the story of A-hoa's first prayer in the following words: "He never attempted public prayer in his life before, and the request came upon him unexpectedly. Immediately he fell on his knees before a rickety old bamboo chair. He was terribly in earnest, and his halting words and broken petitions were charged with most intense emotions. Grasping the arms of the chair firmly with both hands, he shoved it over the hard, uneven floor, making a hideous, creaking accompaniment to his faltering sentences. By the time his prayer was finished he had moved half-way across the room."

Before long A-hoa had three companions who, in after years, rendered much useful service for the Church. One of these was Tan He, who became the first pastor called by the people to a settled pastorate; another was Go Khoan-ju, who for forty years preached in North Formosa. These young disciples became greatly attached to their new teacher and under his teaching made good progress in the knowledge of Christian truth.

On the second Sabbath of February, 1873, almost a year after Mackay's arrival in North Formosa, five converts, in the presence of an astonished and frenzied Chinese mob, publicly professed their faith in Jesus Christ through the rite of baptism. On the following Sabbath, the same young converts sat round the table of the Lord. Thus, through these sacraments, the Christian Church was founded in North Formosa.

The record of incident after incident moves on. The week following, we find Mackay with his converts opening the first Christian chapel at the little village of Go-ko-khi. In this chapel he performed his first Chinese marriage ceremony, a ceremony which even to-day creates much excitement.

Reinforcements Arrive

The North Formosa Mission was now founded, but the task of evangelizing the multitudes in that region was becoming increasingly serious. The medical needs of the people must have led Mackay to feel that the starting of medical work would help probably more than anything else to remove existing suspicions, for he had not been long in Formosa before he wrote home asking that a medical missionary be sent out. In response, Rev. J. B. Fraser, M.D., was appointed in 1874 as Dr. Mackay's colleague, and on January 29th of the following year he and his family reached Formosa. One can readily understand something of the nature of the welcome accorded them by the senior missionary. Dr. Fraser's letters written at that time not only voice his deep sense of the worth of the work, but show that, with a keen and accurate mind, he had a high estimate of the value of medical work in the missionary enterprise. Dr. Mackay's letters, on the other hand, tell of his high appreciation of Dr. Fraser's personal character and of his medical skill. It was a great disappointment, when, on account of the death

of his wife. Dr. Fraser, with his two motherless daughters, had to return to Canada in 1877.

The following year. Rev. Kenneth Junor, a man who had already given promise of a successful career in Bermuda, was appointed as colleague to Dr. Mackay. Mr. Junor, with his wife and their boy, Frank, sailed from San Francisco on April 1st, 1878. Shortly after their arrival, Dr. Mackay wrote of the new missionaries, "I need not tell you that I will never forget the kindness of Mr. and Mrs. Junor. They are getting on famously here. God bless my dear fellow-worker and partner for their care of one so unworthy as myself." Mr. Junor, in turn, was much impressed with Mackay's force of character and his physical and mental energy.

An incident mentioned in a letter from Dr. Mackay reveals a very tender side of his nature. "In the midst of my illness, and when Mr. Junor was suffering from a severe attack of fever, their dear little boy was suddenly prostrated, took convulsions, and on Friday at 2 p.m. was taken home to glory. Dear Frank! Just the evening before he died, he carried a plate with food into my room, got up on the bed and sat beside me. Frank was a real good boy, and now he is yonder, away, away, in the highest heavens, around the throne where ten thousand children stand."

Mackay's Marriage

During the same year two other important events occurred

in the life of Mackay. One was the taking of Bang-kah, and the other, more important still for his whole future career, the taking of a wife from among the Chinese people, a step which he, without doubt, believed would further the cause which was pressing upon his heart, namely, the establishment of a self-supporting and self-governing Church. The following message from Mackay to the Foreign Mission Committee brought no little surprise: "In May I was married to a Chinese lady by the British Consul at Tamsui, and at once returned to the country to visit the stations with her."

Mrs. Mackay from her earliest years possessed a strong and attractive personality. Upon the Christians who constantly came to their home she exercised a wholesome influence. Patient, humble and winsome, she was always a friend to the poor, and those in trouble never failed to find in her a helper. Many others in her situation would have become haughty and overbearing, but it was not so with Mrs. Mackay. She still retains her genial and kindly disposition, and is much beloved both by the native Christians and the missionaries. Toward her husband's successors she has never manifested any jealousy or aloofness. There are few whose fellowship the missionaries appreciate more than that of Mrs. George Leslie Mackay.

◆ ◆ ◆ · · · · · · · · · · · · · ·

𝔇𝔯𝔞𝔭𝔢𝔯

O THOU who dost work in men both to will and to do of Thy good pleasure, we praise Thee for those daring and devoted spirits who have pioneered the way for the Gospel of Thy Son in many parts of the earth. Especially do we thank Thee for this dauntless messenger of Thy grace who in obedience to Thy call fared forth to an island that was far distant and a people who knew not of Thy love, rejoicing that Thou didst count him worthy to suffer loneliness and hardship for the Gospel's sake.

H ELP us through his example to a new appreciation of the gift of Thy Son Who came into our human life and made Himself of no reputation, taking on Him the form of a servant and pouring out His life, despised and rejected of men, in order that we might have fullness of life now and for evermore.

G RANT, O God, that we too may joyfully accept Thy terms of discipleship, day by day, leaving all to follow Thee in any way of duty into which Thy will may lead us. If there be a cross let us endure it; if there be shame let us despise it for the joy that is set before us of winning Thy favor, which is better than life, and of serving our generation by the will of God. For the sake of Jesus Christ, our Lord. AMEN.

CHAPTER IV

MORE ABOUT THE PATHFINDER

First Furlough

THERE were three things Mackay of Formosa never expected to do: he would never sit in a sedan chair, he would never take a furlough, and he would never marry. But he was not the first man who changed his mind and kept his greatness. From the time of Mackay's arrival in Formosa, the Canadian Church was kept constantly informed of the work which appeared to carry so much promise. The Foreign Mission Committee had scarcely time to take in the significance of one report when another, more interesting still, would reach them. As year followed year the work

grew and flourished. In the midst of this remarkable development, the founder of the mission, with mingled feelings, had to face his first furlough. Word was received that Mackay of Formosa was coming home.

Some unfortunate experiences he had on landing in Canada in 1880 marred somewhat the beginning of his furlough. At last he reached his native Province. His home-coming aroused much interest, particularly in the Zorra district. Many there were who wanted to see and hear the man who had slept among savages, had had such hair-breadth escapes, had defied Chinese mandarins and Chinese mobs, and who had brought home with him as his wife a native of Formosa. To see the "Blackbearded Barbarian" who had such a record was no ordinary event.

Among the Churches

After a short rest, calls from various congregations began pouring in upon him. Everywhere multitudes were eager to hear him, and he was worth hearing. It is safe to say that never in the history of our Canadian missions has there been a missionary who could rouse the emotions of his hearers as could Mackay of Formosa. Few could rise to such a high pitch of missionary enthusiasm and genuine eloquence. "We heard Mackay of Formosa and will never forget him" is the testimony to this day of many who then were thrilled by his appeals. His presence on

the platform, his characteristic gestures, his black, piercing eyes, his passionate utterance and his complete selfabandonment moved people intensely. The burning fire within his own soul kindled many hearts. When he spoke of "Beautiful Formosa" it was with a wistful yearning that revealed his love for the island.

Describing the impression he made while on furlough, the *Record* had the following: "Dr. Mackay is a prince among missionaries, possessing, in a marked degree, self-denial, tact, courage and enthusiasm beyond most men. We need not tell our readers how successful he has been." An Assembly report records the interest he aroused in that body: "The presence of Rev. G. L. Mackay, D.D., who has been so pre-eminently useful in Formosa, was a feature of special interest in the General Assembly. His earnest and pathetic missionary addresses will be long remembered by all who heard him." During this furlough, Queen's University very fittingly conferred on him the degree of Doctor of Divinity.

His Chinese wife, who accompanied him whereever he went, created much interest. The reception accorded both was most enthusiastic. By request they visited the Eastern Provinces, where they received a welcome no less cordial than that in his own Province.

Before they left Canada the churches of the Woodstock district held a farewell meeting for them in the Woodstock Methodist Church, at which the Honorable Oliver Mowat was present and expressed his deep interest in Mackay and his work. Mrs. Mackay, on being conducted to the platform, told briefly, her husband acting as interpreter, of her strange and varied experiences in Canada. A still more important event of the evening was the presentation to

Dr. Mackay of $6,215, for the purpose of building in Formosa a training school for preachers.

In November, 1881, Dr. and Mrs. Mackay set sail on their return to their beloved Formosa. Thoughts, retrospective and prospective, filled his mind and stirred his heart as he started on this his second journey to the Far East. He had been home, and on every hand had been shown remarkable kindness and grateful honor. Moreover, he felt that he had been enabled to remove prejudice, to correct false rumors and to arouse the Home Church to a deeper interest and fuller sense of her responsibility. He could now return with the satisfaction of knowing that his first furlough had been by no means unfruitful. There was also the joy that came as they thought of the welcome that awaited them in Formosa.

Back in Formosa

Arriving again in the land of his adoption, Mackay began at once to plan for the new training school. As he had outlined in his mind during the voyage the new "Oxford College," he could almost see the workmen in the quarries cutting out the stone slabs and the men in the forests felling the timbers, and could hear the Chinese shouts as the material was gathered together. His mind was continually occupied, while crossing the Pacific, with the near realization of his long-cherished dream. On the 30th of November, as they neared Formosa, he expressed his feelings in these words:

"Already Formosa's mountain ranges seem to rise up before us. Roll on, wild Pacific! I never expect to cross you again. Winds and waves, favor us still."

The reception given the Mackays by the Formosan Christians was most enthusiastic. The seashore at Tamsui was lined with his spiritual children, waiting to greet their beloved leader and his wife as they landed. As they stepped on shore the shout arose, "Kai Boksu, peng-an! Kai Boksu-niu, peng-an!" — "Pastor Mackay, Peace! Mrs. Mackay, Peace!" It was a happy hour for both of them, to be back again in their home and among their beloved people.

The memory of his experiences in Canada only intensified the enthusiasm of the missionary on his return. Rev. Kenneth Junor had been in charge during his absence, and of the manner in which he had managed the affairs of the mission Mackay spoke in the highest terms. Indeed, one can imagine that it may have been a not unprofitable season for the converts. With the quietness that characterized the different type of leadership, they would have opportunity to realize more fully what they had actually committed themselves to when they accepted the foreigner's religion. The Christians may have learned, too, that God uses varied types of men for the extension of his kingdom.

Building Oxford College

No sooner was Mackay back than hammers were pounding

rocks in the mountain quarries, while saws, axes and planes were at work getting out and fitting beams and fashioning doors and windows for the new college. Stones and lumber came together as by the magic touch of a wizard's wand. The returned missionary changed at once the quiet routine of the mission compound into the old-time activity. The foundations were laid; daily the walls rose higher, and soon the superstructure took on the appearance of a miniature palace to the astonished admirers.

The building was completed and fittingly named Oxford College, after Oxford county, where the money for it had been raised by Mackay's friends. The formal opening took place in June, 1882, just six months after his return from furlough, with foreigners and many of the native converts present. It was an historic event in the history of the mission. Two interesting items on the day's programme were the presentation to the wives of the trained helpers of twenty-four sewing machines which had been given by Mr. Wanzer of Hamilton, and the announcement of a gift from Captain and Mrs. Mackay, of Detroit, of money toward the erection of the Tamsui hospital, and $500 to help in building the chapel at Bang-kah.

Mr. Junor Invalided Home

The college finished, Mackay was keener for work than ever. By this time Mr. Junor was speaking the language fluently, but was

subject to constant attacks of malarial fever. The same disease was giving Mackay also no little trouble.

The policy of living like the people, in order to appear in perfect sympathy with them, may be followed, but nature's laws are exacting and any breach carries its penalty. Time, money and much physical distress are saved by following a reasonable course of self-protection in all Eastern lands. Mr. Junor, broken down nervously and physically, was compelled to return to Canada in December, 1882.

Mass Movement on the Giran Plain

The same year Mackay sent home a glowing account of the work in Giran Plain on the east coast. After describing conditions there, and stating the urgency of the situation, he closed his letter with a request for $2,500 to enable him to build two chapels, that together would accommodate two thousand hearers. "For God's sake, do not refuse, and don't delay." he added. It would have been interesting to have watched the members of the Home Committee as they listened to this story of the mass movement on the east coast, and especially as they heard the heroic appeal for money to build two chapels. What could they do in the circumstances? There was only one thing, and it was done speedily. A cable carried the message, "The money will be sent." Of the mass movement here referred to little need be said. The Pepohoans on the Giran Plain

are fast dying out, or are being assimilated by the Chinese, who on this beautiful plain number one hundred thousand. In the early days, the Gospel had no access to these latter, but of recent years an effectual door has been opened and the work is very encouraging.

Ordaining Native Preachers

We have already noticed that Rev. Kenneth Junor and his family had to return home on account of ill-health. Rev. John Jamieson and his wife reached Formosa the following year. About this time Dr. Mackay seemed to change his policy regarding the sending of missionaries from the home land. He gave his attention more anxiously than ever before to the producing of a native ministry, as his chief hope for the future. In the spring of 1884 he launched out on his long-cherished policy by ordaining two native preachers, both promising and capable men — Giam A-hoa, his first convert, and Tan He, one of the first five who were baptized In the spring of 1873. After ordaining them, he wrote home, "The Foreign Mission Board need not concern itself about sending out another man," and in another letter, "Do not think that the men you send here are superior, I long to see a native church self-supporting." The comment of the Committee on this statement, which appeared in the Record at the time, was somewhat non-committal. "The Committee thoroughly agrees with the editor of the Record, who says Ve are heartily at one with Dr. Mackay in the

belief that the raising of a native ministry is the shortest method of solving the missionary problem,' only we are agreeably surprised to find that he is in a position to inaugurate it so soon."

Dr. Mackay's policy is one with which all his successors would heartily agree, but they fear that with but one foreign missionary, or even two, his desired goal would not be reached for many years or even generations. It is worthy of note that with the increase of missionaries, male and female, self-support has increased more than fivefold. The present attitude of the North Formosa Mission Council may be gathered from the request it sent home, in 1922, for at least fifteen additional missionaries.

The French Blockade

The task of supervising the many outstations, where preachers were seeking to meet the spiritual needs of the converts, was becoming too much for the missionary and his two ordained pastors. Furthermore, a heavy cloud was hanging over North Formosa. French warships were creating much anxiety on the Chinese coast. Rumors were changed to facts when, on the 5th of August, 1885, five French warships approached Keelung harbor. North Formosa was in commotion, and as usual the Christians became the objects of persecution. In October, the French came around the north coast to Tamsui harbor, which they blockaded. The British Consul advised that Mrs. Mackay and children, Mr.

and Mrs. Jamieson, and two English ladies, proceed immediately to HongKong for safety. Dr. Mackay, every inch a soldier, refused to leave his converts to the mercy of unknown perils. After the others had left, and while the French were bombarding the fort and the surrounding district, Mackay was prostrated with a severe attack of malaria from which it was reported he was unconscious for days. He was advised to take the sea voyage to Hong-Kong and from there he was not allowed to return until the blockade was raised.

It was a time of great anxiety, both for the Church and the missionary. Much property had been destroyed. As soon, however, as all fear of the French had been removed, the task of rebuilding and repairing chapels began. Mackay, on sending a request to the Chinese official. General Loo, for indemnity, was granted $10,000. With this money he built chapels in Manka, Shakko and Shinten, and the work of the mission went on as before. ^ It seemed as if every opposition was only a fresh incentive for a further attack on the kingdom of darkness, and a new stimulus to the enthusiasm of the intrepid missionary. After the smoke had passed away, he wrote home, *"Nec tamen consumebatur."*

Arrival of the Gaulds

In 1891 Mr. Jamieson died, after having spent six years in North Formosa, and his wife returned to Canada. Mackay was once

more alone, and finding the task of supervising a growing work too much for one man, he wrote home to the Board asking for a colleague. The Committee responded by appointing Rev. William Gauld, and in 1892, he, with Mrs. Gauld, reached Formosa.

William Gauld was born at Westminster, in the county of Middlesex, Ontario. When a lad of sixteen he and his brother George heard Mackay, when on his first furlough, in St. Andrew's Church, London. After the evening service, while walking home, William, turning to his older brother, said, "I am going to be a missionary." As he grew up the conviction deepened. His mind, however, was turning to India. After serving as public school teacher, he took the course in arts at the University of Toronto, and in theology at Knox College. When the Foreign Mission Board was anxiously looking for a suitable colleague to join Mackay in his work, William Gauld's name was considered for the position. The report of the Committee stated, "That Mr. Gauld had recommended himself by the work which he had done in college, in the home field, and by the interest he had manifested in Foreign Mission work. He was recommended as one well fitted for the responsible position to which he was called."

Mackay's Second Furlough

After the arrival of Mr. and Mrs. Gauld, Mackay prepared to return on his second furlough. Festivities in honor of Dr. and

Mrs. Mackay and family were at once planned by the pastors and preachers. The news spread abroad. Both Christians and heathen joined in the great farewell. No less than seven hundred converts were there to bid their loved missionary farewell. In a letter written at the time, he said, "Heathen and Christian, wealthy and indigent, literary and unlearned, combined to show us respect, and wish us a safe journey to the fatherland, and a quick return. Bands of music greeted us and escorted us from station to station, amid the firing of guns, the waving of banners and the whizzing of squibs. A man awaited us alongside the road with a hundred pounds of beef. Wonderful! Wonderful! The changes these eyes have seen in twenty-one years! As all classes treated me as they liked when making my first tour throughout North Formosa, so I allowed converts and others to do just as they felt disposed on this last trip."

On the 6th of September, nine months after the arrival of Mr. and Mrs. Gauld, Dr. Mackay and family sailed for *Canada on the Empress of India*. On their first furlough there were but two of them; now there were, in addition, Mary, Bella and George, a small Mackay clan, and when in the Highland kilts they made an interesting group. They took with them Mr. Koa Kau, a bright young Chinese student, who in later years married Bella Mackay, and for several years served in the hospital with Dr. Ferguson. He is now an elder in the largest church in Taihoku city.

It was a heavy responsibility for Mr. Gauld, with only a few months experience of the work and with but little knowledge of the language, to be left alone. Mackay, in a letter written just before his departure, expressed his confidence thus: "Mr. Gauld will make his first attempt at preaching next Sabbath. He will visit

the people and preach as he is able, see that all mission property is kept in repair, provide preachers with periodicals... administer the sacraments of baptism and the Lord's supper... This I am sure he will do well and *true*, as he has shown himself earnest and true among us. Mrs. Gauld has her hands full — I consider she is doing her duty, as she has done in her own sphere all along, and with her quiet way, and earnest, sensible manner, her influence will be greater than if she were attempting the impossible."

Mrs. Gauld has now spent over thirty years in Formosa. Few women have got as near the Formosan people as she has during her experience of missionary life. She has nursed them, washed their sores, cured their ailments, turned their mourning into laughter, and endeared herself to them in a remarkable manner. Her happy, buoyant spirit, her passion for music, her love and loyalty have won for her a large place in the hearts of the Christians. She has turned musicians out of what appeared to be most hopeless material, trained young men and women to play and sing in a manner that reflects great credit on her musical ability. By her training of students in our various institutions, a work in which she is still engaged, she has rendered a service of great value to the Formosan Church.

In Canada Once More

The Mackays received a warm welcome on their arrival in

Canada in September, much interest being shown both in the missionary himself and in his family. The following winter was spent visiting the congregations throughout Ontario. Now in the prime of life, Mackay maintained all the splendid vigor and intensity of his young manhood. Very reserved and extremely sensitive, to many ministers at home he was a mystery, but though they might consider him eccentric or peculiar, they admired him.

Mackay was scarcely ever defeated in his purpose. A Highland congregation in Glengarry, however, on one occasion proved more than a match for him. A minister who once labored in that district tells the story of this defeat, which nevertheless resulted in victory. With a map of his beloved Formosa, he visited this congregation. When the elders learned that it was Mackay's intention to spread a map at the service on the Sabbath day, they simply, but emphatically, told him such could not be done. The contention between the session and the missionary can be imagined. It resulted in the Highland missionary being defeated by the Highland elders, and Mackay having to address the congregation without the map. It is not difficult to imagine something of the Celtic fire that burned that morning, and, some passages of the address directed at the session. But the victory? Of these elders, three each left a legacy to Foreign Missions of about a thousand dollars. The clash of arms between the clans resulted, as usual, in favor of Mackay!

It was but natural that there should be a general desire throughout the Church that the missionary pioneer and his remarkable work should be recognized and honored by his appointment to the highest office in the gift of the Church. Accordingly, when the Assembly met that year in St. John, New Brunswick, Mackay was

chosen Moderator, a position that he filled with great acceptance.

The Work Left Behind

Whilst the Mackay family were enjoying a two years' furlough in Canada, the work in Formosa was making quiet, but steady, progress. The fears and misgivings in the minds of the members of the Foreign Mission Committee were removed by the reports received, as the following record indicates: "It is with much satisfaction that Mr. Gauld has entered on his work in Formosa with such sympathy and judgment as encourages us to expect gratifying results. The Committee was somewhat alarmed lest Dr. Mackay's return home would lay upon him a responsibility he might not be able to bear. These fears have been dissipated. Several difficulties have arisen, in which Mr. Gauld and the native pastors and preachers associated with him in the oversight of the work have acted with such wisdom as to assure us that the mission is safe in his hands."

The work thus steadily prospering was thrown into confusion by the war between China and Japan. The taking possession of the island by the Japanese, in 1895, has been dealt with in chapter two. Mr. Gauld was the only missionary in charge at the time. His patience, good judgment, and common sense throughout that exciting and trying period meant very much to the mission. It was a time of great anxiety for the native Church for the Christians

suffered much. We can picture something of the experiences Mackay, so far away from his beloved converts, went through in this their time of trial. The suspense of the Foreign Mission Board can be gathered from the following, which is taken from the preface to their report for 1895 : "The Eastern war caused a good deal of speculation and anxiety as to the probable effect upon our mission should Formosa become a Japanese possession. Of this only can we, at present, be assured, that the God of the Nations will rule over all... In the meantime we gratefully report that Mr. and Mrs. Gauld have been in health and protected from harm... The latest is that all foreign ladies had left Formosa, and that Mrs. Gauld, upon the advice of the British Consul, had gone to Amoy." The report which followed, written by Mr. Gauld, was one of the best in the history of the mission.

In Formosa Once More

In the fall of the year 1895 Mackay and his family reached Formosa. One can imagine how eagerly, after his deep anxiety, he greeted his friends, native and foreign, and sought exact news of the situation. His testimony regarding the manner in which Mr. Gauld and the native pastors had carried on the work during that critical period is a striking tribute — "The work has been kept intact."

In 1899, Mr. Gauld and his family returned to Canada, on

their first furlough. Dr. Mackay was left alone, supervising the work, under a new Government. The changes brought about were gradual. The authorities were friendly disposed towards the Christians, and the work was allowed to go on unhindered. Though unremitting in his labors, the fell disease, which finally proved fatal to the intrepid missionary, was developing rapidly. Mr. Gauld and his family returned in the fall of 1900, and for the first time Mackay welcomed back to Formosa a colleague who had been on furlough. Gripping his hand in an unusual manner, he exclaimed, with quivering lip, "I am thankful you are back to Formosa."

Fighting His Last Battle

When the disease reached a more critical stage he took a trip to Hong-Kong to consult specialists, who pronounced his trouble incurable. He, however, himself did not accept the verdict till almost the very last. Dr. McClure, one of our Canadian Presbyterian doctors in Honan, was sent to comfort the veteran missionary during the last few weeks of his life. To the very end, he fought the disease like a lion recently caged. Those who were privileged to see him in those days claimed they had never seen such vitality displayed in any human being. He could not speak plainly, but he had the lectures read to the students in his presence. One day Dr. McClure gave him a hint that there was a possibility of the disease doing rapid work, and that the end might be near. Leaving him,

he went over to Mr. Gauld's home. From there, looking toward Mackay's house, they saw the dying man on the verandah, pacing up and down, waging the final, desperate fight with the last enemy.

The end came on the second of June, 1901, when the Presbyterian Church in Canada was called upon to mourn the loss of one of her greatest missionaries and the most striking of her missionary heroes. It was a day of deep sorrow and of large significance to the Church in Formosa. But the grief of the Church was not hopeless or despairing. The founder of the mission had been taken away, but the great Head of the Church still remained.

Summary of His Work and Character

Dr. George Leslie Mackay passed away, but his works follow him. The fruitage of his twenty-nine years of missionary service was marvellous. We have seen the conditions under which he began his work. When he died, there were in the mission one foreign missionary and his wife, two native pastors, sixty preachers, twenty-four Bible women, nearly eighteen hundred communicants and sixty chapels, of which more than half were established in Pepohoan villages, although with the passing away of the Pepohoan race, these have practically disappeared. This fruitage is the more remarkable when one remembers that it was the fruitage mainly of the labors of one missionary, together with his native helpers.

The writer never saw Mackay. He has endeavored, however,

to discover all the information possible relating to him and his work, especially from the Formosan brethren upon whom the impression made by their beloved leader was deep and lasting. The estimate given in these two chapters is based upon this information gathered from many sources.

Dr. Mackay was no more nearly perfect than many others. His zeal many times overcame his judgment; he saw wonderful things where many others saw only the ordinary; he had a graphic way of telling stories and describing events; he loved the mountains and gorges and disliked the plains and the common places. His fiery temperament sometimes led him into difficulties, but he could never retrace his steps, or accept defeat. He was a soldier by nature, a commander who seldom consulted his subordinates. He never displayed organizing gifts, for his own inspiring personality was strong enough to be the sum total of the organizing factors of his whole mission work. He created, perhaps, more awe than affection, more admiration than appreciation but this was inevitable in a character so reserved and so far removed from the close companionship of others.

Those were days of Chinese mandarins, of wild robberies, of political oppression, of actual lawlessness. Tenderness and timidity would have been misunderstood and might have been the ruin of the cause. Some men would have wilted in the presence of some of the dangerous situations that the heroic founder of the North Formosa mission had to face. But those days of bitter opposition, of deep prejudices and suspicion have passed away. Methods that then seemed successful would be entirely unsuitable in these days of law and order. Let us be thankful for the day in

which we live, and seek to do our share as faithfully as did those who have left us such an example of loyalty to a great cause and passionate enthusiasm for their Godgiven task.

Mackay seldom, if ever, met a person on whom he did not leave a lasting impression, many of which are on record. In closing this chapter, we cannot do better than quote from some of these:

"High over all other features of his character, redeeming him from littleness, ennobling his nature, adding force to his faith and making his life a factor in the Church's history, was his simple trust in God, his unquestioning belief in an evangelical Gospel, his deep-cut conviction as to his own life work, and as to the mastership of Jesus Christ in the lives of men, unreserved enthusiasm, passionate surrender of himself to Jesus as Redeemer and King. Brave little man ... it is good to know his kind; and to have his face clear in one's memory is to be fore-strengthened against the common men, and the presence of common life."

"He was a little man, firm and active, of few words, unflinching courage and one whose sound common sense was equalled only by his devotion to his Master."

"To me. Dr. Mackay shines out as one of the greatest missionaries of any age. We may thank God for all he was and did."

Dr. Mackay's grave is a beautiful spot in a corner of "Fort Meadow," at the back of the new middle school grounds. It is enclosed by a brick wall, and by his side rests the saintly Tan-he, the first pastor inducted into a self-supporting charge in North Formosa.

Draper

O THOU Who art the Lord of the harvest and hast ordained that except a grain of wheat fall into the ground and die it abideth alone, but that if it die it bringeth forth much fruit, we make mention before Thee of those missionaries in Formosa who have yielded up their lives for Thy sake and the Gospel's; those who in broken health have had to return to their native land and those who still are working yonder, giving up their lives day by day in unstinted service. Fulfil, we pray Thee, Thy law of the harvest and grant an abundant fruitage from this sacrifice of love.

M AKE us worthy to be numbered with them as co-workers together with God for the redemption of the Formosan people and of all mankind. May our hearts burn within us, may a new love for Thee and for our fellow men be kindled in our lives, may we be seized upon by a new enthusiasm for service, as we consider their loyal devotion to Thee.

I T is in obedience to Thine own command that we pray Thee to thrust forth many laborers into this and all Thy harvest fields. May all Thy people have the spirit of the harvest worker, toiling and interceding for the salvation of the peoples of the world, until Thou shalt see of the travail of Thy soul and be satisfied. For Thy Name's sake. AMEN.

CHAPTER V

THE NEW ERA IN NORTH FORMOSA

The New Era in Mission Policy

THE Transition

With the passing of the founder, a new and extremely difficult situation faced the mission. The Formosan Christians were fully persuaded that Canada had no other "Kai Bok-su" to send, for he was so entirely different from any other they had hitherto known. Moreover, they were in a position now to express more freely what had been finding a place in their minds for some time, due no doubt, in a large measure, to the fact that in the South Mission there existed a fully organized

Church under a Presbytery. There was the feeling that they might not need any more foreign missionaries, but that, with the help of Mr. Gauld, the native leaders could carry on the work. It was evident that they had not yet fully realized the greatness nor the seriousness of their task. It was the wise judgment and firmness of Mr. Gauld and the good hand of God on both the mission and the missionary that guided the mission so smoothly and successfully through that critical period.

Coming of Thurlow Fraser

It was but natural that Mr. Gauld should feel more keenly than ever the need of a colleague, and urgently request that a missionary be sent at once to share in the growing burdens of the Mission. In response, Rev. Thurlow Fraser, a graduate of Queen's University, was appointed, and with his wife reached Formosa in the fall of 1902. From the first Mr. Fraser took up language study with vigor and enthusiasm. His free, whole-hearted manner and buoyant spirit appealed strongly to the Chinese, especially to the preachers and students. He made rapid progress in the study of the language, and during his short term of service gained a close acquaintance with the problems of the native Church. It was during his time that an important document of large significance to the work of the Mission was prepared and forwarded to the General Assembly.

Desire for Larger Democracy

During Mackay's later days, Giam Chheng-hoa was his sole adviser. Tan-he, the saintly pastor of Shinten, having passed away some years previously, Giam Chheng-hoa was the only

one who could help in the executive side of the work. No doubt more authority had fallen to his lot than was conducive to mutual good-will. There was a growing dissatisfaction with the policy of perpetuating the rule of a few in Church affairs. The missionaries felt the situation and took steps to meet the nascent, democratic spirit of the infant Church.

An Historic Document

At this juncture, the congregation at Manka sent an urgent request for permission to call as their pastor their young, progressive preacher, Tan Chbeng-gi, son of Tan-he and son-in-law of Dr. Mackay, at the same time promising to make this new charge self-supporting. This request faced the missionaries with the need of establishing a Formosan Presbytery. Considerable time was spent and great care taken in ascertaining the policies prevailing in other missions. The result was the forwarding, on the 9th of May, 1904, of the historic document above referred to, extracts from which are as follows:

"Whereas we believe that the time has come when our Church in North Formosa should be organized into a Presbytery, in order that the brethren may take part in the government and administration of the affairs of the Church, and, by practice, learn the art and acquire the power of self-government, and

Whereas this question has been definitely brought to our attention by the request of one of our congregations for the privilege of extending a call to a preacher to become its pastor, and the expressed willingness of other congregations

to do likewise,

Therefore we, the members of the North Formosa mission staff, petition the Foreign Mission Committee to lay this question before the General Assembly; and we further petition that the General Assembly be requested to form the Presbytery of North Formosa, of which the bounds will coincide with the bounds of the Canadian Presbyterian Mission in North Formosa, within which bounds are resident WilHam Gauld, Thurlow Fraser, and Giam Chheng-hoa, ministers, and also Formosan elders, and

Whereas, we believe that our object should be to build up a native Church rather than to perpetuate foreign control.

Therefore we petition that the Presbytery so formed shall be empowered to resolve itself into a Presbytery of the Formosa Church, competent to receive students of theology on trial for license, and proceed to ordain them, and in general to superintend congregations and sessions within its bounds, without reference to a higher court, until there shall be a native Synod.

Whereas we believe that the time has now come when we should have in our Girls' School competent Canadian lady teachers, and as this question is pressed on our attention by the ever increasing demand for female education.

Therefore, we petition the Foreign Mission Committee to take such action in conjunction with the Woman's Foreign Missionary Society as will result in the sending out of two competent single lady teachers at a very early date.

Whereas, the majority of the students entering Oxford

College to study for the ministry are almost wholly unprepared to begin the study of theology,

Therefore we petition the Foreign Mission Committee to give us permission to erect a building for a preparatory or a middle school."

These extracts clearly indicate that the missionaries fully realized the manifold needs of the mission in view of the changing conditions and the new regime. They reveal also the fact that a new spirit of democracy had taken hold of the mission. Before the Presbytery of North Formosa was organized, Mr. Fraser, who had had a large share in preparing the above petition, had to leave Formosa and retire from the work, owing to the ill-health of his wife.

The New Era in Missionary Reinforcements

Appeal from Mr. Gauld

After his return from furlough, Mr. Gauld recognized that, in order to retain the ground already won, and at the same time carry on a more aggressive evangelistic work among the masses who had as yet been scarcely touched, large additions to the staff were absolutely necessary. Consequently he immediately sent home an urgent appeal for four missionaries — one ordained, one medical, and two lady missionaries. It was a large and courageous request, and reveals how deeply he realized the need of this policy for the

mission. The Foreign Mission Committee was no less courageous or alert to the pressing needs of North Formosa, for the four missionaries asked for were appointed to the field.

New Missionaries Welcomed

It was a great day for the Formosa Mission and for the Church when five young, enthusiastic missionaries set sail for that field. In the month of November, 1905, Rev. Milton Jack, Rev. J. Y. Ferguson, M.D., and Mrs. Ferguson, Miss Janie Kinney, and Miss Hannah Connell reached Tamsui, where they were accorded an enthusiastic welcome by Mr. and Mrs. Gauld and the Formosan Christians. The arrival of this splendid group of missionaries wonderfully revived the spirits of the native pastors, preachers and converts, giving to them fresh evidence of the tender concern of the Canadian Church and added assurance that that Church intended to lay, broad and deep, the foundations of the infant Church in Formosa.

Learning the Language

The two mission houses in Tamsui were now full of life, good cheer and youthful enthusiasm. The new missionaries had before them the task of mastering the Formosan language. Every room that could be spared was turned into a study, in which a missionary and his or her teacher spent every morning and afternoon repeating, with painful monotony, the Chinese tones, all of which, to these beginners, were, for some time, very much the same. Their encouragement was that others before them had acquired a knowledge of the language, and that where others had succeeded

they were not likely to fail. The following year their number was increased. Mrs. Jack arrived in Formosa and enthusiastically joined the rest in the study of the language.

Interest to the Natives

The six young missionaries living on Fort Meadow, the most beautiful spot in the district, formed a group of much interest to the people, particularly when, as their custom was, they went for their walk in the late afternoon along the path that led to the seashore or through the paddy fields. When the two lady missionaries went out together, many took them for husband and wife. It was difficult for the Formosans to distinguish between men and women, for in those days the Chinese scholars strutted about the town of Tamsui in long robes of varied hues, resembling women's skirts, while the women wore trousers. Many amusing, and by no means complimentary, remarks were passed, to the delight of other spectators — remarks which the innocent Westerners were fortunately not able to understand.

As the missionaries made progress in the language, Chinese visitors became more numerous, and the visits more prolonged, oftentimes to the discomfort of the students, whose limited vocabulary was soon exhausted. Where words failed, the hands and facial expression would be called upon to supplement. If the missionaries did not receive encouragement from their teachers, they certainly did not lack flattering words from their courteous visitors, who would tell the missionaries how clever they were and what distinct articulation they had, at the same time turning round to the teacher and asking what the missionary was trying to say.

Just because the Chinese seldom laugh, or even smile, when the missionary makes mistakes, it should not, therefore, be imagined that they have not a keen sense of humor. Follow them home and hear them tell the others the wild blunders of the foreigners. Hear the roars of laughter as they relate the linguistic mistakes of the missionaries. A chapter could easily be written relating the current jokes among the Chinese, at the expense of the missionaries, and it would furnish most amusing entertainment.

The Doctor in Demand

As soon as the Chinese learned that there was a doctor among the new missionaries, it seemed as though the whole town immediately fell ill. They did not wait for an invitation to call. They soon found out the doctor's house, and simply blockaded it at every opening. There are no private rooms in the ordinary Chinese house, and naturally they did not respect any private room there might be in a foreigner's house. The doctor might expect to be accosted in any corner of his house, at any time of the day, by those with sores and ailments who were seeking relief. It was by no means an easy task for Dr. Ferguson to protect the hours set apart for Chinese study. What consideration had a sick Chinese for the time or language study of a foreign doctor? The result was that his afternoons were frequently given over to meeting the needs of the sick and afflicted, with Mrs. Gauld and Mr. Koa-kau as interpreters, until he himself was able to use the strange, new language.

The New Era in Mission Organization

Councils Formed

With the increase of the missionary staff came the need for mutual discussion of mission problems and the framing of common policies. The senior missionary was the only one who had been long enough in the country to know the conditions. Councils were established, problems were discussed, new policies were advocated and adopted, and minutes recorded and forwarded every month to the Foreign Mission Board. Thus the younger missionaries were enabled to gain an effective knowledge of the situation.

By the fall of 1907, the year the writer reached Formosa, the Councils were already directing the regular work of the mission with considerable efficiency, even though the senior missionary was absent in Canada.

Visit of Dr. R. P. MacKay

The visit to Formosa that year of the Foreign Mission Secretary, Dr. R. P. MacKay, was an event of deep interest to the Formosan Church, for it revived, more than anything else had done since his death, the memory of their beloved "Kai Bok-su." They were able to meet and talk with one of whom they had heard their father in the faith frequently speak in the early days of the mission. During his travels in the East, Dr. MacKay probably had no experience that touched his heart more than his visit to the Island Beautiful,

with its lofty mountains and its low-lying plains, and above all, its thrilling memories of the great pioneer he had known so well.

Arrival of Duncan McLeod

In November, 1907, the writer and his wife reached Formosa. During his first two years, spent in language study, he visited many of the outstations. His first travelling companion was Giam Chheng-hoa, the oldest convert and pastor, and the most intimate friend, outside his own family, that Dr. George Leslie Mackay ever had.

Aggressive Evangelism

Visits to heathen villages, in company with the students, soon convinced him that the evangelization of North Formosa was in its very infancy, and that the masses were scarcely touched. The older generation had heard the name of the "Jesus Doctrine," and of "Kai Bok-su," but even of these the younger generation was entirely ignorant — except in places where there was a Christian chapel, and where converts lived. During the last few years of Mackay's life, the work of Oxford College had absorbed most of his time and energy. Pastoral visitation among sixty stations could not be carried on with any degree of efficiency by one foreign missionary and one native pastor, to say nothing of the evangelistic work in the regions beyond. After the passing away of the founder, Mr. Gauld had to teach in the college, help with the pastoral work and attend to the administrative and financial side of the mission. The result was that the work of aggressive evangelism had now to be planned from the very foundation.

More Reinforcements

About this time, four new missionaries were added to the staff
— Miss Mabel Clazie, Miss Lily Adair, and Mr. and Mrs. G. W.
Mackay, bringing the number of duly appointed missionaries in
North Formosa up to ten. The mission had changed not only in
numbers but also in its general character and in its methods of
work, and the outlook was promising.

The arrival of George Mackay, the only son of the founder,
and his young bride, daughter of the well-known minister, Rev.
John Ross, of Brucefield, was an occasion of the deepest interest
to the Formosan Christians. He had been born and brought up in
Formosa and could speak the Formosan language with ease and
fluency. His mother and two sisters, Mary and Bella, were there, to
welcome him back after ten years of academic training in Canada
and the United States. Many of the pastors and preachers had the
happiest recollections of their boyhood days spent with him. But
the happiest person in the gathering was his devoted mother, who,
during his years of absence, had longed to see his face, and had
faithfully remembered his needs in a strange land.

Change of Mission Centre

Several other important events marked the year 1911. With
the increase in the membership of the staff it was necessary to
begin building residences and other institutions. After much
deliberation, the Mission Council requested the Foreign Mission
Board to grant permission to buy land in Taihoku, the capital,
it having been decided that the proper development of the work
necessitated the transferring of the mission centre from Tamsui

to that city. The request was granted and land was bought about a mile out of the city, that would be suitable for the erection of a hospital, a theological college and six mission residences. A few months after the purchase of the land, Mr. Gauld was appointed to the supervision of the building operations on the "Mackay Memorial Hospital."

The New Era in Medical Work

Value of Early Work

From the inception of the mission, medical work has been one of its recognized features. Mackay found its great value, both in removing prejudices against the Christian religion and as an evangelistic agency, to say nothing of its immediate worth as a ministry of healing. During Dr. J. B. Fraser's short period in Formosa, Tamsui hospital was built, as the centre of the medical work. After Dr. Mackay's death, this department of the work was seriously handicapped on account of there being no one to take charge of it. The help that community doctors rendered, though appreciated, was far from satisfactory.

Tamsui Hospital

With the arrival of Dr. Ferguson, the work was thoroughly organized. The Tamsui Hospital was opened, and, though the quarters were cramped, much effective work was accomplished

both for the bodies and also for the souls of the hundreds of patients that were treated each week. The work was carried on along modern lines. This was imperative, because of the rapid progress made by the Japanese in medical science. From the first the officials were sympathetic, and were much impressed with the new doctor's character and skill.

Transfer to Taihoku

For four years Dr. Ferguson carried on his medical work in Tamsui. Every morning over a hundred patients used to wait patiently for their turn to meet the foreign doctor. During those years multitudes were healed in body, many of whom were led to a knowledge of Jesus Christ as Saviour. The actual transfer of the medical work from Tamsui to Taihoku was a simple affair for Dr. Ferguson, but the Chinese men of wealth and influence made it a time for displaying their high appreciation of the medical missionary. A procession of sedan chairs conducted him to the railway station, the doctor's chair being trimmed with red.

Opening of Mackay Memorial Hospital

"Mackay Memorial Hospital," the first institution called after the mission founder, was completed in 1912. The formal opening on December 26th was an interesting event. The Civil Governor and several leading officials were present, and in their addresses expressed their appreciation of the work of the mission founder and that of Dr. Ferguson, in the establishment of such a humanitarian institution in the city of Taihoku, not forgetting to express, in glowing terms, the credit such a building was to the

mission builder.

On the following day, about a thousand converts, from all parts of the field, gathered in the quadrangle of the hospital. The history of the forty years of mission work was reviewed, from its inception, by some of those in whose memory the wonderful record still lived. Among those present was Go Khoan-ju, who was one of the first five converts and who had given nearly forty years to the preaching of the Gospel. Many were the memories of the founder rekindled on that occasion. Such an event made an appropriate celebration of the fortieth anniversary of the North Formosa Mission.

The Test of Medical Missions

The work of medical missions is extremely fascinating to anyone interested in the missionary enterprise. It demonstrates, as few other agencies can, and in a way readily recognized by the non-Christian, the real spirit and practical character of Christianity. At the same time, it is a mighty evangelistic force. Whilst patients are being treated in the hospital, they see the Gospel in action and are made familiar with its story. Naturally the more satisfactory results are secured from among those who remain in the hospital for a longer period, but even to those who come but once the Gospel message is made known. In this way literally thousands hear the Word who otherwise might never be brought into touch with Christianity. Especially was this true in pioneer days.

It cannot be too emphatically stated that the test of the fruitfulness of a mission hospital is not confined to the number of patients reported at the end of the year, and the number of

operations for the removal of physical pain and suffering. A further test is the measure of Christian influence which the hospital exerts and the extent in which it helps in the evangelization of the non-Christian community. If it fails in this, it fails at a point of supreme opportunity, and its claim for the support of any Missionary Society is vastly reduced. In view of this, it is peculiarly gratifying to know that the North Formosa Mission Hospital has always been a strong evangelizing agency. Many stories of the triumphs of medical skill and of divine grace could be narrated.

Furlough of Dr. Ferguson

The completion of the Memorial Hospital was a source of great satisfaction to the Council and more particularly to the medical missionary, who had spent two or three years in preparing plans and regulations, while at the same time ministering with unflagging zeal to the sick. The necessity of having to return to Canada on a well-earned furlough, so soon after the opening of the institution, was a source of deep regret to him, particularly in view of the fact that there was no doctor who had been long enough in the country to have acquired a knowledge of the Chinese language, to whom he could hand over charge of the work.

Medical Recruits

In the fall of 1911, Miss Isabel Elliott, a trained nurse, reached Formosa, and in the spring of 1912, a few m6nths previous to Dr. Ferguson's departure on furlough. Dr. A. A. Gray and Mrs. Gray arrived. When Dr. Ferguson left. Dr. Gray and Miss Elliott assumed the responsibilities of the medical and nursing work of

the new hospital, with Mr. Koa Kau as interpreter to Dr. Gray, and Mrs. Kau, who was Dr. G. L. Mackay's daughter, Bella, interpreter to Miss Elliott. This was a policy that the North Formosa Mission Council is never likely again to follow. It resulted in Dr. Gray's complete physical and nervous collapse, and in his having to be invalided home and finally to resign from the work. Dr. and Mrs. Gray had endeared themselves both to their fellow-missionaries and to the Formosan people. Dr. Gray had revealed a genuine love for the native people and a true missionary spirit, while Mrs. Gray had become a most efficient worker among the women. To their fellow-missionaries their permanent withdrawal was a matter of keen disappointment.

Miss Luscombe's Arrival and Enforced Return

In the fall of 1917 Miss Margaret Luscombe, a trained nurse, arrived in Formosa. She passed successfully her two years of language study in Chinese, but on account of ill-health had to return to Canada in the summer of 1921. Owing to the fact that the Mackay Memorial Hospital was closed for lack of doctors, Miss Luscombe did not have the privilege, even during her short term in the country, of engaging in the work to which she had looked forward with keen interest.

The New Era in Educational Work

New Work Planned

A new step was taken in the fall of 1913, when Mr. Kenneth Dowie, a graduate of McGill University, was appointed to superintend the architectural work and to devote part of his time to organizing Christian work among the Japanese and Chinese young men of the city. He has become a most valuable member of the staff. Though he acquired a good knowledge of both Japanese and Chinese, on account of the depletion of the mission staff he has had to confine his activities to the existing work, having been engaged in the financial, the educational, and, more recently, the architectural work of the mission. He was later joined by Mrs. Dowie, who had been engaged in Young Women's Christian Association work in Japan.

The Middle School Opened

Until the year 1914 there had never been a middle school for boys in North Formosa. From this great lack in the life of the native Church the mission had suffered seriously. In 1902, as we have seen, a petition was sent to the Foreign Mission Board asking permission to open a boys* school, but owing to the lack of trained teachers, the organization of the middle school was postponed till the spring of 1914. Mr. George W. Mackay, who was now on the ground and ready to undertake this important work, was appointed principal by the Council, and in April of that year the school was opened in Oxford College, where his father had spent his best and happiest years.

Its Value and Needs

Since its opening the middle school has amply justified its existence, and has demonstrated its value in educating the youth of the Church and as an effective evangelizing agency. A large proportion of the students come from non-Christian homes. Many of these during the last seven years have professed their allegiance to Jesus Christ. Several, some of whom came to the middle school from heathen homes, have already entered the Theological College. At the present time two capable teachers, or ordained missionaries with teaching qualifications, are greatly needed, especially in view of the enlarged school which will be made possible by the new middle school building, now in the course of erection. The new regulations outlined by the Formosan Government demand the raising of the standards of education. Since the Tamsui Middle School has complied with these regulations, and thus receives government recognition, the institution will become an effective agency for the teaching of the children of our Church, the conversion of non-Christian students and the spread of Christian knowledge throughout the island.

Mr. Mackay was in charge till his recent furlough, during which period Mr. Dowie had charge of the school. Mr. Mackay's perfect knowledge of the Formosan language has added much to his other qualifications, while his Christian character has had a most wholesome influence. Though not an ordained missionary, he has been most successful in directing the minds of the students, among whom the spirit of evangelism is very manifest, to the Christian ministry. Mr. Williams, who arrived in 1919, has been devoting much attention to the deepening of the spiritual life of

the school.

Mrs. Mackay, who has been most untiring in her devotion to the Formosan youth, herself a teacher by profession, has given much of her time and energy to the teaching of English. By having these lads in their home and making them feel that they were interested in them, Mr. and Mrs. Mackay have helped to remove the tendency to regard the school as a Western institution.

The Government's Policy

It is a cause for deep gratitude that the Formosan Government, especially under the civil administration of Baron Dan, has taken a deep interest in the higher education of the Formosan youth. Remarkable progress has been made in primary and public school work for both boys and girls. The serious lack has been in middle schools that would compare favorably with those of the same grade in Japan. The new policy of increasing the number of these institutions and of raising the standard may indicate the possibility of the Government having in view a university for Formosa. Such an institution would render large service in preparing the Formosan youth for the new responsibilities that a more liberal franchise would bring to them. The Christian Church would rejoice if such a policy were carried out. It would make possible a more effective supervision of the morals of her young men. At present, hundreds of Formosan youths are open to the perils of the larger educational centres in Japan. It is safe to say that to no other project would the Formosan men of wealth contribute more willingly and liberally than to an institution of higher learning, such as a Formosa University.

Mr. Jack's Removal to Korea

In 1917 Rev. Milton Jack was appointed to the teaching staff of the Chosen Christian College and with his family removed to Seoul, Korea. Mr. Jack was in charge of the Theological School in North Formosa, for the greater part of the time, from 1907 till 1916. At the beginning of the New Era, during the transition stage, when much executive work had to be done, Mr. Jack, with his keen executive ability and deep interest in the progress of the native Church toward self-support, was an invaluable help, while Mrs. Jack, with her splendid talents, labored most efficiently and faithfully among the Christian women both in Tamsui and in Taihoku.

The Theological College

The Theological College in North Formosa has always been a vital force in the growing life of the Church. For many years the teaching was carried on in Oxford College, Tamsui. When the middle school was organized, the Theological College had to be transferred to Taihoku, where the work was conducted for three or four years in temporary quarters. Mr. Gauld was appointed to draw plans for a new college building, the foundations of which were laid in the summer of 1917, and which was opened in the spring of 1918, a few months before Mr. Gauld left for Canada on his third furlough. This building is large enough to serve the mission for years to come. The work has been suffering seriously, however, from the lack of foreign teachers. The appointment of more ordained missionaries is necessary if this important institution is to render its largest and best service. From its opening the college

has been an attractive meeting place for the pastors and preachers, as well as for Presbytery meetings and general conferences.

For several years the Theological College has been under the charge of Mr. Gauld, while Japanese and Chinese pastors from the city help with the teaching. There is urgent need of efficient teachers, who shall devote their full time to this important work of giving to these young men entering the Christian ministry a thorough preparation. Both the Mission Council and the Foreign Mission Board earnestly desire that this College, in the very near future, shall be thoroughly equipped and supplied with a full and qualified staff.

Kindergarten Work

A new department has been recently added to the mission work in North Formosa. Owing to the fact that henceforth no private primary schools can be opened in Japan, the Mission Council took advantage of the field which presented itself among the children of the larger cities for Kindergarten work. For this special work Miss Jennie Hotson was appointed, and in the fall of 1918 reached Formosa. After spending nearly two years learning the Formosan dialect, Miss Hotson went to Japan to study the Japanese language.

Losses and Gains in the Mission Staff

Retirement of Dr. Ferguson

On account of ill-health it became necessary for Dr. Ferguson, in the spring of 1918, to go to Japan. On his return his health was still so impaired that his leaving for Canada the following year was imperative. The fear that he might not be able to return to the work which he had so ably organized, and to the institution which he had so recently founded, was a matter of grave concern. The subsequent news of his retirement from the work brought deep disappointment to the mission. Dr. Ferguson left a lasting impression on the Formosan Church and on the non-Christian community. He was highly respected by the Japanese officials, especially those in the medical department, because of his sincere character and his medical and surgical skill. A man of few words, of sane judgment and of fine Christian principles, he took the deepest interest in all departments of the work of the mission, and in the many and intricate problems of the native Church.

A Splendid Hospital, but Closed

The Mackay Memorial Hospital has been closed since Dr. Ferguson left in 1919. What this has meant to the mission can be but faintly imagined. To the missionaries, who have to look daily upon their large hospital which could be filled every day in the year with sick folk to whom it could minister healing of body and soul, it is a source of constant and bitter heartache. The situation cannot be remedied until the Church at home makes it possible for the Board to send out doctors in sufficient numbers to warrant its re-opening.

Additions to the Staff

In October, 1919, Mr. and Mrs. Gauld returned from their third furlough. The hearts of the missionaries were greatly cheered by the arrival with them of Rev. and Mrs. George A. Williams and family and Miss Maude Ackison, and, a few months later, of Dr. Kenneth A. Denholm, a graduate of Queen's University, and Mrs. Denholm, who resigned and returned to Canada in 1922.

The latest additions were Miss Mary Haig, who arrived in Formosa in 1920, Rev. W. G. Coates in 1921 and Mrs. Coates in 1922. All of these give promise of much useful service in the years to come.

Present Urgent Needs

The history and progress of the work for which the Women's Missionary Society of the Canadian Presbyterian Church is responsible, will be dealt with in a later chapter. The following summary gives the number of men missionaries which the North Formosa Mission Council have asked for as their minimum requirement to meet the immediate needs:

1. Four ordained missionaries — one for Giran Plain, with its 100,000 inhabitants, one for the Sinchiku district, one for Hakka work, and one for supervising the Sunday School work through the mission.

2. Three medical missionaries for the Mackay Memorial

Hospital.

3. Two teachers for the Middle School.

4. One business manager.

In response to this call who will say, "Here am I; send me"? Or if that is not possible, who with similar dedication will reply, "I cannot go myself, but another shall be sent to represent me"?

𝔇raper

WE give Thee our humble thanks, O God, for the wonders of Thy grace and the victories of Thy Gospel in Formosa. As we survey the growth of the vine which Thy hand hath planted there our hearts are filled with rejoicing and hope and we set ourselves to labor and to pray with a more courageous faith.

FOR every man and woman and little child to whom Thou hast revealed Thyself in Jesus Christ and whose life has been renewed through obedience to Him; for all the homes that He has brightened and purified; for the young Church in which Thy people are finding fellowship for worship and service; for the College and the schools through which minds have been illuminated and enriched, characters strengthened and lives moulded and equipped

for service; for the hospital whose ministries have blessed so many with healing and with the knowledge of the Great Physician; and for all the varied services of friendship which the missionaries have offered in the spirit and in the name of Christ, we thank Thee.

PROSPER these workers in all their tasks and send them reinforcements. Let the beauty of the Lord our God be upon them and establish Thou the work of their hands upon them; yea the work of their hands establish Thou it. In our Redeemer's Name we pray. AMEN.

CHAPTER VI

GROWTH OF THE NATIVE CHURCH

An Indigenous Church Necessary

THE most fundamental phase of missionary work in non-Christian lands is the planting and developing of an indigenous church. It is essential that the missionary constantly bear in mind that his mission is not to transplant to the land to which he goes a foreign institution, but rather to plant there a Church through which the genius of the people may express itself, and which shall be in harmony with the particular conditions under which they live. To perpetuate Western ecclesiastical divisions would be deplorable.

Co-operation between the missionary and the Church leaders, mutual sympathy and the recognition of mutual responsibilities, are necessary in achieving the task of building up a Church which is founded on the New Testament, but which in superstructure is in harmony with the religious history and genius, as well as the social conditions and customs of the people. The responsibility for building up such an indigenous Church must be placed more and more on the native leaders. This calls for the training of men who will be worthy and qualified for this great task. There is reason to be profoundly thankful that the North Formosa Mission has escaped some of the difficulties which have arisen in other mission fields in this connection.

The growth of the indigenous Church must be not only from within, but also from without. If it is to develop, to perpetuate its life and its faith, it must seek both to build up its members in knowledge and godliness and also to carry the Gospel message to the whole unevangelized community. This chapter sketches the story of the development of the North Formosa Church in self-government, self-support and self-propagation during the last fifty years.

Growth in Self-Government

Foundation Work

During the lifetime of the founder, the field resembled a large diocese, with practically one missionary as sole administrator. There

was not yet sufficient material with which the pioneer missionary could build up any elaborate organization. Foundations, however, were laid, but more Canadian and Formosan workers were needed for the preparation of the required material.

The Presbytery Organized

Three years after Mackay's death, the first Presbytery was organized and met for the second time the following year. Rules of procedure were prepared, and committees appointed to consider and report on various departments of Church life and work. This step marked a decided advance. The Church was taking on the appearance of a self-governing institution.

Ordination of Pastors

In the spring of 1906, six new out-stations were opened, some of which were among the Hakka people, and in the following year, the preachers' conferences, more fully dealt with in another connection, were organized. More important still, from the standpoint of self-government and also of self-support, was the ordination, as pastors, of four native preachers. Three of these were inducted into self-supporting congregations, and the fourth was appointed to the pastoral supervision of the Giran Plain, as the representative of the Mission Council. A few months later another preacher, at one time a sorcerer, was ordained and inducted into the largest charge on the whole field, that in the city of Daitotei. One of the four just mentioned, a son-in-law of Dr. Mackay, was called to the famous Bang-kah Church. These events, taking place within so short a period, were as significant of the progress and

stability of the work as were any of those recorded in the more exciting days of the pioneer's life. Were the founder to return he would rejoice to find several of his old students and evangelists settled in pastorates, and assisting in the administration of the Church's work.

North and South Unite in Synod

Shortly after the organization of the North Presbytery, delegates were sent by the South to convey fraternal greetings, a courtesy which was in turn reciprocated by the North. On several occasions fraternal delegates at both Presbyteries expressed their desire for closer co-operation and even advocated the union of the two native Churches. The foreign missionaries, both North and South, strongly encouraged the union movement. Committees were appointed by both Presbyteries. After a unanimous expression of the Churches, North and South, favoring such action, union was happily consummated in the city of Shoka, Central Formosa, in the fall of 1912, and the Synod of Formosa was organized.

Benefits of Union

The benefits that have resulted from this union it would be difficult to tabulate. The adoption of a scale of uniform salaries for preachers, North and South, the production of a small book of "Rules and Order," and a uniform curriculum for educational institutions, have been some of the results. A most important step was the appointment of a standing committee for Sunday School work, which has now been functioning for several years, with devotion and success. This department is regarded as so important

that a request has been made to the Foreign Mission Board for a specialist in Sunday School work. Two years ago the first normal training-school class met in the college in Taihoku. Over thirty Sunday School teachers came together, and for ten days methods of teaching and kindred topics were taught and discussed. The deepest interest was taken in this new phase of Christian work, and the conference will doubtless become a permanent institution.

Recently the Synod authorized the publication of the first hymn book for the Union Church. Formerly there were two hymn books in use, the one in the South being in the South Formosa dialect and differing slightly from the Amoy Church hymn book, which was in use in the North. This unnecessary confusion has now been removed, and a hymn book produced which is larger and much more suitable for general use in church and Sunday School worship.

Last spring the Synod of Formosa, which is now ecclesiastically independent, put itself on record as recommending and urging that the use of strong drink and narcotics in any shape or form be discouraged by all the Christians. The Synod has also decided that the diaconate shall be established throughout the Church.

Growth in Self-Support

Augmentation Fund Created

The growth of the native Church in self-support is no less

conspicuous than its growth in self-government. After the Presbytery had been at work for three years, it recognized, in common with the Mission Council, the necessity of urging upon the native brethren the duty of self-support. The larger and stronger congregations, it was increasingly felt, should come to the help of the weaker. From that time this subject was under discussion at every Presbytery meeting till, in 1910, an Augmentation Fund was definitely established. Since then a new spirit of sympathy and co-operation has characterized the whole life of the Church, expressing itself in a steady annual increase in contributions to all the funds.

Other Funds Established

The needs of the widows and orphans of the deceased pastors and preachers became the object of their next concern. The question was taken up by the Presbytery, and, in a short time plans were adopted for the establishment of a "Widows' and Orphans' Fund," to be followed not long after by the "Aged and Infirm Ministers' Fund," the two funds being amalgamated in 1921. It is to the credit of the Formosan Church that this joint fund has already reached the splendid sum of $3,500, and has done much to remove anxiety from the minds of those who are getting old in the service of the Church. There has also been established a "Home Mission Fund," the interest on which has now been used for several years to meet the expenses of evangelistic meetings for non-Christian people in the neighborhood of the Christian chapels. In addition, liberal gifts have been made every year for outside objects, such as the British and Foreign Bible Society, while for recent famine relief in

China the North Formosa Christians contributed about a thousand dollars. Givings of the Church. The remarkable growth of the Church in the grace of Hberahty is evidenced in the comparison of the givings for 1907 with those of 1921. In 1907, the total amount of the contributions was $2,346. In 1921, after subscribing for the Jubilee Fund about $2,000, the total givings amounted to $14,140, an increase of 500 per cent, in fifteen years.

Growth in the Spirit of Evangelism

Evangelism Defined

Probably the most encouraging feature in the growth of the Church is the progress made in self-propagation or aggressive evangelism. Let us consider what the evangelization of a field means. In Formosa, the masses are in towns and villages, while many live in small hamlets situated on river-banks or on mountain sides, or among clusters of bamboo groves. How is the gospel to reach them and what does the task involve? The year the writer reached Formosa the China Centenary Conference met in Shanghai. At this Conference a definition of evangelization was given which is worth repeating. It was as follows: "To reach every individual in the Empire with such a knowledge of the world-saving mission, the redeeming death and resurrection, and the heart-transforming power of the Lord Jesus Christ, as will suffice for the acceptance of a personal Saviour." This objective includes in its scope every

town, village and hamlet in Formosa, China, or Japan, every class of society down to the coolies on river-boats or in the coal-mines, and every Christian and non-Christian institution. It calls upon all Christian workers, irrespective of their immediate interests, to direct their supreme efforts, to focus their prayers, and direct their purposes on this central task of the Church. Nothing must be allowed to interfere with the final attainment of the great objective, the evangelization of the world.

Christ Our Example

As in all other things, so in this work of evangelism our Lord is our great example. From village to village, on hill-side and lake-shore, to the few and to the multitudes, everywhere and to all classes He went preaching the Gospel of the Kingdom and teaching the "Doctrine." He was never discouraged by adversity nor elated by popularity. In His spirit and with His passion, the missionary must face this task of carrying the Gospel to the ends of the earth. It is here he will always find the largest and most inviting field for his labors.

Converts and Evangelism

It may require a generation or more to produce many men who fully realize the sacredness of the call to the Christian ministry. It may take years for the converts in any large numbers to feel this deep sense of responsibility for their non-Christian neighbors. Unless the sense of sin has entered deeply into their own souls, it is not likely they will be much burdened with the sins of others. They may recognize the folly of heathen superstitions and idolatry, and

yet be slow in grasping the full significance of the Christian faith and the beauty and blessedness of the Gospel as revealed in Jesus Christ. Until they have, and until the fires of Pentecost have burned away much dross, they will not have that passion for the salvation of their own people that will send them forth as flaming evangels.

The Task of the Missionary

It is in this great task of deepening the spiritual life, of leading his co-workers to the higher heights and the triumphant places of the abundant life, that the foreign missionary will, for generations to come, have a large and vital place in the life of the Church. Should he fail here, he will fail totally in his mission. The one who calls men and women to a life of holiness, consecration and service, and leaves them constantly hungering for more of the divine life, ever keeping his own soul sensitive to the Macedonian call, will always remain indispensable to the life of any field of Christian work.

Vital to the Life of the Church

Whatever other qualities may be possessed, the evangelistic spirit is essential to a growing, indigenous Church. Important as even self-government and selfsupport are, they are not enough. The church of Laodicea was self-governing and self-supporting, but was by no means in a healthy condition. If a Church is failing to reach out into the regions beyond, she will not and cannot progress in any vital sense. The situation in China, as summarized by Dr. Donald MacGillivray, of Shanghai, is significant. In closing his estimate of a Symposium on Evangelism, he emphasized the

following four points:

(1) The testimony is overwhelming that aggressive evangelism is characteristic of the Chinese churches, and is responsible for the larger part of the increase in numbers. (2) In the new fields growth must be by fresh inroads on the masses of the heathen. (3) There is danger of slackening in settled charges. (4) There is danger of separation from the heathen community.

Testimonies from leading men conversant with conditions in Japan proper will help us to see how difficult it is for indigenous churches to develop if they fail to accept the responsibility of evangelizing their own territory. At a recent conference the situation was briefly summarized thus: "That Church to which we have transferred, presumably, everything that belongs to a Christian Church, is not, apparently, adequately conscious of its responsibility as an indigenous Church for the Christianization of Japan. This, surely, is no ultimate solution. An independent Church must surely assume the responsibility of carrying on its own extension work. We must leave with each indigenous Church a burning sense of its responsibility for the evangelization of its own unevangelized nationals."

Growth in Organized Evangelism

As far as Formosa is concerned, mission work was in the early years purely evangelistic. The missionary led his evangelists into

the regions beyond the small groups of Christians which he had already won in the towns and villages. Through this method men and women were led into the Christian Church. With the growth of the mission the local work and the teaching of students absorbed the larger part of the missionary's time. During some years there were districts where, for lack of time, the sacraments were not dispensed. The pioneer missionary, specially fitted for evangelism as he was, had to become the general director of a mission plant, with no one to direct the evangelists in the work. Even before he passed away, the workers had lost largely the art of going into the highways and byways and calling the heathen into the fold. After the Japanese occupation, a difficulty arose in that it was scarcely possible for the Formosan preachers to engage in such work without meeting with police interference.

A Suggested Policy

The modern mission, organized as it necessarily must be with its various departments of work, carries the danger of the evangelistic work being neglected on account of the growing demands of pastoral supervision, of the educational work, and of various other departments. Out of a large experience. Dr. Campbell Gibson, the veteran missionary to China, expressed his convictions on the subject thus: "It would be a wise and fruitful policy if every mission would make it a settled point of practice to set apart at least one man at every mission centre to give himself to the work of an evangelist. I am far from thinking that this is work that every man can do, and further still that it can be handed over to the less educated and less gifted of the mission staff. Many seem to think

that such men, while unfitted for school or college, or pastoral work, will do very well as evangelists. It would be deplorable if the Church should ever permit itself to think of evangelism as the dumping ground of the less efficient. On the contrary, let us urge that every mission appoint for each centre either a new man, or, perhaps better, choose from among the best it already possesses a man gifted by nature with a large humanity, by training with a large and living theology, and by grace with an intense spirituality, to be the evangelist of his mission."

Evangelistic Missionary Appointed

It was to this special work of evangelism the writer was appointed in 1907, and to it he has devoted his energies for the last fourteen years. At the time of his arrival he was deeply impressed with a series of articles on evangelism which appeared in the *Chinese Recorder*. It did not take long to convince him of the importance of the work and of the fact that there is a science of evangelism which can be learned only by practice and experience.

Evangelists at Work

As soon as the missionary, appointed to this work, had passed his second-year language examination, he began with his fellowworkers to plan evangelistic work in the non-Christian communities. Street chapels were rented in several districts where preaching was carried on several nights a week. The missionary, with groups of evangelists, preached in towns and villages, on street-corners and vacant lots, in marketplaces and court-yards, and even in heathen temples. In the case of the younger generation

of preachers, who had seldom preached to heathen audiences, the task at first was not an attractive one. It was difficult for the missionary, dull foreigner that he was, to understand their apathy in a work that to him was the all-absorbing mission of his life. The men who, in the early years, had followed Mackay up and down the land were now advanced in years, yet it was among them the most ardent spirits were found. They were reminded of old times, and on these evangelistic trips many were the reminiscences of pioneer days the missionary heard.

District Conferences and Evangelism

One feature of the work contributed largely to the success of this movement. In the spring of 1907 the Presbytery divided the field into three districts, in each of which was established a half-yearly conference for the benefit of the pastors and preachers. At these conferences two days were spent in discussing problems arising out of the growing needs of the infant Church. The third day was given over to the examination of preachers on Biblical and related subjects, under the supervision of a missionary. Every evening the preachers divided into groups, and went forth "preaching the Word." On account of the presence of the foreign missionary, there was no interference from the Japanese policemen. The enthusiasm of the preachers at these conferences was most encouraging. The Christians were stirred and the heathen around became interested. Steadily and persistently the spirit of evangelism grew till "po-so," "planting the seed of the Word," became a most familiar term in the conversation of the Christians.

Evangelistic Meetings in Chapels

It was not long before the leaders in the Church began to realize, with some concern, that a gap existed between the Christians and their heathen neighbors, and that all around their chapels there were multitudes yet untouched by the Gospel. Finally the Presbytery took up the matter, and, after much deliberation, decided that the interest on the "Home Mission Fund," previously referred to, should be used in establishing special evangelistic meetings in twenty or more chapels every year, with a view to reaching the heathen communities in their immediate neighborhood. In order that the best results might be obtained, the Presbytery's Committee on Evangelism drew up the following regulations: (*a*) Printed copies of the week's programme were to be distributed among the people, (*b*) A regular gong-beater was to go round the town every afternoon announcing the place and hour of service, (*c*) Several of the best speakers were to be invited, and asked to forward their subjects, which were to be specially suitable for heathen audiences, to a committee of arrangements, (*d*) The Christians were to be ready to welcome their heathen neighbors, to direct them to seats and to distribute hymn books and Christian literature. They were also to provide for the food and entertainment of the preachers. These special meetings have been kept up for years, with the interest steadily increasing. The chapels have been usually filled, and often crowded, for weeks at a time.

Results of this Work

Direct results have been secured from this method of work, but more farreaching is the changed attitude of the people toward

chapels, evangelists and converts. The wide chasm between the two communities has been gradually closing. The Christians are not now looked upon with the same suspicion and dislike. The pastors and preachers are regarded as worthy members of society, men of all ranks associating with them freely. Leading men, such as town-elders and clerks, though not Christians themselves, often attend these special services, and publicly advise their people to come and hear the Christian "doctrine." They acknowledge the improvement it has brought about in the lives and conduct of many. In Formosa to-day there are many among the more intelligent classes who are seriously thinking of the claims of the Christian faith.

Evangelistic Bands

For some years a few of the more earnest laymen advocated the forming of evangelistic bands, but it was felt by some that the time had not yet come for such a movement. At each of the three Preachers' Conferences the subject was considered, and finally, as the nearest approach to their objective, the Conference districts were subdivided into smaller ones, with an average of five preachers in each. These groups were organized into bands for preaching in heathen villages where there were no chapels and few, if any, Christians. Five consecutive days each month were given to the more distant districts. These bands have now been carrying on this method of evangelism for several years. Until the year 1919 the foreign missionary was largely responsible for their general supervision. It was felt, however, that if they were to do their most effective work, the Presbytery would have to take the movement under its control.

Growth of the Church as Indicated in the Forward Movement

Forward Movement Inaugurated

In the spring of 1919 Rev. A. E. Armstrong, Associate Secretary of the Board of Foreign Missions, visited Formosa. At a large gathering of pastors, preachers, leading elders and deacons, Mr. Armstrong told of the Forward Movement of the Canadian Churches, with the result that, a week or two later, the Presbytery met and discussed the inauguration of a "Forward Movement" in North Formosa. The proposal was enthusiastically received. It seemed most fitting that such a step should be taken in view of the approaching Jubilee of the Formosan Church. Thus the Forward Movement was launched, having as one of its chief objectives the speedy evangelization of the non-Christian communities. A standing Committee on Evangelism was appointed, which took entire control of the evangelistic bands referred to above.

Success of the Movement

From its inception the work has been carried on with enthusiasm and success, as the following extract from the report for 1921 indicates:

"The Forward Movement gathers greater enthusiasm as the year of our Jubilee draws nigh. The twelve evangelistic bands, in addition to conducting their regular church services, preached in

330 outlying villages; and 65,000 people heard the gospel, many of them for the first time. This is an increase of 50 per cent, over the reported hearers of last year. It is impossible to tabulate all the results. Still we do know that fifty-five persons made a definite decision to begin the Christian life, of whom quite a number handed over their idols to the preachers and became regular worshippers at the church services. Besides these special efforts in the heathen villages, evangelistic services were held in twenty-two churches throughout the field. At least 106 non-Christians signed decision cards. Thus the spirit of our Forward Movement is deepening. The most encouraging feature is that it is an indigenous movement, carried on largely by the Formosan brethren who have assumed entire responsibility for its success."

Growth in Numbers

This chapter would be incomplete without reference to the growth of the Church as revealed in its present numerical strength. An explanation ought, however, first to be given, lest misleading conclusions be drawn from comparisons between the past and present which might reflect seriously on the work of the last twenty years. It may be easily gathered from statistical tables that there were more chapels in the days of the founder than at the present time, and almost as many converts.

An Important Explanation

It should be borne in mind that in earlier days it was impossible for one missionary to find out much about the life and conduct of the converts. Discipline was almost impossible. It was extremely difficult for the foreign missionary to obtain information from the Formosan brethren. There was also considerable influx through ulterior motives, such as can be found in many mission fields to-day. Furthermore, lack of sufficient supervision left church rolls unpurged for years. Names of members who had been dead for years were left on by careless preachers. The fact that in the Giran Plain the revision of the church rolls took several years indicates how slow and difficult this process was. During the last fourteen years the numbers reported from the East Coast have been gradually diminishing. With the rapid passing away of the Pepohoan race, over thirty chapels on that plain dwindled down to eight. Almost all these chapels, however, are now in Chinese centres and, with the Chinese converts who furnish a more permanent foundation, the Christian cause in that district is in a much more encouraging condition.

Furthermore, there are now several ordained missionaries, eight ordained pastors, and regular sessions functioning in the general discipline of the membership of the Church. Moreover, the standard of life and conduct and the knowledge of Christian truth is very much higher and the danger of ulterior motives that were peculiar to social and political conditions of the old regime has been considerably reduced.

There are fifty preaching stations or chapels, each of which has a native preacher or pastor. Eight pastors are in self-supporting

charges, while all the rest are partially supported by their stations. In our educational institutions there are several who at one time were pupils in these schools and who, having gone to Japan and graduated from colleges there, have returned as Christian teachers to the schools in which they formerly studied.

Members and Catechumens

At the end of 1921 two thousand three hundred and seventy-four baptized adult members, and one thousand six hundred and twenty-five baptized children were reported. There were nearly three thousand who came more or less regularly to the church services and received Christian instruction. Many of these are on the borderland between Christianity and heathenism. Some of them, while, for various reasons, not yet baptized, have forsaken heathenism and recognize themselves as part of the Christian community. Though heathen superstitions and idolatry have lost all charm for them, they have not yet surrendered fully to the claims of the Lord Jesus Christ. The scarcity of evangelists, who have the power of reaching the consciences of men and who can show the folly of the heathen religions and, at the same time, present the attractive power of the Cross of Calvary, may account for such a large number every year who are still on the catechumen list rather than on the list of members.

Sunday Schools

There are nearly two thousand Sunday School scholars and over two hundred teachers. The preachers, though they have had no special training in this work, have become deeply interested

in it of recent years. They superintend their own Sunday Schools, and among their helpers are many who have gone through our Christian schools in Tamsui. This is a most promising field of labor, for which it is hoped an ordained missionary with special Sunday School training will soon be appointed.

The Christian Comniunity

In North Formosa the Christian community, including baptized adults and children and adherents with their children, may be set at ten thousand. This means that for every one hundred and fifty of the population there is one person who has direct connection with the Christian faith.

Though much progress has been made, especially in more recent years, in the planting of an indigenous Church, the work still to be accomplished is a challenge both to Formosan and foreign workers. There is much cause for gratitude to God for the harmony and co-operation which, throughout the years, have characterized the relationship between the Canadian missionaries and their efficient colaborers, both men and women. The help of the foreign missionaries will be required for many years to come — a fact that the Formosan brethren are realizing more and more, as they become more keenly conscious of the needs, and as they find the missionaries becoming more familiar with the life and problems of the people to whom they have gladly and unreservedly given their life service.

For the present position of the Formosan Church, for its growth in knowledge and spiritual power, in effective organization and in aggressive evangelism, we may well thank God. May the Church

in Canada, by its prayers, its loyal support and the maintenance of an adequate missionary staff, help to hasten the day, that is ever the goal of the foreign missionary enterprise, when the Formosan Church herself shall be able to take over the full responsibility for Christianizing the Island Beautiful.

Prayer

OUR Lord Jesus Christ, we believe in Thee and in Thy Holy Catholic Church. We thank Thee that Thou didst institute a universal brotherhood of believers and we glorify Thee because Thou hast been made Head over all things to the Church. We confess her errors and wanderings, her apathy and worldliness, her strife and disunion, but we rejoice because she is Thy Church, Thy living body, and because Thou art evermore working and expressing Thyself through her.

PARTICULARLY do we thank Thee for the Church in North Formosa, for its increase in numbers, for its growth in energy, for its wise and devoted leadership, for its loyalty to Thy truth, and for its zeal in spreading Thy message. Help it to enter into the heritage of the past and into conscious fellowship with the Church throughout all the

world. May it ever be united and true to Thee, so that it may in nowise withhold or obscure Thee, but may truly express Thee and release Thee among those who have not yet named Thy name. Let Thy special blessing be upon the preachers and Bible women. May every member of the Church give a clear witness to the power of Thy Gospel and by word and life show forth Thy salvation.

POUR out Thy blessing upon Thy Church universal. May she be energized for the great tasks which Thou hast set before her in these difficult and promising days, and in all things may she give Thee the pre-eminence. We ask this in Thy name. AMEN.

Chapter VII

BREAKING NEW TRAILS

MUCH interest gathers round the extension, during the New Era, of the work into new fields. The activities of the mission have not been confined to estabhshing institutions and to organizing and building up the Church from within, important as that work is. New territory has been added to that already occupied. Since 1905 eighteen new out-stations have been opened in North Formosa. Several are in the Hakka territory, three in the Taiko region, seven in Giran, two on the Karenko Plain, two in the Kiirun district, and one in Taihoku. At most of these points churches have been erected, while in a few places the Christians still worship in rented street chapels. This chapter will deal with only one of these districts, but one in which the Christian faith has made great progress of recent years, and in which there have lived some of the most remarkable converts that North Formosa has produced.

Planting the Faith in Taiko

Taiko is a market town with a population of about five thousand, situated in the centre of a large farming district along the seacoast, at the south-west corner of the North Formosa field. Around this town, scattered in every direction, are scores of villages and hamlets. In both the town and villages are many men of wealth and of literary attainments.

Tan Ki Siong, the converted scholar whose lifestory makes up a large part of this chapter, was born in the village of Ma-liong-po, three miles from Taiko. His father was a wealthy farmer who was also a district official, a man of liberal education and good reputation. Tan Ki Siong was the youngest of four sons. The three older brothers were prosecuting their studies of the Confucian classics, but Ki Siong was sent to herd the cattle. He complained of his hard lot and begged to be allowed to study with his brothers and prepare for the examinations. His father sent him to his grandfather, who, on seeing the young lad's earnestness, gave him the permission he sought, on condition that he find a substitute to herd the cattle. He found a poor boy whose highest ambition was to get enough to eat, and this the lad would be sure of in Tan Ki Siong's home.

Whatever faults Tan Ki Siong had, over attention to dress was not one of them. While other young men of ordinary means would be attired in flashing colors, especially when sitting at

examinations, he would appear in common garb. Others might ride on horseback or in sedan chairs; he preferred to travel the two days' journey to the city of Sinchiku, or "New Bamboo," on foot. On one occasion he was made the object of ridicule by two proud youths on the journey. When they reached the city, the examiners, noticing the appearance of these young aspirants clothed in mandarins' costumes, turned on them with the bitterest sarcasm, and, pointing to Tan Ki Siong, declared that he, though the son of a wealthy farmer and an ofhcial, had set them an example of common sense and humility.

His great thirst for knowledge was his outstanding characteristic. In his studies of the Confucian classics he made great progress. But in spite of his many praiseworthy traits, Ki Siong had certain moral weaknesses. Though gentle in manner, he had a very sharp tongue. He was small of stature, slim and sickly-looking, for he followed the example of his grandfather, his father, his mother, and three older brothers, all of whom were opium smokers. Most of the morning he spent in bed smoking opium; in the afternoon he would take a walk around the farm, then return to his room to pass the rest of the day with his classics, his opium and his tobacco water-pipe. He was short-sighted from his youth, a trouble the opium habit only intensified, until at last, from constant rubbing, his eyes became seriously affected.

He was about thirty years of age when Japan took posses-sion of the island. Being a man of means and trustworthy, he was chosen by the Japanese as district official. In this position he not only set his face against bribery, but gained a reputation for settling all matters with such exactitude and justice that evil-doers feared

him. He was also known everywhere for his generosity.

But all this time he was addicted not only to opium but also to liquor, much to the distress of his mother. The following incident he related to the writer: "The Japanese were accustomed to hold many public functions to which the leading men of the district were invited. I was always included and often returned home drunk. One day my mother took me to task, complaining that she was disgraced by my conduct. I felt so grieved on her account, that I pledged myself to total abstinence. On former occasions I rode in my sedan chair, but now I promised my mother that I would henceforth ride on horseback, so that I might be less liable to temptation from liquor. Shortly after I was invited to Taiko to attend a function in connection with the celebration marking the completion of some important public work. In accordance with my promise to my mother, I rode on horseback. During the feast the Japanese official remarked that though the feast was poor, he hoped the guests would not spare the wine, for there was plenty, and urged them to drink freely. Remembering my pledge to my mother, I sank into my seat with a sense of the most painful embarrassment. By my side sat an old scholar, who had never taken strong drink. Fearing that it might injure his weak constitution, he rose with fear and trembling, and addressed the official thus, 'In all my life I have never drunk liquor. May it please your honor to excuse me? By my side is a young friend who is an expert at this business. I am sure he will gladly take my share as well as his own.' As yet I had not touched my own glass. Most earnestly I begged that I also might be excused. The official's persuasion, however, prevailed, with the result that I was taken home in a sedan chair. When I awakened

from my long stupor, my mother was by my side. Later she died. But the habit lived on."

When Tan Ki Siong first came into contact with Christianity his hunger for knowledge was still keen but he was a physical wreck, and was far from peace and happiness. Superstition and idolatry had ceased to appeal to him, while for a mystic and religious enthusiast as he was, Confucianism was a barren field. To secure the satisfaction his heart craved and as a last resort he began the study of vegetarian Buddhism.

In the town of Taiko there were several vegetarian Buddhists who were urging him to enter their sect. These he kept busy with his questions, but could get from them no direct answers unless he signified his readiness to be initiated into their religious mysteries. It was while he was studying their system that, in the providence of God, the way opened for him to gain a knowledge of Christian truth.

At that time there were two or three people in the district who had heard the Gospel in the mission hospital at Shoka, Mid-Formosa. One of these was his own servant, Hiok-a. Every Sabbath morning, before dayhght, Hiok-a, with another young man, would disappear. These two would walk to Sansaho, or "Three-Forked-River," a village twelve miles distant, where a Christian chapel had been recently opened, and after attending two services, would walk the twelve miles of the return journey, reaching home at sunset. Many times had they prayed that God would open a place of worship in Taiko, in order that the people might have an opportunity of hearing the Christian truth and that they themselves might not have to travel so far. One day Tan Ki

Siong asked Hiok-a why he, a poor lad, who could neither read nor write, was so happy, while he himself, a man of means and education, was so unhappy. Hiok-a simply answered, "If you go to hear the Jesus doctrine, you may be happy too."

Early next Sabbath, without the rest knowing anything of their plans. Tan Ki Siong and Hiok-a started for ThreeForkedRiver. On their arrival the servant introduced the master to the preacher, and the whole Sabbath was spent in the chapel. The preacher, though not a scholar, was an earnest man and three times every Sabbath preached to saint and sinner. There was, however, little in the three addresses that appealed to Tan Ki Siong, for he had long before left behind the superstitious beliefs the preacher was earnestly condemning. He remained all night, asking questions till the early hours of the morning. For several Sabbaths he continued coming, and on one of these visits met the first foreign missionary he had ever seen, Rev. Milton Jack, who was much impressed with his singular earnestness and thirst for Christian truth. It was not long before he found that Christianity offered the forgiveness of sins, a doctrine which made a deep impression on his heart.

After travelling to the various chapels and spending whole nights with the preachers, he returned to his first spiritual adviser at Three-Forked-River, and made known to him his decision to be a Christian and his desire to have a rented chapel opened in Taiko. The preacher told him he could not be a Christian and remain an opium smoker. Tan Ki Siong, in his characteristic way, replied: "Have you not been preaching that God is infinite in power? If that is so, can he not help me to give up opium and give me strength to escape the agony of the experience?" Together the preacher and

the enslaved opium smoker went down on their knees and Tan Ki Siong vowed to God that never again would he use opium even if it should mean his death. From that hour he never again touched the drug, and in three days was quite recovered from the usual effects that accompany the breaking off from this habit. It was such a triumph of divine grace that never since has he doubted God's power, or the great reality of the Christian religion.

Tan Ki Siong's Family Become Christian

Tan Ki Siong was a believer for two months before his wife was converted to the Christian faith. Though not gifted, she was a strong character and, on worldly matters, he had always been accustomed to consult with her. It was some time before she could be reconciled to her husband's new religion. She would scarcely speak to him, and would place his meals on the table in silence and with apparent disgust. He, in turn, would just smile that smile which, on many occasions, to those who differed from him was irresistible. Her restoration to health, through his prayers, from a serious illness was the means of her conversion. While at first her grasp of Christian truth was not very clear, in later years many of the women through her heard the Gospel.

His three older sons were attending public school. The eldest was soon to graduate and was looking forward to entering the preparatory course for the medical school. He was bright and proud, and, though respecting his father very highly, was bitterly opposed to his new religion. Through direct answers to prayer, both for his mother who had been ill and for himself, this son was led to accept his father's faith. Later all the members of the family

became Christians.

The first time the writer visited Taiko after his appointment to the pastoral supervision of this district in 1909, he was deeply impressed with the strength of character possessed by Tan Ki Siong, who was outwardly a most insignificant looking man. It made no difference what class of men gathered, rich or poor, preachers or laymen, foreigners or Formosans, Tan Ki Siong, by the sheer force of his character, the keenness of his mind, and his absolute disregard for everything but his newlyfound faith, always attracted attention and commanded a hearing. He had an entirely new way of expressing Christian thought, a way that was striking, and at times amusing, to those who had accepted the Christian faith in the garment of orthodox Biblical theology.

A StreetChapel and its Services

Not long after Tan Ki Siong's decision for Christ, a street-chapel was rented in Taiko and the preacher from Three-Forked-River transferred to this important market-town. The news soon spread throughout the district. When the chapel was opened, several in the district, both men and women, who had heard the Gospel at the Shoka hospital, where Dr. David Landsborough, of the English Presbyterian Mission, for over twenty years has been carrying on a most remarkable work, united with the converted scholar and the new preacher. Every evening the chapel was crowded and as many more stood in the street listening to the new doctrine. Notwithstanding the opposition that was aroused, the number of enquirers increased.

In the little hall, only twenty-five by fourteen feet in size,

with a curtain four feet high separating the men from the women, these preaching services continued. The women would enter by a back door and take their seats in the enclosed area. After two or three addresses were delivered, the congregation would disperse, while the more interested would remain listening to the preacher, Tan Ki Siong and others as they talked quietly on some phase of the Christian message. Oftentimes a little group of converts would continue the conversation till midnight. For sleeping accommodation seats would be drawn together providing space wide enough to accommodate half a dozen men, while for the missionary's camp-bed a corner would be cleared. Not infrequently, however, the odour of leeks and garlic, added to the extreme heat, forced him to find a place for his bed in the street, much to the interest and entertainment of the passers-by. No matter how early he rose, it was impossible for him to escape the curious gaze of the folk on the other side of the street.

The New Church

The growth during the first year was truly remarkable. The number of enquirers steadily increased, and the converts found that it would be necessary for them either to rent larger quarters or to build a church. Through special prayer, they sought the will of God as to what course to follow. Tan Ki Siong soon secured from a wealthy heathen a choice plot of land, and a church fifty feet long by thirty feet wide was erected, for which the converts, though not yet baptized, together with the recent adherents, subscribed nearly a thousand dollars, in addition to several hundred days' labor. At the back of the church was built a house for the preacher, as well

as rooms for the itinerant missionaries.

The Church Opening

The church opening was a great event. In addition to the missionaries and several Japanese officials who were there, people came from all parts bringing various kinds of presents, such as scrolls, clocks and other useful articles. An old Christian woman, eighty years of age, walked fifteen miles from Three-ForkedRiver, where Tan Ki Siong first heard the Gospel, and after the service started back home, the same day, filled with a great joy because of the things she had seen and heard in that heathen markettown, where three years before there were practially no converts.

The following Sabbath sacraments were dispensed for the first time. Tan Ki Siong, Mr. Lim, also a scholar, and many others were baptized, and within a year several elders and deacons were appointed. Though the company of believers grew and prospered, they did not escape trials. The following year a typhoon partially destroyed the main building, the repairs of which cost several hundred dollars. A second typhoon entirely destroyed the room for the missionaries, and again with cheerful hearts the Christians came forward with their gifts for repairing the damage.

North of Taiko are several important towns, and many villages. The story of how the Gospel gained an entrance to Byon, Oanli and Tsusho is most interesting, and reveals in a remarkable way the power of God's redeeming grace.

The Entrance of the Gospel in the Oanli District

First Fruits at Byon.

Tan Ki Siong's deliverance from opium was the talk of the surrounding country. In a village called Byon there lived a barber, an opium-smoker. He began attending Taiko chapel. Every Saturday evening he and his little boy of seven would walk to Taiko, a distance of about six miles, spend the Sabbath in the chapel, and return home on Monday morning. This meant the loss of a day's earnings in the barber shop. The wife, chafing under this loss, took to beating the boy on their return, and, indeed, not infrequently the husband was given similar chastisement. The man was constantly telling how he dreaded going back every Monday, and what a terrible wife he had. The missionary's curiosity was aroused. He resolved to go, with some friends, to Byon, where he would preach the Word and visit the barber's home. This plan met with no hearty response from the barber; in fact all the way to his village he was in constant dread of what might happen should the evil spirits take possession of his wife when this group of Christians arrived.

On nearing the village, the travellers stopped at a shop to sip tea, preached to the passers-by and then proceeded to the barber's home. The mistress of the house was standing in the doorway, but did not return the salutations of the visitors. They entered the general living-room, which was also used as a bedroom, and

found seats wherever they could. After a few moments of awkward silence, the scholar began admonishing the woman, who was still standing on the doorsteps, for her folly in opposing her husband coming to hear the Christian religion. After listening for a moment she disappeared into an adjoining room and returned with a stout bamboo stick, about four feet long, and took her place on the steps again, guarding the doorway. Again there was silence, till the scholar ventured a few more words of counsel. Then the storm broke. In a fit of temper the stout little woman leaped on the floor and beating it madly with the bamboo stick, vowed she would die before she would accept the Jesus doctrine.

It was now the missionary's turn. He arose and, standing beside her, said a few words. So startled was she at hearing a foreigner speak in her own tongue, that for the moment she forgot her temper and listened. "Come unto me ... and I will give you rest" was quoted . The word "peace" arrested her attention. On being asked if she desired this peace, and wished them to pray for her, she answered "Yes." A peculiar hush fell upon the little company as, standing there, they prayed that the God of peace would bring into this stormy soul His own gracious calm.

As the missionary and his friends were about to go, the woman gave them a pressing invitation to stay for dinner, but this was impossible as it was necessary for them to press on to another village. Before leaving, however, the missionary told the woman he would expect to see her next Sabbath, with her husband and their little son, at the Taiko chapel. On turning to go, they found the doorway blocked with a crowd of curious onlookers, who were ready to listen; so advantage was taken of the opportunity to

preach the Word. Conspicuous in the crowd was a large, coarse-looking Chinese, with a pock-marked face, who, at first, was angry, thinking the barber had told the missionary of his misdeeds, but who, on being assured that they knew nothing of his past, listened attentively with the rest.

Next Sabbath, when the missionary entered the chapel, some time before the service, there in a corner sat the barber, his wife and little boy, and the pock-marked Chinese. They remained all day and promised to return the next Sabbath, which they did and continued coming for six months, until meetings were opened near their own village.

Beginnings in Oanli

Byon, where these new hearers lived, was not more than two miles from Oanli. Tan Ki Siong, now an elder and an able speaker, had several friends in the Oanli district, among both the wealthy and the literary class. One day, with the preacher and the missionary, he visited this market-town. They had supper in the house of a young storekeeper who had become interested in the Christian religion through his mother, who on a previous occasion had heard a missionary preach under the shade of a banyan tree, close to her home, and who, at that time, had asked for Christian literature, stating that she was anxious for her son to get a knowledge of this doctrine, as he was in need of reform. This night, after supper, he cleared an unoccupied store, filled it with borrowed seats, and placed at the back several boxes for a platform. The new hearers from Byon were on hand to lend their assistance.

The result of this visit was the opening of a rented street-

chapel and an invitation to Tan Ki Siong to leave his farm, for the time being, and come to Oanli. In the spring of 1913, he moved to that town. After a few months, several decided to be identified with the new converts and an attempt was made to buy a lot in the town, with a view to building a chapel. A number of the townspeople, however, combined to frustrate this plan. Nevertheless crowds came to hear. Several gave up opium and the number of those truly interested in the Truth steadily increased.

Tan Ki Siong and his Water-pipe

The manner in which Tan Ki Siong gave up his water-pipe, to which at this time he was still wedded, will be of interest. While he was living in rented quarters at Oanli, his three sons came home from college on their vacation. The oldest could speak fluently and the second was capable of teaching in the Sunday school. Their father, therefore, took advantage of the opportunity to go back and see how his farm was prospering in the hands of his son-in-law. On the first Sabbath of his absence his sons told the Christians that the missionary was soon going to Canada and that nothing would please him better than to hear before he left that they had given up such unprofitable habits as smoking and the like, and, moreover, that this would make them more effective witness-bearers. Nearly a dozen responded.

The following Saturday, after their father arrived home, a friend dropped in and innocently began talking about the decision of several of the converts to give up their tobacco pipes. On hearing that his own sons had proposed this new plan. Tan Ki Siong was angry. That night Elder Tan went to bed, but not to sleep. It was one

of the most distressing nights he had had for years. His conscience accused him of a habit that weakened his life and example with the converts who were striving to give up opium and other hurtful habits. Before morning he was victorious. He rose a more fully surrendered man, and vowed that never again would he allow this habit to have the mastery over him. That morning he told the story of his interview with his sons, the restless night and the victory through prayer, with the result that several pledged themselves to total abstinence in the future. That morning the elder's sons had the happy task of gathering up nearly a dozen pipes, which they kept to show to the missionary on his next visit.

Growth of the Work at Byon

The work in Byon at first met with much opposition. The barber's wife, who had vowed so vehemently that she would rather die than accept the Jesus doctrine, and later had been converted, was bitterly persecuted, and even beaten for her faith. Difficulty arose in securing a lot for building a chapel and in buying the clay required for making the brick. But again the converts called for special prayer and again the answer came. A lot was bought, a man was found who gave freely all the clay required, and soon a little chapel and a preacher's house were erected, for which several hundred dollars was contributed by Elder Tan himself. Every Sabbath, morning and afternoon, the chapel was filled with converts and adherents.

One of the most interesting of the converts was an old scholar who was a wealthy farmer, but a heavy opium-smoker. This man, after having been led to a knowledge of the Truth, became

an intimate friend of Elder Tan. He was a veritable Nathaniel, manifesting a spirit of remarkable gentleness and meekness. On several occasions the writer, with Tan Ki Siong and an elder from Taiko, has spent a most enjoyable evening in his home, conversing on the absorbing theme of the Gospel. All of these three were Chinese scholars, all had been opium-smokers, and all had had their eyes partially ruined through that habit. To meet these men, now so marvellously transformed, so perfectly happy and so devoted to spreading the Gospel broadcast among their own people, was an experience not soon to be forgotten and a cause for the deepest gratitude.

The first visit of the writer after his return from furlough was on the occasion of ordaining elders and deacons, as well as of dispensing the sacraments. The Tai-kah elders were present to help in the services of the day. Several candidates were received for baptism. Among them was a man who, two years previously, had been cured of a serious illness by the missionary doctor and had become a believer in Christ. His wife had followed him to the chapel, weeping because he was to be baptized. As the service was about to commence, the missionary's attention was drawn to a woman outside, sitting in the ditch with a shawl about her head. On enquiry, it was found that she was the man's wife, bewailing the fact that her husband was that day "entering the doctrine" and would be henceforth lost to her. On being told what his wife was doing, the husband said: "She may weep as long as she pleases, I have delayed two years for her. I want to be baptized to-day." For two whole years this man had been a Christian disciple, and now nothing could hinder him from carrying out his purpose of publicly

confessing his faith in Christ.

This, however, was not the only interesting event that marked the service. After the elders and deacons were ordained, and while an appropriate hymn for the occasion was being sung, an angry-looking woman, above the ordinary size, who had heard that her husband was among those to be baptized that day, came to the door of the chapel and sent an old woman to call her husband out. Immediately on his appearance, seizing him by the neck, she pulled him first to the right and then to the left, pounding his head at each turn. After satisfying her wrath in this energetic fashion, she departed, while her husband, re-entering the chapel, resumed his seat and picked up the strains with the rest of the worshippers, as if nothing had happened.

There is an interesting sequel to this incident. Before the writer returned on his second furlough, he went one evening with a group of converts, men and women, to Oanli to preach. On arriving he found a house made ready for the meeting with a platform built in the outer court, so that people could hear in the street, as well as inside. In a short time the house was thronged with heathen women, while crowds stood outside. After the service, the mistress of the house talked with the missionary enthusiastically about the gathering, when to his surprise he discovered that she was the very woman who, two or three years previously, had beaten her husband at the chapel door. His patience had broken down her prejudice, and now she was a regular hearer of the Gospel.

Triumphs at Tsusho

Tsusho, about five miles north of Oanli, is a town of 2,000 people. Some years ago the missionary and his helpers preached there for three weeks in a rented shop. Early in 1915, a permanent preaching hall was rented, and Tan Ki Siong was given charge of the work there, along with that at Ba-u and Oanli.

In Tsusho there was a teacher of Chinese classics, a man who had become a physical wreck through opium smoking. His wife and children became interested and attended the chapel services regularly. One day the wife invited Tan Ki Siong and the missionary to their home, in the hope that her husband might be influenced and helped. After listening to their message of hope, he promised to try to reform, though he confessed not only his physical but also his moral weakness.

A few weeks later, a wretched looking man came to the door of the missionary's home in Taihoku and told the missionary's wife that he was from Thong-sian and was anxious to give up opium. The missionary himself was absent at the time. Being a stranger, the man had not the courage to go to the doctor in the mission hospital, and so started back home. On the way he thought of his weakness in looking to man for help, and decided to trust God for strength to overcome. He gave the habit up entirely, declared his body and soul were delivered, and ever since has professed his faith in Christ. Later he was baptized, and has since been one of

the leading Christians in the place. Among the other helpers in the work at this centre for several years were a Chinese publicschool teacher, who was an earnest Christian, and his wife, a graduate of the Girls' School in Tamsui.

A new railway is being opened, which passes through Tsusho, Oanli and Taiko, rendering the evangelization of this whole territory more practicable and making it possible for the missionaries to reach with comparative ease whole stretches of country hitherto difficult of access.

The Taiko congregation, which is now selfsupporting with an ordained pastor and devoted elders and deacons, looks upon this whole district as theirs to evangelize. The work is most promising and is a cause for joyous thanksgiving and for earnest prayer that it may continue to increase.

In the opening of these three stations. Tan Ki Siong, the converted scholar, was the moving spirit. Nor did his work end there, for his influence has widened until it has been felt not only throughout the whole field, but also throughout the island. He is a splendid example of what God is doing for the Church on the mission field in raising up a strong, native leadership that shall make possible the indigenous Church for which we all earnestly pray.

Prayer

FORGIVE us, O God, because we so greatly limit and obscure Thee in Thy workings. Our hearts condemn us as we realize how often Thou hast been prevented from doing many mighty works in us and through our prayers, because of our unbelief. Lord, increase our faith, as we consider the wonders of Thy grace in Formosa and among all non-Christian peoples.

REMIND us that however much sin may abound grace does much more abound, that Thy Gospel is the very power of God unto the salvation of those of high or low estate, of respectable or outcast sinners, of the scholar or the ignorant peasant. May we be so convinced of Thy power and willingness to save to the uttermost that we shall, through the prayers of our faith, set Thee free to work Thy miracles of redemption.

WE pray that the Formosan Christians may have a commanding sense of their responsibility to share Thee with their countrymen. Give to them and to the missionaries access to the minds and hearts of the non-Christians. Give them utterance in public and in private, in season and out of season, and beyond all else help them to bear witness by the exhibition of their love and by the eloquence of their own surrendered lives. Continue, O

Christ, to win Thy victories in human hearts in Formosa and in other lands, until the earth shall be filled with the glory of God as the waters cover the sea. In Thy name we pray. AMEN.

Chapter VIII

TO OTHER CITIES ALSO

How the New Doctrine Entered Kinpori

K INPORI is a market-town with a population of three thousand, on the north coast, about three hours' walk from Kiirun. The plain in which the town is situated is surrounded on three sides with high mountains, while on the fourth lies the sea-coast, along which are several fishing villages. About ten thousand people are to be found on this small plain and in the surrounding foothills. It is one of the most isolated spots in North Formosa. At the time the Japanese came the chapel was destroyed, and every vestige of Christianity disappeared. For many years no

missionary visited the place. Go Khoan-ju, who used to live in Kinpori painting temples arid idols, and was one of the first five converts, on several occasions told the writer about the needs of this neglected corner.

Breaking Ground

In 1913 the missionary, with two or three preachers, spent three weeks in this town. On hearing of the arrival of the Christian evangelists, old prejudices were revived, and the gamblers of the town combined to oppose the new doctrine. Difficulty was met with in securing a preaching-hall. At last it was learned that a large house, which had been vacant for some time on account of the reported presence in it of evil spirits, could be secured. When the place was opened the evil spirits, who proved to be a pack of gamblers, slipped out at the back. The house was then prepared to serve both for preaching-hall and dwellinghouse.

For three weeks the preachers carried on their work faithfully. Every morning, the fishing villages were visited, the afternoons were spent in teaching the children of the town Christian hymns and the reading of Romanized script, and the evenings devoted to preaching the Word. The hall was crowded with listeners every night. For three evenings there was organized opposition in the form of a "Punch and Judy" show opposite the hall. The people, however, preferred to listen to the new doctrine. The Japanese official, who spoke Chinese fluently and so could converse freely with the missionary, was very friendly, and expressed surprise that the Christian message had not been preached before at Kinpori. He also expressed a desire that a Christian chapel should be opened,

stating that it was impossible for them to cope with the gambling habit in the district, and that he believed the establishment of Christianity in the town would help the work of reform.

A Second Visit

A year later another visit was made to Kinpori. On this occasion Tan Ki Siong, who was then preacher in the Mackay Memorial Hospital, accompanied the writer. As they reached the outskirts of the town, the children coming from school, recognizing the missionary, shouted, "Jesus is coming! Jesus is coming!" and running home advertised most effectively the arrival of the visitors. That evening a large crowd gathered for the preaching service in the market-place. Two or three men who had heard the Gospel on the previous visit, one of whom had already cast away his idol, were much interested. This man was very desirous that a place should be rented for a streetchapel, but such action at that time was considered premature. The genuineness of his interest was evidenced by his coming several times to Taihoku and the town of Shirin, a distance of about fifteen miles, to hear the Gospel.

A Street-chapel Rented

Early in 1915 the missionary, with two native pastors, paid Kinpori still another visit. They stayed three days, and this time rented a house which would serve both as a chapel and as a home for a preacher. The Japanese official showed his interest by providing them with comfortable quarters during their stay. Already several had become deeply interested and when they learned that a preacher was to be sent to live in their town, they

were much delighted. After the necessary repairs to the house were completed, an earnest preacher was placed in charge of the work. Within six months, forty had become regular worshippers and, while receiving instruction in the Christian truth, had begun the study of the Romanized script. The first year there was much difficulty in getting any of the women or girls to enter the chapel. Gradually, however, their prejudices were removed, some of the women eventually entering the women's school at Tamsui. From its establishment the cause at this centre continued to prosper.

First Baptisms and Present Membership

At the first baptismal service about fifteen men and women were baptized. Now there are over fifty baptized members. The last time the writer visited Kinpori over a hundred Christians and adherents were present at the morning service. These Christians, moreover, have been liberal with their means and faithful in bearing witness to the Gospel among their neighbors. Some of the young lads are looking forward to the Christian ministry, while two or three have expressed a desire to become evangelists to their own people.

An Idol that Spoke Falsely

While space does not permit relating many of the interesting incidents that have marked the history of this promising corner of the field, the story may be told of a family who were converted to Christianity, within recent years, in a village three miles from Kinpori. The husband, a farmer, had been absent from home for several weeks on business. On his return he accused his wife of

unfaithfulness, which she solemnly denied. In a fit of madness he went off to consult the gods. After going through the usual heathen rites prescribed in such a case, he managed to secure from them the information he desired. It is remarkable how these dumb idols can be persuaded to say that which meets the wishes of their devotees! With this assurance from the gods of his wife's guilt, he determined to punish her, going so far as to threaten to kill her.

In the good providence of God, the man heard the evangelists preaching the Gospel. They told of the lying propensities of the gods. This daring accusation arrested him. After thinking it over he decided that he would learn more of the new doctrine. The result was that he was convicted of his folly, of his ill-treatment of his wife and of his own evil life. His wife was anxious to learn of the new religion that had so changed her husband's heart and will. The result was that they both became earnest, happy Christians. One morning, a short time before his return to Canada in 1921, the writer called at their home. When he was leaving, the woman, with her husband standing by, handed the missionary the idol, saying, "Take it, pastor; take it to your country; it nearly cost me my life." Both are now baptized and are living happy Christian lives.

Rebuilding in Giran

The Giran Plain

Giran district is a beautiful plain on the east coast of the island,

a day's journey across the mountains, or six hours by steamer, from Kiirun harbor. The plain has a sea-coast of fifteen miles of an unbroken sandy beach, along which are situated a score of little fishing villages. The mountains form two sides of a triangle, the distance from the sea-coast to the extreme point being about ten miles. On this plain, which is rich and well watered, there are a hundred thousand Chinese, nearly all farmers. In early days there were several thousand Pepohoans in this section, but these have been so reduced in numbers that at the present time there are not more than one or two thousand. In former years all the chapels in this plain were located in Pepohoan villages. The proud Chinese despised the Pepohoans and also their reHgion, particularly in view of the fact that they had received it from the foreigners, the result being that, in religious matters, there was no point of contact between the two peoples. On account of their isolation from the rest of the island, the Chinese were very conservative, extremely superstitious, and would not readily listen to the "Jesus Doctrine."

Method of Work

In 1908, the writer paid his first visit to Giran, with Rev. Giam Chheng-hoa as assistant and guide. He found sixteen chapels, only two of which were in Chinese centres, namely, Giran City and Rato, the latter an important market-town. At that time, in the whole Giran plain there were but one or two Chinese families connected with the Christian Church. The following year, having been given the supervision of the churches on the plain, the writer spent a month there, dispensing sacraments, examining Sabbath schools and, with the preachers, holding evangelistic meetings

every evening in Giran City. This method of work was continued for three or four years. From the very first it was evident to writer that, if the Chinese were to be won to the Christian faith, the chapels would have to be transferred from Pepohoan villages to Chinese towns. A street-chapel had been rented already in Giran City, the capital of the plain, and a native pastor had been stationed at Rato; but as yet the Chinese kept aloof from the "level-plainers." It was a serious case of race prejudice, the Chinese possessing a very marked sense of superiority.

A Chinese Convert

In 1914, after the missionary's return from furlough, he again spent a month in the district and, with the evangelists, preached to the heathen in Giran City every evening. At one of these services, a Chinese, pushing his way through the crowd till he got his shoulder against the doorpost, listened attentively to two addresses. After the meeting he earnestly inquired of the missionary if what they were telling about this Jesus was really true; if He could do all they said He could for men. He was told that it was true. The following evening he came again, and again the third evening, this time bringing his two boys and sitting inside near the front. So earnestly did he listen that apparently he forgot the presence of the Pepohoans. On the Sabbath he and his two boys were present at the morning service, and in the evening his wife slipped in among the Christian women. It was evident that the man was deeply aroused and his heart touched by the truths he had heard.

On the Monday, when the man was away at his work three miles from the city, his wife, having heard that the preacher's

mother had just died, bought a flag and presented it as a token of her recognition of the new religion. This so enraged the mother-in-law that she beat her daughter-in-law most unmercifully. When the husband reached home he went to the ancestral table on which stood the family gods and, taking the central idol, solemnly declared to his mother that he was through with past superstitions and idol worship, as he had decided to become a Christian and, as a sign of his determination to be henceforth a follower of the new religion, he dropped the idol at his mother's feet. He continued to attend the chapel services and was soon able to read the New Testament. The following year he was baptized. Two years later his wife took the same step, and to-day the whole family are in the Christian Church.

Building the Church

Gradually the prejudices of the Chinese, previously referred to, weakened. Many began to venture inside the chapel. All would accept Christian literature, while some would go so far as to buy gospel tracts. For some time it had been known that a gift of several thousand dollars had been made for a church in Giran city. The preparations for building now aroused much interest. Land was bought, but great difficulty arose over getting the thatched cottages removed, for as soon as the owners heard that the foreigners wished to buy, they immediately demanded an exorbitant price. Through the help of the officials, however, the land was cleared and, in a busy thoroughfare in front of the Confucian temple, the "Jane Hunter Memorial" Church was built. A large bell, presented by an old Pepohoan widow, rings out a reminder before every

service, whether week-day or Sabbath, that the Gospel message is to be delivered, and gives an invitation for all to come and hear the "Jesus doctrine." The church, with a residence for the preacher and four adjoining rooms for the use of the itinerant missionaries, is one of the finest buildings in the city.

Soon after the completion of the church. Tan Ki Siong was appointed to Giran to help in evangelistic work, and his oldest son, a graduate of the Theological College, was assigned to Giran city chapel. The new church, the gifted young preacher and his father, as well as the devoted wife and the faithful mother, combined to arouse great interest and enthusiasm in the work. A few months after the opening of the new church, five weeks of special meetings were held. The missionary on this occasion took with him a converted hotel-keeper, who has become one of the most gifted evangelists in the mission.

The Converted Hotel-Keeper

Lau Thian-lai, for that is his name, was a young hotel-keeper, a few years ago, in the city of Taichu, in Mid-Formosa. He was an opium smoker, a gambler, a profligate and a cigarette fiend. After spending some time in Japan in riotous living, he returned home a moral and physical wreck. In vain he visited all the various temples, seeking help and praying to the gods for bodily healing. Finally he went to Shoka, where, in the Christian hospital, under the skilful treatment of the English missionary, Dr. Landsborough, he was healed. While there, he heard the Gospel and compared the helplessness of the gods and the folly of his superstitious beliefs with the new doctrine that was being made known to him. He was

convicted of his sins and of the folly of the life he had thus far led. The change was marked; his conversion was thorough. From that time he never touched opium or cigarettes, and began to preach to others the power and liberty of the Gospel of the Lord Jesus. As soon as he returned home he cleared the hotel of everything that could not stand the light of the Gospel, while to his customers he immediately began to make known the wonderful story. His conversion was the talk of his old companions, the gamblers of Taichu.

It was not long before there was a marked change in his general appearance. In six months one could hardly recognize him. One day an old gambler friend, who had not heard of his conversion, came to the door of the hotel where Lau Thian-lai was sitting fanning himself. The friend, not recognizing him, asked him if Lau Thian-lai was in. On being told that he was, he went through the house shouting for his old companion. Failing to find him, he returned to the man at the door and accused him of telling a falsehood. "Lau Thian-lai is not in!" he exclaimed. The hotel-keeper, with an old familiar smile, looked at him and said, "Which Lau Thian-lai do you want, last year's or this year's?" The man was startled and asked, "What on earth have you been eating?" "I have been eating the Jesus doctrine; sit down and I will tell you about it," he replied.

This was the man who, at the time of the missionary's visit to Giran just referred to, had become an earnest preacher, while still the owner of the hotel. He had been deacon in Taichu for two years, and at the time of this visit to Giran was an elder.

An Interesting Conversion

The special meetings in the new church were well attended. A few nights after they began a Chinese woman was led to hear the Gospel, with results that were singularly interesting. She was the wife of a Japanese registrar, who had wasted his substance by drinking and gambUng. The wife being a gambler also, they soon reached the end of their resources. The man decided to cast his wife and their young daughters out of the house, while he kept the sons. The woman was thus practically on the street, without a home, when the Christians invited her to come and hear the Gospel, assuring her she would receive peace. The first night she entered by a back door and, being much taller than the average Chinese woman, bent down in her seat the whole evening while looking up steadfastly at the speakers. The following evening she came again and on the third invited her husband to attend. At first he laughed, but finally, out of curiosity, he came, intending simply to stand at the door and listen. He was, however, led up to the front seat, where the text above the pulpit arrested his attention. The following evening he returned, and again on the third evening, this time bringing a large Japanese colored napkin, full of objects of worship, belonging to himself and to his wife, his whiskey vase and what was left of his cigarettes. Thus, in one act he gave up the past and trusted God for his whole future. Siong-tian Him-hi never drank or smoked again, and entered on the Christian life with remarkable earnestness. On the band of his hat he wrote the word "Christian," so that others might know that he had passed from death unto life and that he had changed masters. He understood the Gospel, trusted Jesus implicitly, and consecrated his whole life to

God and to the extension of His Kingdom.

The following year, the writer had the happy privilege one Sabbath day of baptizing the whole family, together with nine or ten Chinese converts. Soon afterwards, Siong-tian Him-hi was the means of the conversion of a Japanese official, who had been a drunkard, and given to beating his wife when under the influence of liquor. This official and his wife were both led to Christ through the faithful witness-bearing of this earnest convert, and at the following communion season were baptized in the Chinese Church. He was afterwards promoted and transferred to Taihoku, where he joined the Japanese Congregational Church.

The conversion of the Japanese registrar and his family deeply stirred the Christians. From that time the work prospered and old prejudices gradually disappeared. Siong-tian Him-hi was ordained an elder two years after his conversion, and in that office has served faithfully and has given liberally of his time and means. Recognizing the value and power of Christian literature, he bought one hundred and fifty dollars' worth of Christian books for distribution among those who, he thought, would make good use of them. A Sunday-school class for Japanese children was started, which he took charge of every Lord's day. He is a striking illustration of the power of the grace of God.

Gospel Triumphs at Rato

The work at Rato, a town of three thousand Chinese, five miles distant from Giran city, has been truly a testing of faith and patience. For years the prejudice against Christianity was very strong, and until quite recently there was not a single Chinese convert in the town. Ten years ago there were half a dozen chapels in the neighboring Pepohoan villages. It was, therefore, necessary to concentrate efforts on Rato, in the hope of gaining converts from the Chinese community. Though a Chinese pastor, an able and delightful character, had lived there for a year or two, so far as could be judged no impression had been made.

Tiu-a-pu, the Town Clerk

Among these proud Chinese of Rato no one despised the Jesus religion more than Tiu-a-pu, one of the town clerks. He was strong physically, coarse in manner, and had an uncontrollable temper and a blasphemous tongue. A most superstitious devotee of the gods of China, he went over to Foochow city on the mainland, in 1914, in company with three other pilgrims, to visit the famous temples and seek happiness, protection and prosperity. Five hundred dollars were spent on this futile trip. At every noted shrine they burned incense and finally decided to bring the sacred fire from one of the famous temples back to their own town in Formosa. This was by no means a simple undertaking, for on no account must the sacred fire be allowed to go out. They were all seasick crossing the Formosan channel and on arriving in Kiirun they found they had missed the boat. This necessitated the crossing of several ranges of mountains which in such stormy weather was an exceedingly difficult task. But being a strong man, Tiu-a-pu undertook this journey and was

successful in bringing the sacred fire to Rato. After first burning incense on his own ancestral hearth, he went proudly and lit the incense sticks in the temples of the town.

The sacred fire from Foochow, however, could neither avert nor drive away misfortune from the town clerk's family. Never before had there been so much sickness in his home. Not a month passed without his having to call in a sorcerer to drive off some evil spirit. About this time a rented preaching hall was opened near his home, and his little daughter started coming to the Sabbath school, where she soon learned some Christian hymns and the Romanized script. The mother also became interested. She formed an acquaintance with the preacher's wife, and began attending the services. Her interest in what she heard increased, much to the alarm of her husband. The little daughter made such progress in the Sabbath school that the preacher proposed that she should be sent to the Tamsui Girls' School. The mother was willing for her to go, but the father most strenuously opposed it.

While this proposal was under consideration, special evangelistic meetings were opened in the Rato chapel, in connection with which Tan Ki Siong, his son, the hotel-keeper, Lau Thian-lai, and other preachers were called in to help. The town clerk, Tiu-a-pu, was persuaded to come and for the first time hear the Gospel, against which he had so often spoken and the converts of which he had so thoroughly despised. The first night he expressed astonishment at the good teaching he heard. He continued coming every evening while the special meetings lasted, with the result that the little daughter was allowed to go to Tamsui. Indeed, it was her father who took her across the very

mountains over which two years before he had travelled with the sacred fire from a Foochow shrine. In the course of a year his wife was baptized, while he himself became a regular attendant at the church services and started to learn to read the New Testament in Romanized colloquial. It was not long before he believed, and at once became a faithful witness of the Gospel of God's grace.

On one occasion Tiu-a-pu visited the writer in Taihoku. He came to tell the missionary an incident that had made a profound impression on his mind, and that had aroused in his heart the deepest gratitude to God for His goodness in delivering him from the power of superstition and idolatry. That day he had been looking after the burial of one of the men who, two or three years before, had gone with him on that fruitless pilgrimage to Foochow. Three days previously the man had gone to the famous temple at Pak-kang, in Mid-Formosa, where, while burning incense before the goddess Ma-tso, he had suddenly fallen down dead. The body had been brought to Tai-hoku, where the policemen had hired coolies to carry it to a graveyard on the outskirts of the city. Here the coolies had left it in a hole full of water. Some one had sent word to Tiu-a-pu, the converted town clerk, who immediately responded and saw that proper arrangements were made for his friend's burial.

Tiu-a-pu is no uncertain Christian. Even before he was baptized he observed family worship in his home. His liberality may be illustrated by the fact that he has offered as much land as may be necessary for chapel grounds from a large plot he has bought in the centre of the town. There are now in Rato several Chinese Christian families, who, with the Pepohoan Christians

from the surrounding villages, have united in establishing one church in the town. Thus hath God wondrously wrought by His vSpirit in the town of Rato.

A Mission Station Needed at Giran

Interesting incidents in connection with the opening of preaching halls in other Chinese centres in the Giran field could be related, but space does not permit. Throughout the plain there is much need of missionary supervision. The Mission Council is looking forward to opening, in Giran city, a mission station with an ordained missionary and two lady evangelistic workers. Such a station in Giran would provide more thorough supervision for the Karenko plain, about sixty miles to the south, in Mid-Formosa.

Water-Lily Harbor

Karenko, or Water-Lily Harbor, is a town on the north of this plain, with a population of some two thousand Japanese and about the same number of Formosans. The harbor, which affords anchorage for Japanese steamers, is an open shore upon which heavy waves roll, producing a very restless surf. On the least

provocation from an adverse wind, this surf becomes so heavy that no boats can venture out.

Landing under Difficulties

Landing in a harbor such as this is, of course, at times, extremely precarious. On the beach nearly a hundred savages, men and women, are lined up to help load and unload the boats which move back and forth from the steamers anchored a few hundred yards beyond the surf. Many of these savages are expert swimmers. Dexterously they plunge through the high waves, rising several feet above them and, swimming out to the boats that await their chance behind the breakers, they snatch light ropes attached to heavier ones and ride in on the top of the waves to the sandy beach. As soon as the larger ropes reach the shore, the savages grasp them and wait impatiently for the call. In the meantime the boats behind the surf come as close as they dare. Then at the command of the skipper, they are turned around, stern shoreward and the call is given. Immediately the savages, with a characteristic yell, pull the boats on the top of the high waves and land them high up on the beach. The feelings of the passengers can be better imagined than described, as during the thrilling landing they squat on the bottom of the boats. The writer once saw a boat turn perpendicular, capsize and split in two on the beach. The men escaped, but the mail-bags were scattered over the raging surf. That day there was no landing in WaterLily Harbor, and the steamer had to seek a safer anchorage.

Successes at Phoenix Grove

From Water-Lily Harbor to a point sixty miles to the south a light railway has been built. Thirty miles south is the town of Horin, or Phoenix Grove, the most remote preaching station in the territory of the Canadian mission. Some years ago a few Christians settled in this vicinity, some on farms, others in the neighboring foothills for the purpose of distilling camphor, and a few in the town. While supervising the building of the new church at the north harbor, the writer, with a preacher, visited Phoenix Grove. The Christians were most enthusiastic and asked that a preacher be sent to them, a request which was granted the following year.

In 1915, successful evangelistic meetings were held at this point, when three preachers and the missionary spent a week visiting villages during the day and preaching to the heathen in the town every evening. Much opposition was met with on the part of the more influential Formosans.

A young man, the bookkeeper of the Camphor Company, who had never heard the Gospel before, told the town elder that he was going to hear the Jesus doctrine. The elder advised him not to go and tried to discourage him by saying many uncomplimentary things about the new religion. The young man, however, was not to be discouraged, but was present the first evening. He was intelligent and courteous and from the first was deeply interested. The following evening he was at the street-chapel before the

meeting opened, and sought an interview with the missionary. The third evening he stood up in the middle of one of the addresses and enquired if he might ask a question. Then, turning round to the audience he said: "I have heard now for three nights and while I do not understand much yet, I believe, from what I have heard, that these men are telling the truth. I do not believe this foreign missionary would come all these thousands of miles to tell us what is not true." Then, turning to the missionary, he asked, "What guarantee have you that this Jesus can forgive sins? I have not lived a good life and I want to know more about the forgiveness of sins." No heathen in that town had a better reputation than the bookkeeper, but that night his heart was touched; the truth entered and found good soil.

After his conversion, he wondered how his parents would take the news of his having become a Christian, for they had never yet heard the Jesus doctrine. It was not long, however, before they too followed his example and became believers. A few months later he wrote a letter telling how thankful he was for having heard the Gospel. A year afterwards he was baptized and we heard that he had been ordained a deacon in one of the South mission stations.

The Christians at Phoenix Grove were greatly encouraged by the bookkeeper's conversion. A number of heathen gave up their idols and several names were added to the list of adherents. Their next step was the erection of a church. The Japanese official gave a large plot of land in the centre of the town for this purpose, and the town elder, who had advised the bookkeeper not to go and hear the Gospel, sent in a contribution of twenty-five dollars to the building fund. The Christians themselves raised nearly seven

hundred dollars, in addition to the labor they gave. In 1921 the church was completed. There are now about a hundred names on the list, including communicants and adherents. Prejudices are being gradually removed and the prospects for the future are most encouraging.

The Passing oj Tan Ki Siong

The announcement of Tan Ki Siong's death has recently been received. This chapter ought not to close without a brief record of the closing period of this remarkable man's life. In 1918 he and his oldest son, who was then the preacher at Giran, removed to South Formosa. This son was called to Tainan as preacher to the largest congregation in the island. His second son is still in Japan attending Kyoto University, preparing to enter the Christian ministry. The third son is a preacher in Mid-Formosa and the fourth, a young lad, is in Japan attending school.

From the time Tan Ki Siong left Giran till his death he preached throughout the South mission stations, spending most of his time, however, in helping his son in Tainan. Though not in good health, his mind was constantly planning for the extension of the Kingdom of God. One of his cherished plans, to which he gave much effort, was that of establishing a band of laymen who would give of their time and means for the evangelization of Formosa. Throughout his fourteen years of Christian service, he devoted himself to personal

work, encouraging weak congregations, preaching to heathen audiences and giving freely of his means wherever the need was greatest.

From the time of his conversion, he was deeply desirous that all his sons should enter the Christian ministry. How far this desire was realized has already been indicated. His family had great respect and affection for him; indeed, we have rarely seen more obedient children. The love was mutual, for he sacrificed much in order that his sons might be well educated and fitted for useful service for his Lord and Master.

Few among the Christians of Formosa have possessed such unwavering faith, such surrender of heart and life, such consecration of means, such enthusiasm for the evangelization of his own people and such respect and affection for men of another race as Tan Ki Siong, the converted scholar. Formosa can never be the same without him. He has gone to his reward; his influence has been farreaching and his works do follow him. There, in yonder glory, a trophy saved by grace, he finds a fitting place in that throng seen in vision by the apostle John — "After this I beheld, and, lo, a great multitude, which no man could number, of all nations, and kindreds, and people, and tongues, stood before the throne, and before the Lamb, clothed with white robes, and palms in their hands."

Draper

O THOU great Shepherd of mankind, we thank Thee that Thy concern and love include us and all men and that Thy heart is moved with compassion for those whom Thou dost see scattered abroad without a shepherd across all the meadows and mountainsides of the world's life. We thank Thee, too, for all the men and women who have so shared Thy compassion as to go with Thee into difficult and remote places seeking those that were lost.

ESPECIALLY do we thank Thee for those who have gone from our land to Formosa. Encourage their hearts more and more as they see the triumphs of Thy Cross in the cities and hamlets of the Island. May they and their Formosan coworkers be given health and protection and the daily renewal of Thy Spirit, so that fruit may increase to their account. Grant that the new converts may be established in faith and in godly living, and that the young Church may grow in zeal and spiritual energy and may rejoice in a great Ingathering to its fellowship.

WE beseech Thee, O God, that we In our homeland may be genuinely concerned for these other sheep that are not of our fold. Give to each one of us a passionate desire for their salvation and a spirit of intercession in their behalf, until all shall

be broughtIn and there shall be joy In the presence of the angels of God and in the heart of the Good Shepherd. For His Sake. AMEN.

Chapter IX

WOMEN'S WORK

Beginnings of Work for Women

THE first reference to definite Christian work among the women of North Formosa is found in the report of 1879. The Women's Missionary Society for several years forwarded a definite sum of money to Dr. Mackay to be used in the education of the Christian women. In 1879 Mrs. Junor assisted Dr. and Mrs. Mackay in the instruction of a number of women converts. In 1881, Dr. Mackay sent home a request for a grant of three thousand dollars for the erection of a Girls' School building. The request was granted and in 1882 the building was completed and opened,

with an attendance of forty-five pupils, mostly from Giran Plain.

The First School

There was considerable difficulty in getting the Chinese converts to send their daughters to the school, so much in fact that it had to be turned into a combined school for women and girls. The school was built on the same beautiful plot as that on which Oxford College stood. The absence of a high wall around it led the Chinese to hesitate to allow their daughters to attend an institution so unprotected, and in such striking contrast with the seclusion that marked the life of the Formosan girls in those days. However, the school at that time met a great need. Preachers* wives and preachers' widows and a few girls from Christian homes made up the happy family on Fort Meadow. Dr. Mackay had the general supervision; Mrs. Mackay, Mrs. lap and other Christian workers, taught the women, while the godly Tan He, a capable teacher and a man of devoted spirit, conducted the Bible study. Every morning and evening the whole family met in Oxford College. Those days are still to many a delightful memory.

Co-operation of the W.M.S.

There was, however, a general feeling that much more was needed for the women and girls of North Formosa. The Women's Missionary Society's report for 1894, in discussing the work in Formosa, indicated that from the very first the Society had been ready to provide whatever was required to make the work effective for the evangelization of the Formosan women.

First Women Missionaries

During her furlough in 1900 Mrs. Gauld spoke at W.M.S. conferences and presbyterials, strongly emphasizing in every address the great need of women missionaries for North Formosa. After her return to the field, she wrote back urging the Women's Missionary Society to send out workers. The petition forwarded to the Foreign Mission Committee in 1902 contained a strong appeal for two unmarried lady missionaries to be sent out to reorganize the Girls' School. In response to the request, two teachers were appointed and sent to Formosa in the fall of 1905, Miss Jane M. Kinney and Miss Hannah Connell.

School Work

After two strenuous years spent in acquiring the Chinese language, these two devoted workers began to plan for the opening of the Girls' School. The deep interest of the Formosan Government in all the educational institutions established in the island was an important factor in the situation. In order to secure the largest possible efficiency, the two lady missionaries, before opening the school, visited the sister missions both in South Formosa and on the mainland, studying most carefully policies and methods of work.

Girls' School Opened

The opening of the new Girls' School, in October, 1907, was an historic event for the womanhood of North Formosa. That such was possible so soon after the arrival of the missionaries, who had not had two full years of language study, was a tribute to their faithful and efficient work. One can imagine the fear and trembling that seized the twenty-four timid girls who arrived in Tamsui, when they found themselves not only inside the school, with a wall six feet high surrounding them, but actually locked in the grounds, much to the comfort, however, of the parents who were leaving their daughters in the care of these foreign missionaries. Soon, however, the timidity passed away. The mutual love between teachers and pupils grew steadily, and in a short time these Formosan girls would not have exchanged their new home on Fort Meadow for any other in the island.

The following year the parents were invited to the closing exercises. It was interesting to see their amazement at the comforts of the school, the neatness of the rooms, the care taken of the morals and health of their daughters; and as they looked at that six foot wall, their doubts all vanished and they felt their daughters were, indeed, in safe keeping and in good hands. They were not slow in discovering that Tamsui Girls' School was the safest place morally, the most wholesome socially, the most instructive religiously and educationally, and, what was no less important, the most profitable financially in North Formosa.

The New Building Completed

The old school building, erected in 1883, was now becoming

dilapidated and utterly inadequate to meet the growing needs. Accordingly, in 1915, it was torn down and on the same site a more commodious building erected. The formal opening of the new School, in May, 1916, was marked not only by a large and interested gathering, but also by the presence of leading educationalists and the civil governor, who gave an address on education.

High School Department Added

Advantage was taken of this opportune time to add to the regular course a high school department. The standard of this new department corresponds to that in similar Japanese schools for girls, with the addition of definite Christian teaching. The most of the work is carried on in the Japanese language. Thus students who wish to proceed to Japan for more advanced work are well fitted to enter schools of higher education there.

The Only Woman Doctor in Formosa

Mention should be made of a bright young Christian girl, who, after graduating from the Tamsui school, went to Tokyo, where she studied medicine for several years. In 1920 she graduated and returned to Formosa, the first and only woman doctor in the whole island. She is an earnest and attractive young woman and desires to spend her life helping her own people. At present there is no opening for her in our mission, as the hospital is closed. In the meantime she is engaged in medical work in the government hospital at Taihoku.

One Product of the School

On the outskirts of Tamsui is a palatial home, owned by a very wealthy Chinese. In accordance with the usual custom of the rich, he has taken to himself three wives. He is well-educated and, though not a Christian, he appreciated the advantages of a Christian education for his daughter and sent her to our Girls' School. At first the wives, who were all heathen, were not in favor of her being sent. Gradually the Gospel found a lodging in the girl's heart and she became a true believer. At once she was concerned for her family. Little by little, through her influence, the three wives became favorably disposed toward Christianity, and welcomed the Bible woman as she came regularly to the home. Before long, all three were attending church, and soon learned to read and write Chinese in the Romanized form. Now they are all professing Christians. The father as yet has given no signs of becoming a Christian, but we dare to hope that ere long he, too, will be won for the Kingdom. The daughter, after graduating from the Girls' School, went to Japan for further study, and thus to fit herself for still larger service for her own people. As we think what her life might have been — one of ease and luxury, with marriage, doubtless, in time, into another wealthy heathen home — and contrast that with what it is, one of usefulness, happiness and service for others, we thank God for the Girls' School.

Their school duties made it impossible for the two missionaries to give much attention to the heathen women throughout the district. During the summer holidays trips were made to the country, but these trips had to be occupied largely with visiting the homes of the pupils and their friends, endeavouring to increase interest in

the school and to secure more pupils.

Women's School

It soon became apparent to them that a great need existed for a Bible school where women could receive instruction and be prepared to go out and teach their own sisters. In 1910 the Women's School was built and Miss Connell appointed to take charge. The women came from non-Christian as well as Christian, from poor as well as wealthy homes. Since then many of the preachers' wives have taken advantage of this training and have come to the School, some for shorter and some for longer periods. A few have taken a full two years' course and graduated as Bible women. Many have been able to take only a shorter course, and have returned to their homes not only to become better wives and more intelligent mothers, but also to take an active part in Christian work in their own communities. The school, too, has been a direct evangelistic agency, in that many who entered as heathen have gone out decided Christians.

Instances of the Work

Among the instances that might be given of work of the school, two are of special interest. Peng-a-chim was the wife of a well-to-do heathen, an opium smoker, who lived in Taiko. She was taken ill and went to the mission hospital at Shoka, which was not far distant, where she was brought under the influence of the Gospel and became an earnest believer. To her joy, on her return home, she found a chapel had been recently opened and crowds were coming to hear the Word. She began attending the meetings,

but in this was much opposed by her husband, who went so far as to beat her on some occasions. She persisted, however, in coming.

In the course of time his opposition ceased and, though he did not become a Christian, he gave her permission to go to the Women's School. Here she made splendid progress. By the time she had finished her course it was very evident that she was well fitted, in many ways, for definite Christian service and so was appointed as a Bible woman. Her husband had already taken in another wife. Peng-a-chim was therefore free to engage in Christian work. For eight years she has worked with untiring energy in the hospital, in chapels, and as travelling evangelist with the lady missionaries. Refined and attractive in manner, she has won her way into the homes of the rich, while her humility of spirit and her love and sympathy for her own people have made her a welcome visitor in the homes of the poor.

"Peaceful Heart."

Another graduate of the School, whose story is of special interest, is An-sim. When a little girl, An-sim, or "Peaceful Heart," was sold for a few dollars by her heathen mother. As she grew up she was passed on to another home and finally became the second concubine of a wealthy farmer, on the outskirts of Taichu city in Central Formosa. In the meantime her mother had become a Christian. She was constantly thinking of her lost daughter. The day came when the wealthy farmer died and An-sim, knowing that life henceforth in that home, for her, would be intolerable, determined to spend the rest of her days in a Buddhist temple. With only the clothing she wore, she stole away. On her way to

the mountain temple she passed through her home town, and her mother, hearing news of her, brought her to her home for the night.

It was a singular providence that led the writer on this occasion to the city of Taichu to have an interview with Lau Thian-lai, the converted hotelkeeper. That evening a few Christians were invited to a prayer-meeting in his home. Among them was the woman referred to above who came with the daughter, now a young woman of twentytwo, whom she had sold sixteen years before. The missionary knew nothing of the circumstances, but the message, from Romans 12: 1-3, was specially suitable to one who was about to dedicate her life to Buddha. Peaceful Heart had never heard the Gospel before, and at once responded. The result was that, a few days afterward, instead of going to the Buddhist temple she came to the Women's School. While there she revealed a keen mind and was very receptive to Christian truth. The missionaries spoke of her as one of the most promising women who had ever passed through the school. She graduated in the spring of 1922, and at once went out to bear the good news of peace and deliverance to others. The Union Young People's Society at Humesville, Manitoba, has undertaken her support as a Bible woman.

Faithful Women Workers

It is fitting that mention should be made of two other most faithful women who are still in active work. Mrs. Iap was a teacher in the old School for Girls in the days of Dr. Mackay and, after the lady missionaries had reorganized the school, continued teaching for some years. During the last few years she has been a Bible woman in the city and has accompanied the missionaries on their

country trips. Her knowledge of the Bible and her long experience as a Christian have made her a most valuable worker. Refined in appearance and manner, she has no difficulty in gaining an entrance to heathen homes, where her message is always appropriate and helpful. Her daughter has been teacher to one of our missionaries, while for several years her son has been a dispenser in the hospital.

For the last four years Mrs. Lo has been used in a singular way in winning others to Christ. Naturally she is very reserved and before becoming a Christian was seldom seen outside her own home. Even after she became a believer, it was with diffidence that she ventured out among the Christian women. After her husband's death she attended the Women's School and manifested special fitness for Christian service. She not only understands Christian truth in a remarkable way, but is able to convey her knowledge very effectively to others. She has a peculiar gift for personal work and in her quiet, earnest way is reaching many hearts with the Gospel message.

The Missionary Staff Increased

Miss Mabel Clazie arrived in 1910 and Miss Lily Adair in 1911, but owing to the needs of both the Girls' School and Women's School, as well as the hospital, it was impossible to organize the evangelistic work among the women in the country. Both were needed in these institutions to reHeve others. Owing to lack of missionaries it was not till about 1914 that definitely organized plans were undertaken for country work among the women.

Medical Work Among the Women

A Successful Soul-winner

The work for women carried on in the hospital has been most encouraging. When Dr. Ferguson reorganized the medical work in Tamsui, one of the first to come under his care was a poor widow, Mrs. An. She was an interesting character, and one whose name has been familiar in the hospital and in many chapels for the last fifteen years. When she came to the hospital she was advanced in years and diseased almost beyond remedy. Mrs. Gauld, who knows the Chinese language and understands Chinese women as few do, helped to look after her. A small corner was given her in the outer court of the hospital. Through the skill, patience and perseverence of the doctor she finally recovered. After having learned to read the Chinese in the Romanized form herself, she began teaching other in-patients and soon became an active personal worker. Among others who shared her ministry was Bok-a, a blind young man, a heathen, who had come to Tamsui Hospital. Mrs. An cared for him and taught him Gospel hymns. He became a Christian. After recovering his health, he was helped to go to Tainan "School for the Blind." where he graduated as a masseur, since which time he has been able to earn a livelihood. He is now in the city of Giran, where he and his wife, his father and his mother, are all members of the Church.

Other instances of the work Mrs. An is doing might be given.

The report of the Women's work for 1921 has the following item about her: "Mrs. An is far from attractive in appearance, and shabbily dressed. She has one desire, to win souls for Christ, and has had the joy of winning not a few. Among others this year was a woman of seventy-two, who had been a vegetarian Buddhist for fifty years." As one looks at Mrs. An, the words of Paul come readily to mind: "And base things of the world, and things which are despised, hath God chosen."

A Transformed Life

Another of the fruits of the medical work among women was the conversion of the saintly Mrs. Ban Heng. About twelve years ago she came to the hospital in Tamsui. Here she heard of the love of Jesus, and by it her whole life was transformed. She soon learned to read and at once began to attend the women's weekly meetings and to visit heathen homes with the missionaries. But her strength was gradually failing and eventually she was confined to her bed. Her tiny bedroom, a dark, dingy room with uneven mud floor, opened off a small living-room. The only light that entered it came through the door, a small opening in the wall, and some small panes of glass in the roof. A miserable home-made structure, on which she lay, served as a bed. The only other furniture was a table and a bench. On he walls were posted Bible pictures taken from Scripture rolls. Here she lay for over six years.

She greatly desired to lead her husband to Christ and for a time was hopeful. But, alas, he grew tired of a sick wife, and brought a second wife into the home, which did not further her hopes nor add to her comfort. Her sick-room was visited by many, including

the missionaries, all of whom recognized that here was one to whom the Saviour was so precious that bodily ills and discomforts counted for little. Always patient and bright, she was ever ready to speak to others of the love of Jesus. During those years of illness many a neighbor heard the Gospel from her lips and even learned to read and memorize hymns.

At the time she was confined to her bed, she had not yet been baptized. When she learned that she could be baptized and receive the sacrament of the Lord's Supper in her little room, she was very happy, for she had long wished for this, but had been reticent about making the request. One Sabbath, after communion service, the elders, a missionary and his wife and Miss Connell went down to Mrs. Ban Heng's home. It was an experience those present never will forget, so manifest was the presence of the Spirit in the simple baptismal and communion service. Her joy was inexpressible. She felt she had now obeyed the command of her Lord and was ready to go. From that time on, at the close of each communion service in the Tamsui church, a little group of three or four, with the pastor, went to her home and there, at her bedside, the simple feast was held that commemorated the love of Him who had brought such peace into her life.

A time came when she appeared to be growing a little stronger. She had a great desire to go to the Mackay Memorial Hospital in Taihoku, not only in the hope that she might be helped, but also with the thought in mind of the opportunities she would have there of speaking to other afBicted ones. Dr. Ferguson made all arrangements necessary for the train journey, and himself accompanied her to the city. She lived there for some months, able

to move about the hospital wards, speaking to the women patients, a blessing to many, a wonder to all and a bright, happy witness for her Lord.

But her mission on earth was about finished. She returned to Tamsui, and not long afterwards God called her to himself. Hers is a crown of many jewels won for her Saviour. None of us who knew her can ever forget the fragrant influence of her life. "She being dead, yet speaketh."

The Nursing Department

On the opening of the Mackay Memorial Hospital in Taihoku, the Woman's Missionary Society became responsible for the Nursing Department, which, in the fall of 1912, Miss Isabel Elliott was appointed to superintend. In former years there were neither foreign nor Formosan women nurses; relatives of the patients came to wait on them, under the supervision of male dispensers and ward coolies. With the opening of the new hospital everything was changed. The foreign nurse, however, soon discovered that much patience was required, for it was no easy task to make the Chinese respect the sanitary laws observed in Western institutions. As Miss Elliott had to commence her duties in the hospital before she had learned the language, an interpreter was required. This position was very ably filled by Mrs. Koa, formerly Bella Mackay. Several young women who had attended either the Girls' School or the Women's School were received in training, graduated in due course and, through the good services of Dr. Ferguson, received government diplomas.

A Promising Work Closed

During these few years a most promising work was carried on among the women in the wards of the hospital. There were many cases of remarkable healing, not only of body, but also of soul. Not only were Christian hymns taught and Scripture texts memorized, but many of the patients learned to read their Bibles in the Romanized script. This necessary and promising work has been stopped and the hospital closed since 1919 on account of the Board not being able to send medical missionaries. Since then Miss Elliott has been engaged in country work among the women. The closed hospital, with its splendid equipment, is a mighty challenge to the home churches to make it possible for the Foreign Mission Board to release the ministrations of this agency that carry such large possibilities for the Kingdom of God.

Work Among the Women at the Outstations

The Woman Missionary Necessary

No work in the mission is more fruitful than that among the women in the outstations. In earlier days it was difficult to get women and girls to listen openly to the Christian message. When the male missionary and the Formosan evangelist entered a heathen home, the women would generally disappear and, through half-open doors, from behind bamboo partitions, or from some secluded corner, would listen to what the missionary or evangelist had to

say. The woman evangelist with her Bible woman, however, could gather them into the central hall and converse with them with the greatest freedom.

Changing Attitude of Women

Of recent years the attitude of the women is greatly changing. With the passing away of foot-binding, the women go out much more than formerly. To-day they reveal a new interest in affairs outside their own homes, and everywhere they are ready to listen.

The Woman Missionary at Work

The woman missionary arouses curiosity wherever she goes. After a stay of from one to three weeks in a centre the curiosity changes to real interest, not so much in her, personally, as in the message she brings. Part of her work is the organizing of the Christian women into classes for definite instruction in the Bible and for teaching them to read the Romanized colloquial. Usually the mornings are spent with these classes, the afternoons in house-to-house visitation, and the evenings in evangelistic services in the chapels. Thus the number of Bible readers among the women is being steadily increased, the Christian women are being strengthened and many of the heathen are being influenced for Christ.

One of the greatest joys in the country work is that of meeting those who were formerly in the schools, but who are now wives of preachers or other workers, taking their places faithfully in the service of the Church. Some of these are in remote and lonely corners, and to them the cheer and encouragement given by the

visit of the woman missionary means more than can be expressed. The friendship of school days is renewed and strengthened, as together they talk over and engage in the work of the home community. These former pupils are always ready to accompany the missionaries and, in many instances, have already paved the way to heathen homes as well as to the homes of the needy. The great regret is that because there are so few missionaries free for country work, such visits can be made only infrequently.

Work Among the Women in Taiko

In the town of Taiko work among the women has developed, in a few years, in a remarkable way. This town has been visited several times by both the married and unmarried women missionaries, and classes for the women have been held from two to four weeks at a time. The women showed much enthusiasm in learning to read and in memorizing Scripture. Their response to Christian truth was surprising. Nine years ago a weekly Bible class was organized and in all that time the class has never missed its meeting. The pastor's wife, who at one time attended the Women's School and is now the devoted mother of eight children, has been largely responsible for its signal success. The women also have organized a Saturday house-to-house visitation for the purpose of inviting their heathen sisters to come to church, with the result that there are more women than men now attending the Sunday services.

One cannot think of the native workers this district has produced without rejoicing and looking forward with confidence to the yet greater things of the future. At the present time more Christian workers are to be found in the church in Taiko than in

any other part of the field. It will be of interest to know that not only the pastor's wife, but also the doctor's wife, who is himself an elder, a deacon's wife, a preacher's wife, and a Bible woman, all rendering faithful service in the Taiko congregation, are graduates of either the Girls' or the Women's School. Other places might be mentioned where the progress is equally encouraging.

It is a cause of much joy that two new women missionaries are preparing for country evangelistic work, the most needy department of the mission. One has been appointed specially for the Hakka district.

Other Forms of Women's Work

The latest department in the women's work is the kindergarten. In connection with the chapel in Daitotei, a kindergarten Sunday-school class was organized two years ago, which has created a great deal of interest and enthusiasm. There are three centres — Taihoku, Sinchiku and Giran — where kindergarten schools could be opened to great advantage.

Though the wives of missionaries are not appointed by the Mission Board in the same way as the other members of the staff, they are among the most active of the missionary force. In addition to the multitudinous duties that fall to them as missionaries' wives, all of which contribute in large measure to the life of the mission, some have taught music and others general subjects in the

Middle School or in the Women's School, while others again have conducted Bible classes in Tamsui, in Taihoku and in outstations, or have accompanied their husbands on evangelistic trips in the country.

Some years ago the wife of one of the missionaries started a weekly Women's Bible Class in the village of Hokuto. A poor widow lived there whose chief means of making a living was gathering firewood on the edge of the mountains and selling it in the village, earning thereby about fifteen cents a day. Her only child, a daughter of nine or ten, accompanied her regularly to the Bible class. From the first the missionary was drawn to the little girl, who was bright and attractive and took a keen interest in the Bible lesson. She was a promising pupil, and soon steps were taken to provide the necessary means for her education in the Girls' School. Part of this she earned herself by working in the school several hours a week. In the course of time she graduated and for a time was teacher to one of the lady missionaries. Now she is a teacher in the Women's School, trusted and faithful, with one overmastering desire, that of helping her own people.

Call to Meet Present Needs

For several years repeated and urgent requests have been sent to Canada for women workers, teachers, evangelists and nurses. Again the opportunity for the investment of one's life in the task

of training young women and of bringing light, life, and happiness to these sisters beyond the seas is presented and the challenge thrown out. Who will respond? At present, the following women are urgently needed:

A University Graduate with Normal Training,
A Domestic Science Teacher,
A Music Teacher for the Girls' School,
Seven Women Evangelists for Country Work,
Five Women Evangelists for Hakka Work,
Two Women Evangelists for the Hoklo District,
Two Nurses for Mackay Memorial Hospital.

"Whom shall I send and who will go?"

Draper

O THOU Who art light and in whom is no darkness at all, we recognize Thee as the only answer to the gloom of sin and sorrow and death in the world. We bring Thee humble and hearty thanks for the brightness which Jesus Christ has brought into the lot of womanhood. We bless Thee, Son of Mary, that wherever Thou hast been made to prevail in human relations Thou hast lifted woman from neglect to loving care, from limitation to privilege,

from degradation to an estate of honor.

BLESS, we beseech Thee, the women of Formosa. Reach them with Thy Gospel of emancipation and enlightenment. Open their hearts to Thy truth. Be with the women missionaries that are at work among them as they proclaim Thee in the homes, by the wayside, in chapel, school and hospital. Give Thy blessing richly to the Bible Women. Grant that they may be abundantly equipped through instruction and personal experience, so that they may give their witness in demonstration of the Spirit and in power.

MAY Thy gracious blessing rest upon the Woman's Missionary Society that has been the means of conveying Thy message of love into Formosa and other lands. In larger measure may the Christian women of our homeland joyfully claim the privilege of sharing Thee with their sisters throughout the world, for the glory of the Name which is above every name. AMEN.

CHAPTER X

WHAT OF THE FUTURE?

THE Christian Church has made remarkable] progress in Formosa, both in the North and in the South, during the last fifty years. The work, however, is but begun . For every Christian in the Island Beautiful, there are one hundred and twenty-two non-Christians, and among a population of 3,500,000 only 150 preaching stations. The inadequacy of this is even more apparent when we are reminded that Formosa has 4,500 villages with a population of from 300 to 500 each, and 900 with from 500 to 1,000; 1,000 towns with a population of from 1,000 to 3,000, 82 with from 3,000 to 5,000, and 20 with from 5,000 to 10,000; and 11 cities with from 10,000 to 60,000. This list does not include the thousands of small hamlets scattered over the mountain-sides, among the bamboo groves, and in the little nooks throughout the island. Unless the progress of the last fifty years is greatly accelerated, generations will pass before Formosa's people are

won for Christ.

We need to remember, however, that the area of the island and the size of the population, while helping to constitute a tremendous task, are neither of them overwhelming; that in Formosa there is but one united Christian Church, without any sectarian divisions to interfere with progress; and that the two Missionary Societies at work there, representing the Presbyterian Church of England and the Presbyterian Church of Canada, have been for many years co-operating in their efforts for the speedy evangelization of the island. In view of all this, granted the required increase in consecrated native workers and an adequate staff of missionaries — teachers, medical workers and evangelists — and above all with the mighty working of an Omnipotent God, the "Evangelization of Formosa in this Generation" may be regarded, not as a fanciful motto, but rather as a challenging watchword to the fulfilment of which we may look forward with confidence.

The rapid changes in the commercial, social and religious life of the Formosan people call for serious attention and speedy action on the part of the Christian Church. No nation is undergoing more radical changes than Japan. Politically she is facing a crisis. Her religions are already in the crucible. Nevertheless, Christianity is making progress in the Empire. The anti-Christian attitude is weakening with the years. In Formosa many Japanese Christians are in important positions of trust, and as the number of these increases the effect on educated Formosans will be to dispose them more favorably towards the Christian faith.

What of the Hindrances?

New Hindrances for Old

The old hindrances to progress, such as ancestral worship, superstition, conservatism and illiteracy, are giving place to modern problems. With the neglect of the Confucian Classics, ancestral worship is passing. Indeed, in Formosa, the whole Confucian system is falling to pieces. The rapid progress Japan has made along modern educational lines is responsible for the rising generation of Formosans seeing the emptiness of many of their old beliefs. To a large extent, however, Japanese and Formosan teachers are agnostic in their attitude toward religion, with the result that, while the young people are growing up with their faith in the old superstitions shattered, nothing whatever is being given to them to take its place.

Idolatry Entrenched but Declining

Idolatry has still a firm hold on the masses. Belief in the malign activities of evil spirits and in the influence for good of the idols, which represent the spirits of the virtuous sages of the past, still exists. The masses still believe that the neglect of worshipping the idols will arouse their anger and bring misfortune and that paying them homage will be rewarded by good luck, good crops and general prosperity. The younger generation, however, is getting beyond the childish credulity of their fathers. Many

temples are falling into disuse. Only few are being repaired and few are patronized with any measure of enthusiasm. The waste of money on their reHgious festivals is being discouraged by the Japanese. The influence of the Japanese rule has certainly broken the backbone of old Chinese conservatism, while the introduction of all kinds of Western goods is greatly changing the attitude of the entire nation toward the outside world. All this has contributed in no small measure to the decline of idolatry.

Illiteracy Being Removed

One of the great hindrances to real progress has been illiteracy. Probably no nation of modern times has done so much in removing this hindrance from its national life as Japan. In Japan proper at the present time only five per cent, of the population are illiterate. In Formosa, in earlier days, only six in a thousand could read, and the ignorance of the people was appalling. With the establishment of public schools in the island by the Japanese, this has been entirely changed and a condition created much more favorable to the rapid spread of the Christian faith. This is evidenced in many ways. The sale of Christian literature and the number of tracts and Bible portions distributed is increasing steadily. Two colporteurs are now in the field, while one of the missionaries is to be set apart for the work of translation and the preparation of Christian literature. All the young people in Formosa who have gone through the public school are bilingualists. What they cannot read in the Chinese character they can read in the Japanese script, while all Christian young people are able to read the Romanized colloquial. The daily newspapers are issued in both the Japanese and the Chinese

languages. Thus the illiteracy of the people is being removed and with it one serious hindrance to national and religious progress.

But though some of the old hindrances to progress are disappearing in a measure, there are to-day many grave problems that imperil the true advancement of the people of Formosa.

Social Hindrances

Among the main hindrances the Formosan Church has to contend with at the present time are those common to all lands. One could wish that Japanese rule in Formosa were marked by a larger measure of social reform. Though crime has been reduced to a remarkable extent, much to the credit of the Government, the vices of opium, gambling, intemperance and prostitution still remain, with their debasing effects upon the life of the people. It should be stated that opium and gambling are on the decrease. On the other hand, while so many of the nations are effecting important temperance reforms, in Formosa breweries are rapidly increasing. The Japanese are fond of liquor. Many of them, indeed, have been ruined through intemperance. Unless the curse of strong drink is removed from their national life, one sees nothing ahead for them but disaster. In their addiction to this evil, the Formosans are beginning to imitate them. There are no restrictive measures in the island. One may buy, sell, or treat as he desires, or he may possess any quantity of liquor without interference. It is only fair to add that one rarely sees a Formosan under the influence of strong drink. The Christian Church is taking no uncertain position on this question, as may be gathered from the reference already made in a previous chapter to the action of the Synod regarding strong drink

and narcotics.

Intellectual Hindrances

Intellectual hindrances that cannot be ignored have been created by the introduction of modern education. The coming in of Western non-Christian literature is helping to undermine belief in the spiritual. The false conclusions of anti-Christian philosophy and science are being read by the students, while science and Christianity are regarded as mutually antagonistic by many of those in Japanese university circles. Hundreds of Formosan students are in Japan, and through them these ideas are filtering in to the island.

The Hindrances a Challenge

These hindrances, however, which are not peculiar to the East alone, should not be regarded as causes for discouragement. They constitute a fresh challenge to the reality of our evangelical faith that has stood the stress and storm of the centuries. We know that victory is sure, that love and truth will be triumphant, for Christ is on the throne. There can be no conditions, no hindrances, whether in the East or in the West, that will remain a perpetual problem to Jesus Christ. If He is revealed in the lives of His followers, if His Gospel is fully preached and His principles faithfully applied to all social, moral and religious conditions, there need be neither fear nor question of the final result. The challenge is to us.

What of the Encouragements?

But we must review some of the encouraging features and incentives to progress which are to be found in Formosa at the present time.

Individual Liberty

The presence of law and order, together with complete religious liberty, encourages people to think independently. The individual can follow more freely the dictates of his own conscience without being threatened by paternal, social or political authority. Christianity is being recognized as a source of social good, a force that makes for the moral uplift of the people. Many who, for various reasons, do not wish at present to become Christians are glad to have their children receive Christian instruction. A spirit of freedom is abroad.

Christian Morals Recognized

Furthermore, the evils which are placed under ban by the Christian conscience are now recognized as real evils and detrimental to public life. Everywhere the pastors and preachers are looked upon as surpassing in education, in life and in conduct the priests of the non-Christian religions. Sorcerers, fortunetellers and necromancers are considered not only useless, but even detrimental to the true progress of the community. The Christian preachers are

often invited by Japanese officials to give addresses on problems of moral reform before audiences made up entirely of non-Christian citizens. Christianity is thus coming to be recognized, not so much as a foreign religion, as one of the religions of the people and a force for individual and national righteousness.

Regard for the Missionary

The fifty years that the missionary has been in North Formosa have shown how utterly false and foolish were the accusations that in the early years were charged against him. He can now associate with all classes without any sense of embarrassment or aloofness being created, and is appreciated as one who has come to the island seeking the good of the people. In 1921, the writer was in an accident in a midnight express train, when the engine was badly battered by a freight train and a fireman killed. Early in the morning, as the passengers viewed the wreckage, they expressed much surprise that there had not been more loss of life. Recognizing the missionary in the crowd, one of the Formosans shouted, "The missionary was on board; that is why we were not killed." Fifty years ago, or less, he would have been blamed for the whole disaster.

New Attitude Toward the Christians

In the earlier days many wild stories were circulated concerning those who connected themselves with the foreign religion. They had given up their parents. they were "rice Christians," they worshipped neither spirits nor Buddha, they had lost all their natural endowments, they were no better than pigs or dogs — these

and many accusations wilder still were freely circulated. To-day all is changed. It is surprising how generally those things which mark the Christians are being recognized. They are not afraid of evil spirits, they worship God every Sabbath, they are happier, the men have only one wife, there is less quarrelling in their homes — these distinguishing marks of the Christians are recognized freely and remarked on by the non-Christians.

One of the most interesting things which the heathen observe about the Christians is that they are less subject to disease. Many cases of remarkable recovery among the Christians have become known to them. The fact that healing has been obtained through the use of natural means does not lessen their belief that it is due directly to the Christians' God. It is true that the percentage of Christians who succumb to epidemics is smaller than that of the non-Christian community. Statistics bear out the statement. In 1919 the Mackay hospital was used for three months by the Japanese medical department, to meet the critical situation that had been created by the scourge of cholera. Both Japanese and Formosans were treated. Several deaths occurred every day. All around the hospital were Christian families who were allowed to meet every Sabbath in the chapel, while others were prohibited from assembHng in large gatherings, and even the schools were closed. During this scourge hundreds died; yet, to the knowledge of the pastor and preacher in that district, there was not a single death among the Christians, who followed the instructions given by the authorities while the heathen simply ignored them. The cheerfulness and general bearing of the Christians during this epidemic was a striking contrast to the fretfulness, despondency

and anxiety of the heathen. Every Sabbath morning they met, a happy band of people, delivered from the bondage of ignorance and superstition, and praised God for His protecting care in the midst of the plague that was threatening their lives. Fifty years ago the Christians would have been blamed for the presence of the plague.

Changes in Social Customs

Nowhere in Formosa are changes more apparent than in the social customs of the people. Many of these changes may be classed among the encouragements, while others increase the difficulties in the path of true progress. Social functions have become a source of much expenditure, both of time and money. If the Formosan youth can afford it, he spends a great deal in entertaining his friends in tea-houses and even in more objectionable quarters. Western ways, Western food and Western style of clothing, though more costly, are being copied. In regard to their funeral processions and their marriage customs, on both of which more money is expended than in former years, the Formosans might well imitate the simple and unpretentious ways of the Japanese.

The influence of Christianity upon social customs may be seen in the conduct of funerals. The quietness, orderliness and solemnity that mark the Christian funeral procession, at the head of which flags or banners bearing appropriate texts of Scripture are carried by boys from the Sabbath school, is in striking contrast with the noisy and disorderly funeral processions of the heathen, marked as these are by the beating of drums, the weird music of chanters, and the procession of mourners in sackcloth. This contrast is making its

appeal to the more thoughtful among the non-Christians. Probably nothing more strikingly illustrates the outstanding difference between Christianity and the heathen religions than the Christian attitude toward death, the funeral procession of the Christians and their burial of the dead. Increasingly, Christianity is having its effect upon the social life and customs of the people.

Conditions Affecting Women and Girls

Womanhood is acquiring a better status in Formosa. This is a social fact of the greatest significance. In the matter of foot-binding, the Japanese have been very tolerant with the Formosan women. They have never forced them to unbind their feet. Among the young, however, the custom is forbidden, and it is only a matter of time till this injurious practice will be a thing of the past. At the present time cloth and leather shoes are commonly worn. The doing away with this custom will mean very much to the womanhood of Formosa. The old secluded life of the Formosan girls is passing away. In increasing numbers they are attending public schools, where, both in the classes and on the playground, they mingle with the boys. The young women travel on trains with the utmost freedom and often attend the Christian chapels with their friends, particularly during seasons of special evangelistic services. In this way non-Christian women are coming into closer contact with the Christian women, and so the opportunities are steadily increasing for the exercise of Christian influence.

The Industry of the People

Still another encouraging feature is the industry of the

people. Formosa's population of over three million has only about six thousand square miles of the island for occupation, the remainder being mountainous and covered with primeval forests. Nevertheless, the problem of unemployment is never even heard of. There is work for all. Japanese administration, which is strongly opposed to social parasites, urges every person capable of earning to engage in some means of making a livelihood. As soon as a young lad is able to work, he has to do his part toward the upkeep of the family. One fact to be mentioned in this connection is that, except in the high schools, the love of healthy sports has not yet been developed in Formosa. For the pleasures that mark Western life, the majority of the people have but little time, while many of those pleasures as yet make very little appeal to the Formosans or other peoples of the Orient. There are signs, however, that the place of recreation and physical development is coming to be recognized in the lands of the East.

What of the Challenge?

The Challenge of the Future

Notwithstanding the marks of progress and the encouraging features that have been reviewed, one cannot think of the future of modern Asia, of which Formosa is a part, without feelings of supreme concern. Its rapid development in recent years, its vast resources both in material and in men, its tremendous possibilities

either for weal or for woe to the rest of the world, constitute a challenge that the West dare not ignore — a challenge that demands that the East should know, without a shadow of uncertainty, the redeeming and regenerating power of Him who alone is the Author of world salvation, world peace and world brotherhood.

The Challenge of the Jubilee

Fifty years of missionary history and service in Formosa now challenge the Church in Canada. The devotion and labors, the heroism and successes of Mackay, the pioneer, and all the missionaries who have followed in the noble succession, surely call for a devotion on the part of the Home Church equal to that of the foreign workers. The growth that God has so graciously given to the mission during these fifty years is a challenge to larger faith and increased effort. Then there was the solitary missionary who was regarded as a "foreign devil;" now there is a staff of twenty Canadian missionaries and fifty-six Formosan workers, nine of whom are ordained, with open doors on every hand and invitations to come and establish churches. Then the pioneer had yet to win his first convert; now there is an adult membership of 2,264, with 1,563 baptized children, and 2,942 unbaptized attendants. In 1912, the North Formosa Church contributed towards self-support 7,154 yen, or nearly $3,600; in 1921, that amount had grown to 26,020 yen, or over $13,000.

Then there were no schools or hospitals; now we have a Theological College, a Women's Bible School, a Boys' Middle School, a Girls' High School, and the Mackay Memorial Hospital. During these fifty years the Canadian Church has been loyally

investing its money in support of this work. The only way by which those investments can be protected and the dividends increased is by the Church giving to this work a larger and more adequate support.

What of the Need of Workers?

Some one may say, "But why ask for more missionaries? Why not depend upon the native workers for the evangelization of their own countrymen?" It is probable that, were the missionaries to be withdrawn, the island would eventually be evangelized, but the accomplishment of the task would thereby be pushed into the indefinite and distant future. The missionary is needed in Formosa and will be needed for many years yet, for leadership and direction, for training workers and for projecting into the various agencies that aggressive, dynamic force so essential to the success of the work and which, as yet, is not possessed in any large degree by many of the native evangelists. Were any suggestion made to withdraw the missionary, the first to rise in vehement protest would be the native leaders. Any step that would weaken, in any measure, the institutions where workers are trained, where they get their knowledge of Christian truth and a deeper sense of their responsibility for the welfare of their own people, would be disastrous to progress and a most serious hindrance to the speedy evangelization of the island.

Workers Needed for the Hospital

The Mackay Memorial Hospital, a splendid building with excellent equipment, has been closed for the past five years, not only on account of lack of doctors, but because the Board has lacked funds to send doctors. Does not the closed hospital — which after all is but a shut door to an open need — with all it might mean to the Kingdom of God, ring out a challenge that must be answered?

For the Theological College

During the fifty years of the mission's history the Theological College in North Formosa has never had, on account of the smallness of the staff, even one missionary whose time has been entirely devoted to the teaching of the students. The missionary has always had to carry other responsibilities. Consequently, the college has suffered seriously. There is no doubt but that, if this policy is continued very much longer, it will be difficult to attract students to the institution. Already those who are graduating from the Middle School and have acquired a knowledge of English are beginning to look to the higher schools of learning in Japan. It would be a serious mistake to let the young men who have the ministry in view, go out of the country for their theological training. The missionaries and Formosan teachers, specially fitted for this work and familiar with the conditions which prevail in Formosa, can give them the training required much better than can any teachers in Japan proper.

For Evangelistic Work

What of the need for missionaries for evangelistic work?

Missionary statesmen differ in their opinion as to the approximate number for which one missionary should be considered responsible. Some say 25,000; others 50,000. Even at the 50,000 rate, thirty missionaries would be required in North Formosa. As a matter of fact, there has never been more than one missionary whose time has been entirely devoted to pastoral and aggressive evangelistic work, and when any one ordained missionary was home on furlough, that field of work was left vacant.

Although the outlook was never so hopeful, the needs were never so great. Giran, with its 100,000 of a population, an average of a thousand to the square mile, has never had more than a brief visit from the foreign missionary. At the present time, seven Formosan evangelists are seeking to meet the spiritual needs of those people. One ordained missionary and two women evangelists are urgently required for the task of their evangelization. An effectual door has been opened. The Taihoku plain has a population of over 100,000 in the city and another 100,000 in the surrounding towns and villages. One missionary for the city, and one for the towns and villages is a very modest request for such a field.

For Work Among the Aborigines

One of the, as yet, untouched parts of the Formosan field is that of the aborigines or Hill tribes, often known as Head Hunters, to whom reference was made in Chapter two. These untamed savages inhabit the mountainous region of Central Formosa and seldom come into contact with the outside world except to barter for goods which they themselves cannot produce. The total number of these people, as estimated by the Japanese authorities in 1920, was

130,000. An earnest attempt is now being made by the Government to persuade them to accept a higher form of civilization and abandon their barbarous habits. Already 25 schools have been established with 105 teachers and 3,695 pupils. One thing, however, is lacking and that the supreme thing, a knowledge of Jesus Christ. Now is the opportune time for an aggressive campaign of evangelism among them. The fetters of the past are being broken. The dawn of a new day is casting its first faint rays of light upon them. What shall that day bring to them?

For the Hakkas and the Hoklos

Reference has already been made to the 250,000 Hakkas in the Sinchiku district, to the south of the railway. There are eleven preaching stations among these people, but, they have never had a foreign missionary who could preach in their own dialect. This district needs at least one ordained missionary and two women evangelists. The Sinchiku plain has a population in the city of 20,000, and three times that number in the surrounding villages. In the city a fine plot of land has been bought, and a mission station is to be opened in the near future. Several missionaries should be located here to carry on the work among the Hakkas and the Hoklos of this extensive territory.

For Formosa's Women

Through the schools, the hospital, the women's classes and other agencies, many of Formosa's women have heard the gospel and not a few have come to know its power and freedom. The task remaining, however, the responsibility for which faces the women

of the Church in Canada is great and challenging.

During the last eighteen years the Women's Missionary Society has sent out nine women missionaries. This does not, however, represent the actual working force on the field. Among this number there is now one vacancy and always some are absent on furlough. Nine workers! What are these among the multitude of women and girls in North Formosa, especially in these days when old customs and prejudices are fast breaking down, when large numbers of women and girls are desiring education, and when their minds and hearts are opening to Christian truth as never before?

The needs are clamorous. For women's work alone the Council is now asking for fourteen new workers. A modest request surely, in view of the present staff, so terribly overworked and so inadequate in view of overwhelming opportunities.

For Formosa's Children

Dare we forget the children of Formosa? The opportunities for influencing the non-Christian children are steadily increasing. The children of the Christians meet with them in the public schools, where, owing to the passing away of bitterness and prejudices, much closer friendships than in the past are being formed. For this large and promising field, an urgent appeal has been made, for the last two years, for a missionary specially trained for this particular type of work.

For the Awaiting Harvest

The field is white unto the harvest. There are no longer political barriers nor social hindrances. Religious prejudices are

being gradually removed. Thousands of villages are awaiting the coming of laborers, Christian institutions, the coming of teachers, and the sick the coming of the medical missionary with his skill and sympathetic touch. The Formosan people are kind, hospitable and sociable, ready to appreciate benefits received and to pay back love and sympathy in kind. They are still worshipping at their old shrines, powerless to get rid of their religious instincts. To them the Gospel, which alone can bring them satisfaction and meet their needs, must be made known. If we delay or if we fail in adequately responding to the urgent and inviting call that Formosa now makes, we may find that centuries of missionary effort will not be able to redeem the lost opportunities of the present hour.

But the Church in Canada dare not and, with God's help, will not fail. Realizing the farreaching significance of the present situation, with a new faith, a new courage and a new devotion to her Lord she will respond to His call until throughout the Island Beautiful His name is known and His Kingdom is established.

> He has sounded out the trumpet
> that shall never call retreat,
> He is sifting out the hearts of men
> before His judgment seat.
> O be swift, my soul, do answer
> Him, be jubilant my feet,
> Our God is marching on!

Prayer

OUR Father Which art in heaven, hallowed be Thy Name. Thy Kingdom come. Forgive us that we have offered with so little sincerity the prayer which our Lord has taught us and have withheld from Thee our means and our talents, our intercessions and our lives, so that to-day there are lands that know little of Thy love and isles that wait for Thy law. Remind us that in spite of our failures, our selfishness and our disloyalty Thou art trusting us still to make Thy message known to all mankind.

MAY all our confidence be in Thee as we recognize the difficulties that confront us and the opportunities that lure us to renewed endeavor. Forbid that Thy people should hold Thee back in any way from revealing Thyself as the only Redeemer of the world's life. May those whom Thou hast chosen for missionary service joyfully answer Thy call; and let none of us fail Thee in this day of Thy power.

DEEPEN our gratitude for the victories of Thy Gospel in North Formosa and give us courage and faith as we face the unfinished task in the Island. Pour out Thy blessing upon the missionaries there who represent Thee and us and on the leaders of the native Church. May the glad tidings of Thy love go swiftly

throughout that region and throughout all lands, until every knee shall bow to Thee and every tongue confess that Jesus Christ is Lord, to the glory of God the Father. AMEN.

THE ISLAND BEAUTIFUL

FORMOSAN FACTS AND FIGURES

Population of our Field (the northern part of the Island)

Chinese	1,278,500
Japanese	76, 000
Aborigines	17, 500
Total	1,372,000

Staff and Membership

Canadian Missionaries	20
Formosan Ordained Men	9
Formosan Unordained Men	47
Adult Membership	2 ,264
Baptized Children	1 ,563
Unbaptized Attendants	2,942

Schools and Hospitals

1 Theological College
1 Women's Bible School
1 Boys' Middle School
1 Girls' High School
1 Mackay Memorial Hospital (closed for four years because of lack of doctors)

Self-Support

Contributions of N. Formosa Church in 1912, Yen 7,154
Contributions of N. Formosa Church in 1921, Yen 26,020 (One yen is equivalent to fifty cents)

NEEDS

Men   8 Ordained Evangelists
3 Doctors
3 Middle School Teachers
1 Chemist
1 Director of Religious Education
1 Business Manager

Women   5 Evangelists
1 Doctor
3 Nurses
1 Music Teacher for Girls' School
1 Domestic Science Teacher

The Presbyterian Church in Canada

L'Église presbytérienne au Canada

The Life and Mission Agency

April 15, 2020

Dear Ruth Chueh,

Thank you for contacting us about the exciting translation and publication project you have started. And please extend our best wishes to the members of Vancouver Taiwanese Presbyterian Church on the celebration of the congregation's 35th anniversary.

It is with pleasure that we assure you that there is no objection from The Life and Mission Agency of The Presbyterian Church in Canada to VTPC creating and circulating an edition of *The Island Beautiful, The Story of Fifty Years in North Formosa* by Duncan McLeod in English and Taiwanese.

We ask that you note the following in your publication: "The original English version of *The Island Beautiful, The Story of Fifty Years in North Formosa* by Duncan McLeod was published by the Board of Foreign Missions (now the Life and Mission Agency) of The Presbyterian Church in Canada". Additionally, we would very much like a copy of this remarkable project commemorating such remarkable events.

We will also be anxious to hear Canada Post's response to your petition asking for the creation of a Mackay postage stamp in 2022.

Again, many blessings as you celebrate many years of faithful ministry in Vancouver.

Sincerely,

The Rev Ian Ross-McDonald
General Secretary, The Life and Mission Agency

NOTES

NOTES

NOTES

NOTES